THE CREATIVE ART OF
BONSAI

THE CREATIVE ART OF
BONSAI

Isabelle & Rémy Samson

WARD LOCK

First published in France in 1986 under the title
Comment Créer et Entretenir vos Bonsai
by Isabelle and Rémy Samson

© Bordas, Paris 1986

Photographs © Alain Draeger, Isabelle Samson, Christian Pessey and Jeanbor

Illustrations of pests and diseases by Danièle Molez
Other illustrations by Valerie Ducugis

First published in Great Britain in 1986 by Ward Lock Ltd
Villiers House 41-47 Strand.
London WC2N 5JE

Translated by Derek Hanson and Judith Hayward in association with First Edition, Cambridge.

English text © Ward Lock Ltd., 1986
Reprinted in 1989
First English paperback edition, 1991
Reprinted in 1991

Printed in Italy by New Interlitho, S.pA., Milan

British Library Cataloguing in Publication Data.

Samson, Isabelle
    The creative art of Bonsai.
    1. Bonsai
    I. Title.   II. Samson, Rémy.   III.
    Comment créer et entretenir vos bonsai.
    English
    635.9'772   SB433.5

ISBN 0-7063-7024-4

CONTENTS

Chinese juniper (*Juniperus sinensis sargentii* 'Henrii'). 15 years old. Height 20 cm (8 in). 'Hokidachi' style. Photograph taken in June.

Page 1. Azalea (*Rhododendron lateridum*). 20 years old. Height 25 cm (10 in). 'Han-Kengai' style. Photograph taken in June. Outdoor bonsai.

Pages 2-3. Fig (*Ficus retusa*). 50 years old and 6 years old. Height 45 and 12 cm (1 ft 6 in and 5 in). 'Tachiki' style. Photograph taken in September. Indoor bonsai.

Wisteria *(Wisteria sinensis* var. *'Daruma')*. 35 years old. Height 40 cm (1 ft 4 in). 'Tachiki' style. Photograph taken in April.

Yew *(Taxus baccata)*. 70 years old. Height 45 cm (1 ft 6 in). 'Nejikan' style. Photograph taken in June.

Publisher's note
This work deals with experience and conditions in France, as regards the cultivation of bonsai, which can range from a continental climate of extremes in the interior of the country to the milder Mediterranean coasts and other maritime regions. The hot sun in summer time, in many parts of France, can ripen the wood of flowering subjects in a way that many people in Britain must envy.

No attempt, therefore, has been made to adapt the English translation to the very varied climatic and geographical conditions of the British Isles. To have done so would have been a well-nigh impossible task in view of the multitudinous microclimates that exist in these islands. One would also have to consider the effects of altitude and length of daylight according to whether growers of bonsai lived in Cornwall, say, or the north of Scotland. Individuals will, therefore, be the best judges of how to adapt the experience of the authors to their own local conditions; indeed, work suggested, month by month, must necessarily be taken as a general guide to be applied according to whether it is to be carried out at an altitude of 300 m (1000 ft) or at sea level, or in an exposed or sheltered position. For example, the authors point out the variable hardiness of *Pinus parviflora* as between the Mediterranean region and more northern Europe, whereas few bonsai growers in Britain would have reason to doubt that plant's constitution.

Readers in the southern hemisphere should note that the months cited in the text apply to the northern hemisphere. It is hoped that the following table will prove useful to them:

Northern hemisphere	Southern hemisphere	Northern hemisphere	Southern hemisphere	Northern hemisphere	Southern hemisphere
For January, read	July	For May, read	November	For September, read	March
For February, read	August	For June, read	December	For October, read	April
For March, read	September	For July, read	January	For November, read	May
For April, read	October	For August, read	February	For December, read	June

The publishers are extremely grateful to Mr Alan Roger, Chairman of the Bonsai Kai of the Japan Society of London, for his invaluable help and patient advice in editing the English text of this translation.

Note to readers
The advice we give in the following pages is the fruit of fifteen years spent patiently and attentively caring for these miniature trees. We hope that we shall succeed in sharing with the reader not only our experience but also our enthusiasm. But we still have a lot to learn. The general guidelines we give must, of course, be adapted to the particular tree in relation to the climate, its geographical situation, the temperature and the season. It is often a good thing to leave room for intuition within the framework of strict rules.

How to choose a bonsai

Choosing a single plant

Make sure that the roots do not cross each other and that they are well spread out around the trunk. Lift the ball of earth out of the pot to make sure that the rooting is satisfactory, that the root hairs are clean and dense, and that they are not flabby. Next, examine the trunk: see that its curves look natural, that there is nothing wrong with the way it rises from the soil, that its bark resembles that of the full-sized trees of the same species and that it looks healthy. Now, check the layout of the branches: they should not cross each other. They should be firm and solid, ranged elegantly round the trunk. The leaves should be small, plentiful, and the right colour for the season of the year. If you are choosing a deciduous tree it is best to do so in the winter, when the absence of leaves makes it possible to see the silhouette clearly and to note its good and bad points. If the tree is bearing fruit, or is in blossom, look carefully at the fruit and the blossom to make sure that there is nothing wrong with them and that they are reduced in size; even if the scale is not exact, they should be small. This, however, does not hold good for wisteria, because it is not possible to produce small blossoms on this plant. There is no fundamental genetic difference between the bonsai and the full-sized tree.

When you have looked at all these details, note the general appearance of the tree from the topmost branches down to the collar. Look carefully at the crown in relation to the foot of the tree and in comparison with the whole. Look to see if there is any moss at the foot of the tree, which might mean that the potting was done some time ago. Lift the moss to check the state of the soil. If there is no moss this might mean that it has only recently been potted. The tree which has only just been potted is more fragile, its roots are less developed. To check that the potting was carried out some time ago and that the roots are sufficiently well developed, wait until the ball of earth is dry and then take the tree out of its container: the ball of earth should not come apart, the earth and the roots should be firmly joined and form a single unit.

If you are choosing a group of plants

Examine each tree individually (as you would for a single tree) and then look at the group as a whole. The general appearance should be aesthetically satisfying and natural. Think of the perspective: the trees should lean in the same direction, the curves should be parallel and complimentary. Compare the diameter and the height of different trunks. They should be varied and well balanced. The branches of one tree should not get in the way of, or across, the branches of a neighbour.

If you are choosing a tree on a rock or a landscape

Pay special attention to the rock and to the roots; you will be able to tell that the latter are placed well if they sweep gracefully down the side of the rock, in harmony with the shape of the tree. The base of the plant should be wedged firmly into the rock. Check the layout of the miniature plantations of grasses or bushes; these should be at different levels, according to how thick and how tall they are. The colours of the plants and their fruits or their blossoms should match well.

Finally, satisfy yourself that the container is big enough, and that it has got a hole at the bottom to allow excess water to drain away. See that the drainage holes are not blocked up, and that the container and the tree go well together.

There should be some affinity between the tree and the person who buys it, so follow your first inclination and choose the tree which first caught your eye even though you might not be able to explain exactly why. The bonsai is something which is alive and it needs to be loved and respected if it is to flourish and to grow ever more beautiful.

Part 1
GENERAL PRINCIPLES

Rémy Samson's bonsai garden at Châtenay-Malabry, near Paris

1 INTRODUCTION

What are bonsai?

Bonsai is a miniature tree grown on a tray. The word *bonsai* is Japanese. The word is derived from the contraction of bon-sai which means 'tree on a tray'.

To grow a bonsai is to create a work of art. But, unlike other art forms, this one can never be brought to completion: it is a living form and the work of shaping it lasts a lifetime, since the artist's hand is visible, for good or for ill, in every inch of its growth. Thus, it is capable of becoming a perfect work of nature, with the result that man is transformed into a creator.

Success in growing bonsai only comes to those who deserve it: it does not freely give itself to any chance comer, but demands constant care and attention. This requires a great deal of time and can only be achieved by the utmost patience. It is a two-way process, for the tree exercises an influence on man at the same time as man exercises an influence on the tree. In Chinese poetic thought the tree is conceived as providing a link between Heaven and Earth. Whatever its size, it is the vehicle of a spiritual meaning. For the equilibrium which they seek to establish is a means of restoring the harmony of nature, this they embody in a symbolic form which, though frequently beyond the grasp of the western intellect, is a sign which has a fundamental cultural significance.

History
FIRST IN CHINA

The first mention of the art of bonsai goes back to the Tsin era (third century BC): on the tomb of Zhang Huai, the second son of the Empress Tang Wu Zetian, there is a figure of a woman carrying a bonsai in both hands. Then, during the Tang dynasty (which ruled China from 618 to 907) and the later Song dynasty (960-1276), public records refer to a man who 'had learnt the art of creating the illusion of immensity enclosed within a small space and all this contained within a single pot'. At the same time, between the tenth and the twelfth centuries, the Buddhist monks are said to have carried the p'en-tsai (trees taken from the natural surroundings and replanted, just as they were, in ornamental pots) throughout the Far East.

During the Song period, many Chinese artists painted pictures of trees which, through the action of the forces of nature, had been reduced to dwarf size, and had been subsequently replanted in ornamental pots. But it was only in the twelfth century, during the Southern Song dynasty, that there appeared, little by little, by virtue of much hard work and of many slight modifications, the bonsai as we know it today. At that time this art was the exclusive preserve of the rich, for whom it provided relaxation. During the Yuan dynasty (1276-1368), an official is said to have fled the rule of the Mongols and gone to live in Japan with some p'en-tsai together with a number of texts elucidating the art, and this is how, so the story goes, they were introduced into Japan.

Next, the Ming (the imperial dynasty which ruled from 1368 to 1644) placed great importance on the highly ornamental pot which contained the tree which was left untouched. The eye of the observer would inevitably find in the landscape of China those meanings which architecture had first placed there: sand would evoke water, the well-spring of life; rocks reminded the onlooker of mountains, the framework of the earth. These stood for the creative power of the soil, but as for thought, this was pure flow, just as life was flow. These truths, it was the task of trees to hint at. In every plantation, there was one particular plant which embodied Wisdom. In China, as subsequently in Japan, this role was filled by the bamboo.

From the Song period onwards (960-1280), artists begin to represent dwarf trees which have become so through natural causes. They are shown growing in pots which rival each other in the splendour of their ornamentation.

During the Tsing dynasty (which held sway after the Ming), the *p'en-tsai* ceases to be a pastime enjoyed only by the nobility, and now becomes accessible to everyone. At the same time, a number of *p'en-tsing*, complete landscapes of dwarf trees, were also planted in China.

Sageretia (*Sageretia theezans*). 110 years old. Height 40 cm (1 ft 4 in). Most sageretias are descended from trees that have been collected from the wild in China.

NEXT IN JAPAN

From our twelfth century onwards and up to the middle of the fourteenth century (the period of Kamakura), the first refer-

A servant carrying a *p'en-tsai*. A mural painting of the Tang period (eighth century) in the tomb of Princess Zhang-Huai at Xian

And then this art became forgotten. During the eighteenth century, it had been popularized to a certain extent by sailors coming back from the colonies with plants ordered by collectors, apothecaries or gardeners. It was a curiosity which was all the rage for a short while but did not last long; a momentary whim of the pampered rich!

In the nineteenth century, bonsai were rediscovered. Serious essays appeared on the means employed by the Japanese to obtain dwarf trees. Both in France and in England there developed an interest in this art so new for Westerners. Hypotheses were formulated, which proved to be sound. In 1889, J. Vallot wrote an article published in the *Bulletin de la Société de Botanique de France* on 'the physiological causes which bring about the stunting of trees in the Japanese cultivation of plants'.

Paul Claudel, during his period as French Ambassador in Japan, was surprised, overwhelmed and absorbed when confronted by a forest of maples wrought into the form of bonsai. He contemplated these trees with their deciduous leaves and explained that he could not help imagining himself in one of these maple woods, and, in imagination, could hear the chirping of the birds on the branches.

Between the two world wars, the Parisian florist, André Baumann, brought a number of bonsai to Paris to satisfy the demand of those people attracted by Far-eastern culture. Japan was once again in fashion but that was short lived.

Japanese engraving by Hiroshige (the Kaei period 1848-53) representing a landscape painted on a pot

ences to bonsai begin to appear in Japan. There is, for example, the famous scroll of the Buddhist monk, Honen, which is decorated with bonsai and which dates roughly from the twelfth century. Later, Seami (1363-1444) created a drama based on the story of the Regents of Kamakura, Hojo Tokiyori, for whose benefit a poor man called Tsuneyo had burnt three bonsai, which represented the sum total of his earthly goods...

The period of Edo (1615-1867) coincided with a growth in interest in highly wrought, colourful trees grown on trays. The *bonkei* were whole landscapes on trays and bonsai trees grown in pots. In the former, one finds the essential elements of nature (water, mountain, sand, vegetation). In the latter, the foreground is occupied by Being that is to say the world of creatures. The well-to-do classes in Japan gradually formed an attachment for bonsai. The trees which they succeeded in growing took pride of place in their homes. From that point onwards, the cultivation of bonsai is a hobby which spreads slowly through the various social strata, the last to adopt the hobby being the common people, and that after a century or more had passed. But today the cultivation of bonsai is practised throughout the whole of Japan.

AND ALSO IN EUROPE

Bonsai appeared in Europe in the fourteenth century, introduced by travellers who were discovering the East and had made eastern art fashionable. Booklets, with a certain amount of unconscious humour, dealt with the art of bonsai in a rather naïve way, but not without poetry. They bore titles such as: 'Japanese Curios', 'Essays on Japanese Horticulture', 'Japanese Gardens'...

Today, the countries of Europe are acquainted with all forms of bonsai. Associations or clubs have been set up where amateur gardeners can meet to talk to one another about their absorbing interest, exchange their bonsai or swap recipes. The United States, also, has its own amateurs and specialists in the art of bonsai. Each of them is busy trying to transform the species of his own country into bonsai.

The first collections of bonsai to be exhibited in Europe appeared at the World Exhibition in Paris in 1878

2 BONSAI CHARACTERISTICS

As regards the dimensions of your bonsai, no one size is any better than another. Everything depends on the judgement of the individual, whether he likes his miniatures to be more or less small, and how much space he has available. What matters is that the general shape must always be that of a well-balanced and harmoniously formed tree. Certain Japanese masters are of the opinion that there are five classes of bonsai, others maintain that there are only three, for the intermediate classes are really not very much different from the others. Some specialists say that the maximum height should be 1.20 m (4 ft) but this is hotly disputed, not least because if you are lucky enough to be invited to the Imperial Palace, you can admire bonsai which are taller than one metre twenty. People in Japan also speak of a Lilliputian size, known as 'Keshitsubu'. Special pots are made for bonsai of this size. However, these plants are extremely rare.

From left to right:
Japanese maple (*Acer palmatum* var. *'deshohjoh'*). 15 years old. Height 30 cm (1 ft). 'Tachiki' style. Photograph taken in May.
Japanese pine (*Pinus parvifolium* var. *pentaphylla*). 300 years old. Height 1 m (3 ft 3 in). 'Tachiki' style. Photograph taken in May.
Chinese elm (*Ulmus parvifolia*). 10 years old. Height 12 cm (5 in). 'Nejikan' style.

Classification of bonsai

In the present work we shall only consider the three main classes of bonsai, as these are the most in vogue.

The *mini bonsai*, known as 'Mame bonsai', which can be held in one hand. It ranges in size from 5 to 15 cm (2-6 in) the Japanese call it 'Shôhin'. Some of these are very young plants while others are very old. Trees this small are produced by being placed in very small pots and by regular trimming of their branches. They are repotted less frequently than the other bonsai. The pot, which is quite small, contains little earth, and for this reason the tree is more delicate. Special attention has to be paid to watering and the siting of the plant. In fact, this kind of bonsai is very vulnerable to sun, wind and frost.

The *classical bonsai* ranges from 15 to 60 cm (6 in-2 ft) in height. This class is sometimes divided into two: the bonsai from 15 to 30 cm (6-12 in), known as 'Katatemochi' or 'Komono', and the bonsai from 30 to 60 cm (1-2 ft), known as 'Chûmono'. But more usually these bonsai are included in a single class. To carry these you need to use both hands. They can be from five to several hundred years old.

The *great bonsai* ranges from 60 cm to 1.20 m (2-4 ft) or more. For this bonsai you need four hands, as it usually needs two people to carry it. It is known as 'Ômono'. It is often of venerable age. In the olden days, in Japan, it used to have the place of honour at the entrance to aristocratic houses as a sign of welcome or, more simply, as an indication of wealth. Nevertheless, it is possible to find some of tenderer years, being no more than about fifteen years old.

The size of these bonsai is calculated vertically from the tip of the tree to the base of the trunk, not counting the pot. It is difficult to assign cascade or semicas-

cade bonsai to a particular class because they rise initially and then sweep back down again. The semicascade kind are often almost horizontal. The solution is to measure these trees from their tip at the highest point, that is to say at the bend which is formed by the trunk before plunging down again.

The 'Mame bonsai' are the only ones which present difficulties because of their small size. They are fascinating, but must be looked after with extreme care. Certainly, they are less hardy. Their earth is apt to dry out quickly; it is therefore necessary to water them frequently. But if they have too much water they will immediately die as their roots will go

mouldy. They cannot stand frost and live in fear of strong winds. As for the other bonsai, the extent to which they should be exposed to the sun depends on the species. Nevertheless, this kind is very popular with collectors, on the one hand, and with amateur growers, who do not have much space, on the other.

Thus, apart from the business of watering and the need to take great care in choosing the exact location for the mini bonsai, we can say that the three kinds of bonsai are developed and cared for in much the same way, requiring the same kind of care – trimming, repotting, wiring, watering, temperature, ventilation and fertilizer. See also p. 27 and pp. 28-31.

Symbols

Certain plants, linked by common associations, are placed in the soil together to provide New Year's gifts for friends. This is an ancient tradition which is still practised in Japan today. These plants cannot be expected to last, but they have a special meaning and bring great happiness to those who receive them. Nowadays, they are given both at the New Year and at Christmas time. The plants are collectively called 'Shô-chiku-bai', which means pine, bamboo and Japanese apricot tree which, respectively, stand for happiness, long life and virtue. The apricot tree should be in flower when it is given as a present. The reason for this is that, previously, the New Year was in February. Today, for an apricot tree being given as a present to be in flower on the first of January, it is necessary to force its growth for, in its natural state, it flowers in the second fortnight of February. To get an apricot tree to flower you must place it in a warm room (20°C, 68°F roughly) for a fortnight and spray it once or twice a day with water at room temperature and this will cause it to blossom.

To these three fundamental species, one may add ferns or grasses with red berries which symbolize wealth. Sometimes small flowering plants may also be added, whose blooms have been forced for the occasion: miniature bamboos, Nandinas, for example, in harmony with the three fundamental types of tree. Some people also plant an orchid to enliven the whole.

For the people of Thailand, bonsai lost its original meaning and became a form of evocation: the treatise on the tree or 'Klong-Tamra Mai-Dat' speaks of the tree metaphor. The forms of the tree become magic and are reduced to signs, evoking human attitudes or characters.

In Vietnam, trees became the bearers of man's earthly misfortunes: thus it was that there was a tree which symbolized a tortoise, a sacred animal which supports the earth on its shell.

Thai signs

According to the K'lông tamra mal-dat, the treatise written by a Thai poet of the nineteenth century

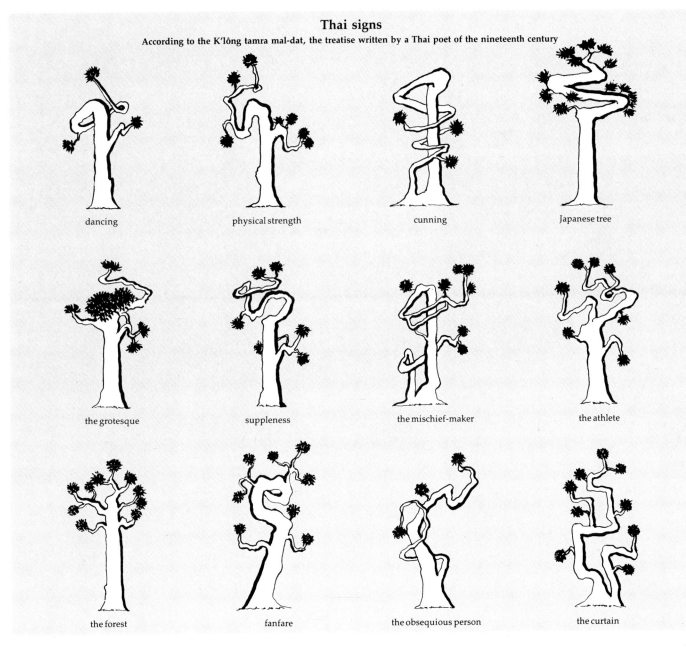

dancing

physical strength

cunning

Japanese tree

the grotesque

suppleness

the mischief-maker

the athlete

the forest

fanfare

the obsequious person

the curtain

Styles

In every bonsai, you will find the shape of the triangle. Bonsai joins Heaven and Earth, it becomes a concrete allegory by leading Man along the pathway of spiritual values. The story is often told how an old sage used to explain his smooth and youthful features by his devotion to bonsai: when he contemplated his work, he could not grow old, because 'while flowers may fade in Winter, in his home they were always in bloom'.

Bonsai, inward image, symbol of eternity. In fact, it abolishes time. Thus it reflects the harmony between Man and Nature, between Heaven and Earth. And, in every bonsai, you will find the ever-present triangle: God-Earth-Man. The slope of the triangle varies from one tree to another. This is the essence of style in these dwarf trees. Style is defined, in fact, by the number of degrees in the angle formed by a vertical line traced from the top to the bottom of the trunk. The trees may, therefore, be classified according to their style as defined by the silhouette of the tree. There are four main styles, the other styles stem from these. Also they may be classified according to whether there is one or more plants in a single container.

Thus there are four main groups:

GROUP 1: A SINGLE TRUNK

The Chokkan style this is the Formal Upright style: the tree grows straight up towards the sky.	直 幹	
The Shakan style the trunk bends and may do so to the extent of being a semicascade style.	斜 幹	
The Kengai style or the cascade style, plunging downwards.	懸 崖	
The Bankan style the trunk winds round itself like a twisted cord. These four styles are the main ones.	蟠 幹	

Styles derived from the above:

The Tachiki style Informal Upright.	立 木	
The Han-kengai style semicascade.	半懸崖	
The Bunjingi style or Literati style the tree rises obliquely, with a trunk which is bare except at the top.	文人木	

The Hôkidachi style the tree in the form of a broom.	箒立	
The Sabamiki style the trunk is split, torn, bare in parts.	娑羅幹	
The Saramiki style the trunk is stripped of its bark like a dead tree.	娑婆幹	
The Fukinagashi style the Windswept style – the tree resembles those which grow along seashores, beaten down by the wind, with their branches on one side of the trunk.	吹流	
The Neagari style the roots are exposed.	根上	
The Sekijôju style Root-over-rock style – the roots grip the rock and penetrate the earth.	石上樹	
The Ishitsuki style the tree is planted on a rock.	石付	
The Nejikan style the trunk is partially twisted	捩幹	
The Takozukuri style the 'octopus' style.	蛸造	

GROUP 2: MULTIPLE TRUNKS FROM A SINGLE ROOT

The Sôkan style double trunk.	雙幹	
The Kabudachi style trunks grouped around a single root.	株立	

The Kôrabuki style multitrunked style.	甲羅吹	
The Ikadabuki style Straight-line style – the stump is formed by the horizontal trunk.	筏吹	
The Netsunagari style Sinuous style – several trunks grow from a single sinuous root.	根連	

GROUP 3: MULTIPLE TRUNKS/ GROUP PLANTINGS

Except for trees planted in pairs, bonsai are always planted in an odd number (3, 5, 7, 9 ...).

The Sôju style twin trunks.	雙樹	
The Sambon-Yôse style three trunks.	三本寄	
The Gohon-Yôse style five trunks.	五本寄	

The Nanahon-Yôse style seven trunks.	七本寄	
The Kyûhon-Yôse style nine trunks.	九本寄	
The Yôse-Ue style multiple trunks, more than nine in number.	寄植	
The Yomayori or Yomayose style a natural grouping.	四間寄	
The Tsukami-Yôse style Clustered group style – multiple trunks springing from the same place.	摑寄	

GROUP 4: THESE ARE NOT BONSAI IN THE STRICT SENSE OF THE TERM

Bonkei landscapes.
Kusamomo or Shitakusa grass plantations or bulbs.
Grass plantations and seasonal plants

Style 'Ishitsuki': *Juniperus sinensis* (Chinese junipers) between eight and thirty-five years old, planted on a rock

3 PROPAGATION OF BONSAI

Since bonsai are trees of sacred origin, the work of propagating and looking after them involves a rigorous ritual with its own inflexible rules. The first bonsai were trees taken from their natural environment. In fact, bonsai exists in the natural state. It is a tree which, for one reason or another, has been unable to develop normally; the unfavourable growing conditions have resulted in its becoming stunted: drought, wind, avalanches, herds of browsing animals have arrested the growth of the tree. To remove the tree from its natural habitat, part of the roots were cut over a period of two or three years, in the spring. This was an art in itself. Today, in Europe as in Japan, to remove such plants from the forests or mountainsides is forbidden, and that is why we shall not give any further details about how it is done. Nevertheless, it is possible to grow your own bonsai in various ways.

Propagation from seeds or seedlings

This method requires much patience and care, but it produces particularly fine trees. Almost all bonsai may be obtained from seeds. There are no special bonsai seeds. Seeds can be taken from bonsai or from 'normal' trees. These seeds can be bought from a dealer or be harvested from the trees themselves. They are collected in autumn: all kinds of fruit, acorns, berries, beechnuts and other nuts bear seeds which may be harvested and planted to give, five to seven years later, beautiful miniature trees in the desired form.

The conditions for germination are different for each of the various kinds, from the moment of sowing. Some seeds should be planted straight away, for they germinate immediately after their harvesting. Others should be preserved in a fresh and dry environment before being planted. Certain seeds, however, can germinate in the autumn or the winter but, so that they retain their ability to germinate, should be buried for a few days in damp sand. Many of these seeds need a period of rest. They should be stratified (that is to say they should be

placed in layers) in damp sand from six months to a year, and protected from frost and heat. For each particular seed, see Part 2.

Some seeds may quite simply be preserved in the vegetable container of the refrigerator. The length of time may range from one day to a month; after this they should be steeped for twenty-four hours in warm water. There are two particularly favourable moments to sow these seeds: either in the spring, or at the end of the summer and in the autumn. For each tree, we shall see in Part 2 when and how to sow the seed. A seed with a hard shell may have slits cut into it to assist the process of germination. Seeds of different species should not be sown together because their requirements with regard to water, heat, light, may be different.

To sow, first of all, get hold of a small seed tray with holes at the bottom to allow excess water to drain away. Fill it with compost, which should be a mixture 50 per cent peat and 50 per cent river sand. This tray should be three-quarters full only and should not be heaped too high in

order to allow air and water to circulate. When this sifted mixture has been placed in it, the seeds should then be sown therein, well spaced out. Cover them with the sifted mixture, lightly spread, then water abundantly with a fine sprinkler. Next, cover the tray with a glass and place it in the shade and protect it from frost.

As soon as the first shoots appear (which occurs sooner for some species than for others) half open the glass in order to allow the air to circulate. Remove it completely as soon as the first leaves appear. In the spring, when the stem has thickened, plant each seedling in a flowerpot that can, bit by bit, be introduced to the sun. After two years, you will be able to begin shaping this young shoot into a bonsai by trimming the branches (in spring and in summer) and the roots (in spring). Three to five years later, the tree thus obtained from the seeds will have the desired form and be graced with an elegant silhouette with no unseemly cut or swelling on the trunk; its branches will be harmoniously balanced.

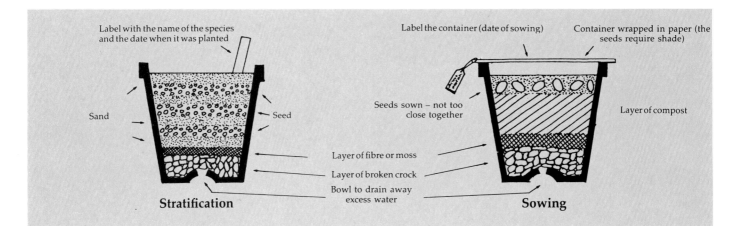

Label with the name of the species and the date when it was planted

Sand

Seed

Label the container (date of sowing)

Container wrapped in paper (the seeds require shade)

Seeds sown – not too close together

Layer of compost

Layer of fibre or moss

Layer of broken crock

Bowl to drain away excess water

Stratification

Sowing

Propagation by seeds

1 You will need a sieve to make sure that the soil mixture in which the seeds are sown is fine enough

2 Filling a traditional terra-cotta pot with the mixture of sieved soils

3 The seeds, which have been stratified, are laid on the soil mixture

4 The thickness of the layer of earth covering the seeds depends on the size of the seeds

5 If, as here, the seeds are quite big, it is a good idea to heap up the earth covering them. For this you should use a traditional 'trowel'

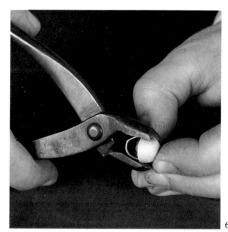

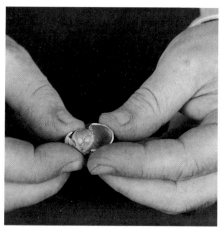

6 If the seeds (here ginkgo) are protected by a shell, you will have to break this with a pair of pliers

7 Once the shell has been broken, you must gently remove the seed from its protective envelope

8 The seeds removed from their shell can now be sown. Since they germinate easily, they do not need to be stratified

9 A paper disc is placed on the surface of the soil

10 This disc prevents the earth being disturbed when watering takes place

Propagation from nursery seedlings

It is also possible to gain good results from plants bought as nursery seedlings. These will be between two and three years old and may have an interestingly shaped trunk or silhouette. Choose examples which are not too tall and which have a good set of branches. Trees not suitable for sale or ornamental gardens make good bonsai.

They must be unpotted, and their roots must be trimmed to two-thirds their original size. The new pot in which they are placed must be quite big. The best season for this is the spring. The treatment then continues as for a tree that has just been repotted. What is important here is the trunk and the roots. As regards the latter, one must be careful to see that they spread out from the trunk like a fan without resting on one another. As for the trunk, it is necessary early on to cut back the low branches, bearing in mind that in doing so you are creating the silhouette of the tree as it will finally be. This silhouette will almost immediately dictate the style of the tree. As for its height, this is also determined at this time because the tip of the tree is removed. The wood will take some time to harden, the degree of hardness varies from species to species. When the wood has hardened, it should be bound or wired so that the lines of growth of the tree are fixed. This process may take up to six years. After this it will have assumed the shape selected for it and may now truly be called a bonsai.

Propagation from cuttings

This method requires less time and patience than the one mentioned above. As is known, propagation from cuttings consists, by definition, of planting either directly into the earth, or after a period spent submerged in water, stems of plants that have no roots and have been cut from the parent plant. This method also holds good for bonsai: when the branches are pruned, it is possible to obtain cuttings about 10 cm (4 in) long. There are in existence hormones, in liquid or in powder form, which make it easier for the cutting to take root if it has been dipped in them for a period of time. The reader will know

Cuttings from indoor bonsai

All the materials necessary to get cuttings to take: earth, sand, bowls, hormones to encourage the cutting to strike and, of course, recently taken cuttings

The mixture of soil and compost used to encourage the cuttings to take is made up of sand and compost; shake them up until you obtain a uniform mixture

Before placing the cuttings in the soil, you should ensure that the soil is well watered

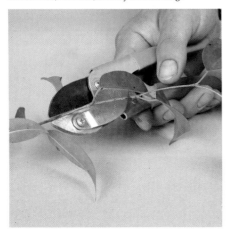

The cuttings should be no more than 12 cm (4¾ in) in length. The illustration shows a cutting from a *Ficus*

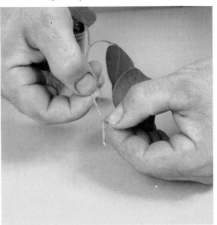

The leaves at the base of the cutting (the part which will be placed in the soil) should be removed

Removing part of the leaves from the cutting. This should be done with a pair of very sharp secateurs so that the plant tissue is not damaged

Deciduous cuttings

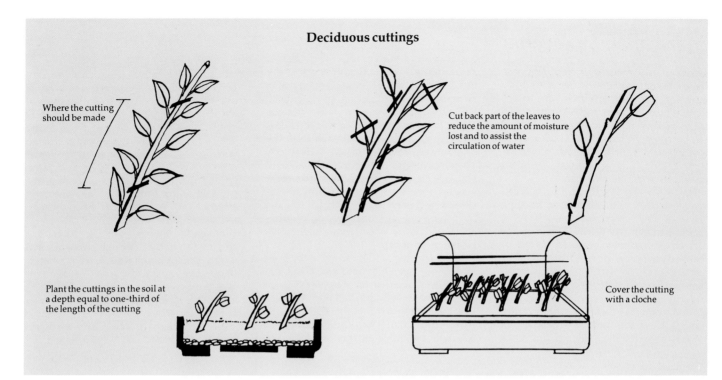

Where the cutting should be made

Cut back part of the leaves to reduce the amount of moisture lost and to assist the circulation of water

Plant the cuttings in the soil at a depth equal to one-third of the length of the cutting

Cover the cutting with a cloche

Coniferous cuttings

how to prepare a cutting: the branch of the parent plant must be cut just above the point where a leaf is about to develop; the soft part of the cutting is also trimmed back. The stem which is retained should have six to eight leaves on it, and not be more than 10 cm (4 in) in length. It should then be inserted to a depth of 3 cm (1¼ in) in a receptacle containing sand and peat inside a flowerpot. The cutting should be abundantly watered and covered for its protection with a sheet of plastic wound round the top of the pot. In order to grow, it requires light but must be kept away from the sun and frost. To keep the soil humid enough, it is necessary to spray it regularly.

When new shoots appear on the stem, roots are developing and the cutting has taken. Now is the time to take the plastic away and allow the new plant to get used to the sun. Apply a little fertilizer in spring and protect it carefully from frost the next winter. After one or two years, the cutting should be shaped to make it into a bonsai. Be careful that you do not cause the cutting and the young roots to rot by watering too much. You must control the amount of water it receives, and this is where the difficulty lies. Propagating by cuttings is possible throughout the whole year with certain species. But cuttings taken in the spring and early summer take better and much more quickly than those taken at the end of the summer or in autumn because the sap flows much more freely, and there is more of it, when the plant starts to make leaf again.

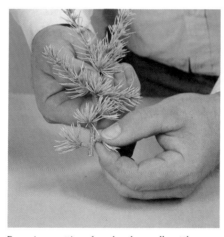

Preparing a cutting of a cedar: the needles at the bottom are removed

The lower part of the cutting is dipped in hormone rooting powder. In this way the chances of the cutting forming roots are considerably improved

Make a hole in the earth with a pencil, then insert the cutting

Firm the soil around the cutting to make sure that there is a perfect contact. Water thoroughly and firm the soil again

17

Propagation by layering

Layering is the method of obtaining new plants from runners, suckers or side branches, these coming from the parent plant, which are then partially covered in earth; by this means rooting occurs. The link between the two plants is cut and the new plant is now completely independent. By extension of meaning, the word 'layer' refers to this new plant.

Simple layering is carried out, in particular, on trees with flexible or hanging branches. The branch selected for layering should be bent over towards its base, the part which is about to be buried should be stripped of leaves or needles, either by using clippers to sever the leaf from its stem, or by taking them between finger and thumb. Make a cut in the lower part, about 5 cm (2 in) in length, to assist rooting. Cover the branch with soil.

Make sure that the earth remains moist by watering it as soon as it starts to dry out. The number of times the plant has to be watered and the amount of water used depend on the region and the climate. When new roots have developed, it is possible to separate the branch from the original tree, severing it with a clean cut. Then replant this branch in the mixture of soil which is right for this particular species (see Part 2). From now on, it should be treated as a tree which has just been repotted, and the specific requirements of that particular tree should always be borne in mind.

Aerial layering is most suitable for trees with more upright branches. It has the great advantage that the tree may be pre-shaped while still attached to its parent tree. This process normally takes place in April. You should not choose a branch which is too thick as this will not root easily; choose, rather, a branch about 5 cm (2 in) in diameter. Aerial layering is obtained by a vertical cut in the limb of about 4-5 cm (1½-2 in) in length. It is necessary to bind a piece of wood to the cut or apply a little moss to stop it from healing too soon. It is also necessary to place above it a plaster of peat and damp sphagnum contained in a plastic bag pierced with holes, but hermetically sealed at top and bottom. After three to five months, the roots will have developed sufficiently: now remove the plastic bag and cut the runner through cleanly with a small pair of secateurs or scissors, depending on the thickness of the layer and the hardness of its wood. Immediately it must be potted in a compost which is right for that species. Then the same sequence of events occurs as if it were a bonsai which had just been repotted.

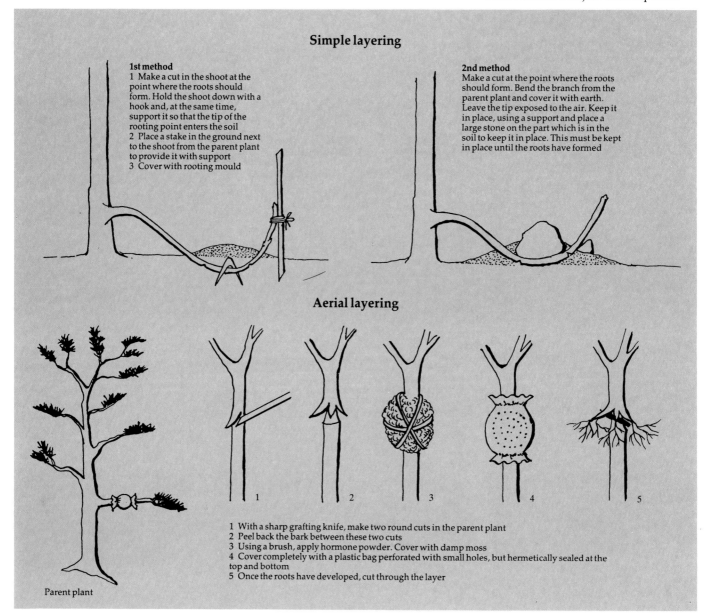

Simple layering

1st method
1 Make a cut in the shoot at the point where the roots should form. Hold the shoot down with a hook and, at the same time, support it so that the tip of the rooting point enters the soil
2 Place a stake in the ground next to the shoot from the parent plant to provide it with support
3 Cover with rooting mould

2nd method
Make a cut at the point where the roots should form. Bend the branch from the parent plant and cover it with earth. Leave the tip exposed to the air. Keep it in place, using a support and place a large stone on the part which is in the soil to keep it in place. This must be kept in place until the roots have formed

Aerial layering

1 With a sharp grafting knife, make two round cuts in the parent plant
2 Peel back the bark between these two cuts
3 Using a brush, apply hormone powder. Cover with damp moss
4 Cover completely with a plastic bag perforated with small holes, but hermetically sealed at the top and bottom
5 Once the roots have developed, cut through the layer

Parent plant

Propagation by grafting

Grafting consists of implanting a plant (stock) with a segment of another plant (scion) which will subsequently replace, either completely or partially, the aerial part of the stock, while allowing the original tree to retain its individuality.

In the great majority of cases, the scion and the stock must belong to the same species. Nevertheless, in Japan, white pines are often grafted on to Thunberg pines, to obtain more rapid growth.

The best moment for grafting is when the sap is rising, that is to say in the spring. This method has both advantages and disadvantages. The results are never all one could wish for. In fact, where the grafting has been made on the trunk, swellings appear. Nevertheless, arboriculturists use this method most frequently for their fruit trees. It also makes it possible for flowers of different colours to be produced by the same plant. In particular, *Prunus* is capable of producing white, pink and red flowers at the same time.

Grafting is frequently the means used to save bonsai whose roots have been damaged. It is also the method that must be used for certain plants that cannot be reproduced in any other way. Another advantage of grafting is that, whereas with seed reproduction, variations may occur, reproduction by grafting retains all the original characteristics.

Grafting compound protects those parts of the tree which have become exposed against inclement weather and the attacks of parasites or disease. The graft must then be wired and the way this is done will depend upon their shape. The wiring should be both flexible and yet not too loose, so that the graft does not slip or damage the bark and, in general, the whole should be kept together. It may be necessary to provide a support for trees which have received a graft, to protect them from the wind.

There are many different ways of grafting: here we mention only those which differ significantly and which are the most common. (Many different ways of grafting only vary with respect to the way in which the cut is made.) The most frequently practised are:

- cleft grafting
- lateral grafting
- inarching
- root grafting
- shield grafting
- crown grafting

Cleft grafting

Cleft grafting makes it possible to implant new branches in the tree. This method may only be used with slender branches. In the spring, make a vertical slit in the stock about 3-5 cm (1¼-2 in) long and slip a branch which has been cut to a point about 5 cm (2 in) long, either taken from the same tree, or from a tree of the same species. When the scion is firmly in place it should be bound up and smeared with grafting wax.

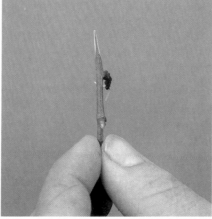
Use the grafting knife to cut a double chamfer in the lower tip of the graft

A cleft in the rootstock made with the blade of the grafting knife, ready for a traditional cleft graft. Disinfect the blade by placing it in a flame

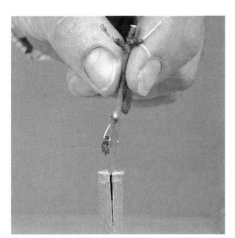
The graft, or the grafts, should be inserted in the vertical cleft made in the rootstock. This cleft should not be too deep

When the graft is in place, bind it with raffia

The graft should be smeared with grafting compound. Use a piece of wood for this purpose

Lateral grafting

Lateral grafting is made on evergreen trees. In summer, make a notch about 5 cm (2 in) in length in the lower part of the trunk of the stock, shape the branch (scion) to obtain a chamfered edge and slip it into the notch (so that, later on, the earth will hide the point where the graft has been made). The scion will start growing in the following spring. The stock should then be cut obliquely, above the scion, to separate the two.

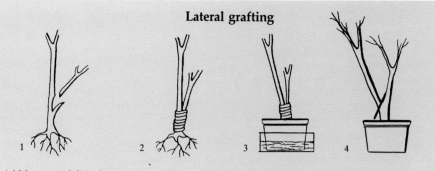

Lateral grafting

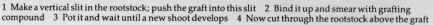

1 Make a vertical slit in the rootstock; push the graft into this slit   2 Bind it up and smear with grafting compound   3 Pot it and wait until a new shoot develops   4 Now cut through the rootstock above the graft

Inarching

Inarching which copies nature's practice directly is therefore the oldest and simplest method. This method makes it possible to unite two trees, in order later to replace branches which are missing or to provide protection for plants which are difficult to obtain using other methods. Inarching should take place at the end of the spring, in order to conform to the cycle of nature. The scion should be left at-tached to the stock until the two are completely united. Scion and stock may come from the same tree. Peel the bark of the scion and that of the stock back for about 3 cm (1¼ in). Bring them into contact, placing one over the other. Next, cover with grafting wax and wrap it round with raffia. The scion will have taken by the end of the autumn. Now separate the scion and the stock, by making a cut as near as possible to the stock to avoid too large a swelling occurring. Every time you make an incision as part of the grafting technique, smear the branch with a healing compound to allow the cut to heal up more quickly and to ensure that pests and other forms of blight do not gain a hold.

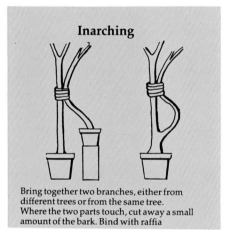

Inarching

Bring together two branches, either from different trees or from the same tree. Where the two parts touch, cut away a small amount of the bark. Bind with raffia

Root grafting

Root grafting should be carried out in spring. This is necessary for trees with damaged roots. It helps cuttings which are growing to take off if you graft them on to the roots of another species, and reduces the rate of growth of a tree in which the trunk has become too long in relation to the branches.

Choose roots with well-developed and healthy root hairs. Proceed exactly as you would for cleft grafting, replacing the branch with the roots. Wire and add healing compound. When the graft has taken (the roots are developing), trim the upper part of the rootstock.

Sometimes you can use the inlaying method. In this case, the graft is made on the root, and there is no need to cut off anything. But these are, essentially, techniques used by professional growers.

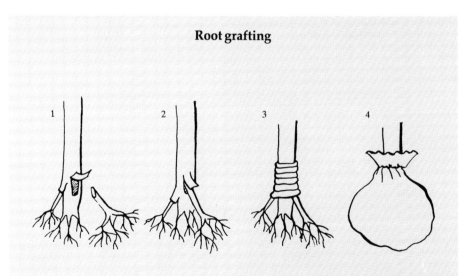

Root grafting

1 Make a cut in the bark   2 Insert the graft   3 Bind up with raffia   4 Spread a mixture of sand and peat around the graft and cover with a plastic bag

Shield grafting

Shield grafting is one of the most frequently used methods. This technique makes it possible to unite a male and female tree in order to obtain a composite tree which will give fruit. This grafting should take place when the buds are swollen and the sap is rising. When the stock has been well moistened by spraying, it should then have a T shape cut into it. Next, implant a bud taken from a branch of the scion. Smear with grafting wax and bind the scion with raffia. Be careful not to drain the bud during this operation. When the leaf stalk falls (generally the next spring), you will know that the scion has taken. It is possible to make grafts in different places to make it more likely that the scion will take and to obtain more branches.

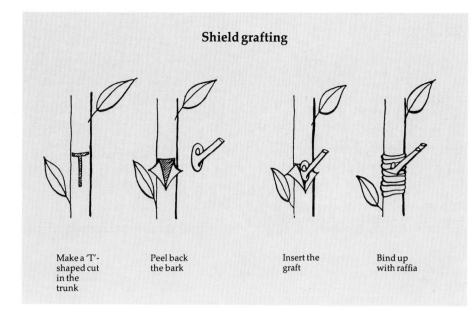

Shield grafting

Make a 'T'-shaped cut in the trunk

Peel back the bark

Insert the graft

Bind up with raffia

Crown grafting

Crown grafting is only used with large trees. This is the method used to obtain bonsai with multiple trunks and to improve the appearance of old trees. This should be done in the spring. The diameter of the scion should be smaller than that of the stock. Make an incision in the trunk of the stock about 3 cm (1¼ in) long and insert the scion. In this way several scions may be inserted into the stock. Place grafting wax on the join and then bind it round with raffia.

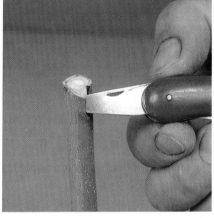

Using the grafting spatula, prise open each vertical cut made in the bark

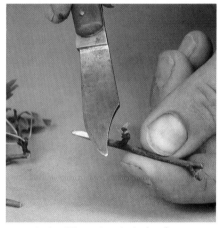

The grafts should be cut in a single chamfer at one end, to allow them to come into contact with the cambium of the rootstock

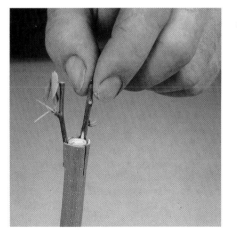

The grafts should be placed gently in the vertical clefts made in the bark of the rootstock

As for the cleft graft, binding is best done using raffia

Here also, the graft should be smeared with lime. The compound will assist the healing process and protect wounds from parasites and diseases

4 HOW TO CARE FOR YOUR BONSAI

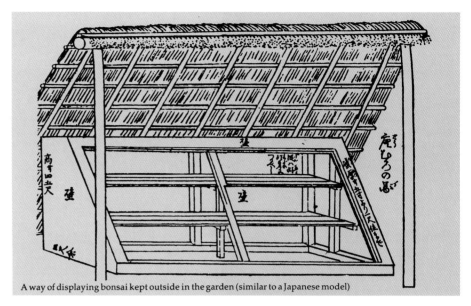

A way of displaying bonsai kept outside in the garden (similar to a Japanese model)

Once you have got your bonsai, you must think carefully about the best place to put it so that the tree can flourish; you must also choose a pot that will show it off well. Find out which tools you will need to keep it in trim and what you have to do to look after it all the year round.

The first thing is to decide whether you have an outdoor or an indoor bonsai. This question, of course, has to be considered in the context of the place where you are living. The five-needle pine (*Pinus parviflora*, synonym *pentaphylla*), which would be an outdoor bonsai in a Mediterranean climate would be an indoor bonsai in the coldest parts of Europe. When the environment, the temperature, the amount of sunshine and all the atmospheric conditions of your region are very different from those of the natural environment of the tree, you must try to reconstruct those conditions – or at least the input they provide for the tree. This requires extreme care: man's contribution goes hand in hand with the natural elements.

The indoor bonsai come from tropical or subtropical regions where they would be growing outside. But they are capable of adapting to conditions in European homes. In 1979, the authors were responsible for introducing indoor bonsai into France. Since then, they have been increasingly successful. They make it possible for many people who have no garden, terrace, balcony or even window sills, to have their own bonsai. Outdoor and indoor bonsai pose different problems.

Outdoor bonsai should be placed high up on shelves or on high stands: if they are placed on ground level they run the risk of attack from parasites or even being damaged by a household pet. In addition, bonsai roots do not penetrate the ground and, if you are going to look after them properly, it is easier to have them at eye level.

Indoor bonsai should be placed in the light, in a room heated to a normal temperature. The warmer it is, the more often you will have to water the plant. Choose a container which will show the bonsai off to the best advantage and which will harmonize with the colour tones in the rest of the room. It must fit in with the rest of the room and give the room an atmosphere of serenity. You should get ready in advance the tools you will need for the upkeep and general development of the bonsai, which only seeks to grow and flourish throughout the year. Get a table, a pedestal table or some other piece of furniture which will enhance the appearance of your plant. To prevent it leaving any marks on this piece of furniture, place a tray, a saucer (without water) or a piece of cloth on it. If you have several bonsai, they can be arranged on a set of shelves intended for just this purpose. Make sure that the shelves are far enough apart so that the top of the tree does not touch the shelf above and that it has enough space to contain it and to allow it to breathe.

On no account must you allow a household pet to spoil indoor bonsai. Never expose them to draughts, because they can easily be harmed by these. They do not like being moved round continually. In fact, they need a certain time to adapt to their new location. When a bonsai first arrives in a new place, it begins by producing a few yellow leaves which it then sheds. But after a fortnight it will settle down and get used to its new place. Do not forget that the corners of rooms, even near a window, are dark. Try to place the trees as much as possible in the light. Avoid extremes of temperature: they like a constant temperature. Never leave them near a source of heat which is too strong, for example, on a mantelpiece above an open fire . . . they will soon dry out.

Indoor bonsai can be adapted to suit all kinds of furniture. But if, in addition, you have quite a lot of greenery in the room, make sure that you do not place the bonsai in the middle of the other plants, or they will not stand out. And if you have a plant infested by pests or suffering from blight, the bonsai will be affected.

A display of indoor bonsai. Photograph taken in November.
From left to right, at ground level Serissa (*Serissa japonica*). 6 years old. Podocarps (*Podocarpus macrophyllus Maki*). 7 years old. *On the shelf* Ophiopogon. Bamboo (*Bambusa multiplex*). Fig (*Ficus retusa*). 10 years old.

A selection of bowls

Some of these bowls were chosen by Rémy Samson in Japan and in China; others were created by French potters

Choosing the right spot for your bonsai

Sunshine Outdoor bonsai, which are species which grow in our climate, have the same requirements as trees growing in their natural state: some species prefer to be partially in the shade, others in full sunlight. Indoor bonsai need more or less light according to the species. As the reader will know, all that is required to reduce the amount of light in a room is some ordinary net curtains. In any case, all tender species dislike direct sunlight and you must be careful not to put them too near sources of heat, for example, on a mantelpiece above an open fire.

Ventilation Outdoor bonsai which have become used to the rigours of our climate are better equipped to deal with the ill-effects of the wind; nevertheless, for certain species it is preferable to find a sheltered location, especially in winter, if you want the tree to grow well: this will avoid both the dangers of dehydration and the sudden onslaught of cold caused by gusts of wind. For indoor bonsai, draughts should be rigorously avoided.

Temperature Outdoor bonsai are species which grow naturally in our regions. Nevertheless, some species, more closely related to orange trees, are somewhat delicate, while others are more hardy and are capable of surviving the inclemencies of the weather. The outdoor bonsai are well adapted to the seasonal cycles of our regions. You may be tempted to bring the more delicate trees inside during the winter if they are threatened by frost; these will include certain species of orange tree which are susceptible to cold weather. But whatever you do you must not leave bonsai indoors for more than three days at a time in winter. If you do, the heat of your room will cause the sap to rise. After three days inside, deciduous trees start to bud and leaves appear. Obviously, this artificial spring will be fatal for the tree, because it will exhaust all its reserves and it will not be long before it dies. As a general rule, the greater the difference between the outside and the inside temperature, the more dangerous it is to bring the tree inside.

In summer, too, you should not keep an outdoor bonsai inside the house too long. One week is the maximum, and even then you must spray the tree every day and make sure that it is in the light. If you bring a bonsai indoors, you must not put it in front of an open window or take it out at night. Of course, when it is inside, the tree no longer experiences the temperature fluctuations which occur beween day and night and neither is there any dif-

ference in the degree of moisture in the air: as a result, it will soon start wilting. As far as is possible you must respect the natural daily and seasonal cycles of the tree if you want it to remain healthy.

In winter, however, when the temperature goes below freezing, the roots of the bonsai, protected only by the small amount of soil in the pot, are at risk from frost. For this reason, when the temperature is below −5°C (23°F), the container should be wrapped round with paper, wool or straw, right up to the base of the trunk, or you might add dead leaves to keep the roots warm and protect them from frost. Another thing worth doing is to put the tree in an upright case, which thus acts as a niche, if possible sheltered from the icy winds.

You could also dig a hole in the earth and place the tree and its container in it so that only the base of the trunk and the part above is showing. Another possibility is to bury the tree with its pot. A simpler solution is merely to bring the bonsai into a cold room, even one that is not very bright, during the periods of more extreme cold. But in this case, you must make sure that the earth is damp enough and water it lightly as the need arises, and also spray the plant. For indoor bonsai, the problem is quite different: they can survive high temperatures, but are unhappy if the room gets any colder than 12°C (54°F). In Mediterranean regions, some species may be put outside in the summer, provided that they are sprayed and watered.

Type of pot Pottery is not only something useful, it also has an aesthetic value which merges with the beauty of the tree.

The material By tradition this will be terra cotta or stoneware. But if the sides are to be porous, the inside must not be glazed. On the other hand, glazes may be used on the outside with colours such as whitish beige, chestnut colour, willow green, and in particular cobalt blue, occasionally black.

Colours and motifs The choice of the colour and the motifs depends on the kind of tree that has been selected. Some pots are plain. Chinese pots are often ornamented with painted or sculpted motifs; if you can arrange it so that there is a link between the tree and the motifs the result is all the more attractive; if the opposite occurs, the motifs may destroy the elegance of both tree and pot.

The shape Like all flowerpots, the pot has a hole in the bottom (or several depending on the size). Thus any excess water can drain away. Their shape, of course, must be in harmony with the shape of the tree – and must suit the taste of the owner. Certain species look best in deep containers; the shape may be oval, rectangular or round. Certain styles of trees require certain shapes of pot: a tree whose branches sweep down to the ground should be in a deep pot, generally

The size of the pot in relation to the size of the tree

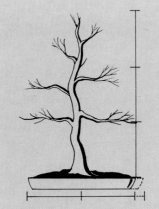

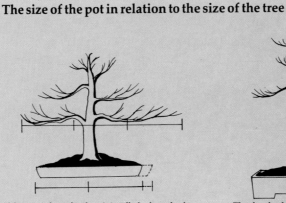

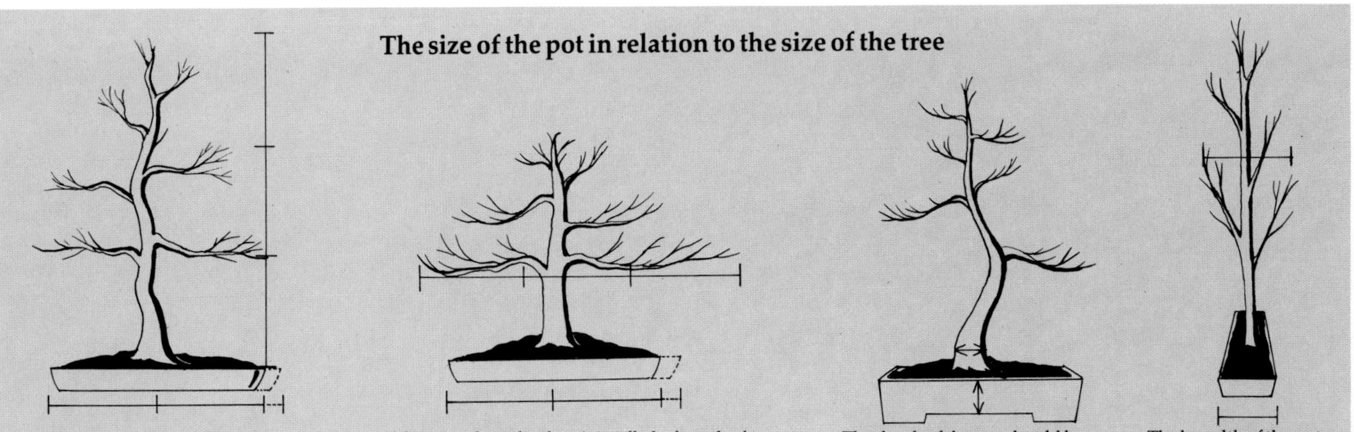

As a general rule, the length of the pot must be slightly more than two-thirds of the height of the tree

If the tree is broader than it is tall, the length of the pot should be slightly more than two-thirds of the breadth of the tree at its widest point. It must never be equal to the breadth or the height of the tree

The depth of the pot should be equal to the diameter of the trunk, except in a case of the cascade style and where there are multiple trunks

The breadth of the pot should be a little less than the breadth of the tree at its widest point

round, square or hexagonal; a plant shaped more like a broom should be in a very flat oval pot; a forest should generally be potted in a container whose breadth is equal to two-thirds of the height of the biggest of the trees. As a general rule, the breadth of the pot should be equal to the average breadth of the branches of the tree; however, it can sometimes be bigger.

Size The pot should show the tree off to its best advantage and be of the same scale. It is necessary that the laws of proportion should be rigorously observed. A container which is too big will not allow the roots to absorb all the moisture in the soil, and this will mean that they are in danger of rotting. But a container which is too small will cause the roots to become stunted, and in addition, the tree will be receiving too little nourishment.

Cleaning If you want to keep your bonsai looking healthy and attractive, you will have to keep them tidy: regularly remove dead leaves, and do the same for the conifer needles which have turned yellow, using a small brush and your fingers, brush the earth, and remove weeds. All these activities should be carried out as part of the routine of tidying the plant. Cut through dead branches with clippers; always spread a healing compound in and around the wound area or the places where the incisions have been made. Sprinkling the leaves is another part of the tidying-up process; this is not just done for appearance, it helps to keep the tree healthy, preventing it being infested with parasites and blight while also airing its leaves and its subsoil. By this means the tree and its foliage are rendered free from dust and pollution.

How to control growth

Growth Bonsai are living trees and, as such, they continue to get bigger (this is why it is necessary to cut them back). Generally, conifers grow more slowly than deciduous trees and, among the latter, some grow more rapidly than others, this is why they must be trimmed to a greater or lesser extent. The rapidity of growth varies from tree to tree and this question will be dealt with, considering each tree individually, in Part 2.

Repotting Naturally, bonsai, a dwarf tree, has only limited growth. Nevertheless, it does increase in size so each time you repot the plant it should be placed in a larger pot*. The best time to do the repotting is in the spring when the plant is beginning to grow new leaves. This should be after a period of:

- from three to five years for conifers;
- from two to three years for deciduous trees;
- from one to two years for fruit trees;
- from two years onwards for indoor bonsai.

How often you repot depends upon the age of the plant: the older a bonsai is the less it needs to be repotted. The time to repot has come when you feel that the roots are forming ridges and attempting to go beyond the span of the branches. As we have already stated, a pot that confines the tree too much will no longer provide it with sufficient nourishment and consequently it will die. When you are repotting you will have a good opportunity to clean up the roots by trimming the rootlets.

Take the tree out of the pot, having made sure that the earth is dry and then allow the soil to crumble by gently shaking the ball of earth; this will make the roots supple again so that they can continue to grow. The next pot you use should be just a little bigger than the old one. You should cover with a plastic netting the hole at the bottom which allows the water to drain out. At the bottom of the new pot scatter some small stones covered with a layer of fairly large lumps of soil, then by a second layer of medium-sized lumps. Prior to this, you should have trimmed anything from one- to two-thirds of the root hairs, using clippers, being careful not to damage the main root or roots. When you put the tree back in its pot you can, if you wish to provide it with support, attach it with a copper wire. In this case, the wire will run from underneath the pot entering by the drainage holes and coming out inside the pot. Now you should fill up the pot with soil whose grains are medium sized, making sure that it goes well down between the roots. Spread fine earth on top, and this should be slightly heaped up to allow the air and the water to circulate. The earth on the surface should go through a very fine sieve and be well watered, but with a very fine spray. The state of the tree will be delicate for about six weeks. Protect it from the sun and from any night frosts which may still occur, by covering it.

Soil Here are some principles concerning the soil mix. For each tree, more precise details will be given in Part 2.

For conifers ⅓ leaf mould, ⅓ loam, ⅓ river sand.

For deciduous trees a mixture of loam and river sand in equal proportions.

For fruit trees and flowering trees a mixture in equal proportions of loam and compost.

For trees requiring leaf mould the proportions should be ½ leaf mould, ¼ compost and ¼ peat.

For indoor bonsai ¼ compost, ¼ leaf mould, ¼ river sand and ¼ loam.

Pruning Pruning consists of cutting back young shoots, leaves and branches. Pruning is an activity which is basic to the art

**The advice to pot on into a larger pot each time is contrary to normal practice in Britain. As a rule, this is only done during the early trimming period and until the desired basic size of the bonsai is reached. Thereafter, the plant is returned to the same container for the rest of its life, each time it is repotted, subject only to some special circumstance intervening.*

of bonsai. It is this which gives the tree its shape and preserves it: pruning is, in fact, an activity which has to be repeated often. Pruning not only serves to strengthen the plant, but also to limit its growth. It allows the sap to flow more freely. There are different kinds of pruning.

Nipping off the buds consists of cutting back the new shoots as they begin to sprout. It is mainly carried out on conifers and on deciduous trees of slow growth.

Stripping the leaves should be carried out in summer if the tree is healthy, every two or three years, but never in the same year that it has been repotted. It is a way of creating artificially a second spring, and the leaves which will be produced in this way will clothe the tree with all the finery and splendour of autumn. Cut all the leaves with a good pair of scissors, and protect the tree from too much wind and sun. It is also possible to cut half the leaves of trees that have big leaves to encourage these leaves to become smaller. Finally, it is possible to cut off some of the leaves on a bonsai whose foliage is too dense, in order to make it possible for the leaves to breathe, and to prevent the middle part of the tree from deteriorating.

Pruning the branches Because sap has a natural tendency to rise, this kind of pruning allows the lower branches to receive a greater quantity of sap. Pruning in this way allows the sap to flow through all the branches and prevents the tree from growing too tall. As a result, you will

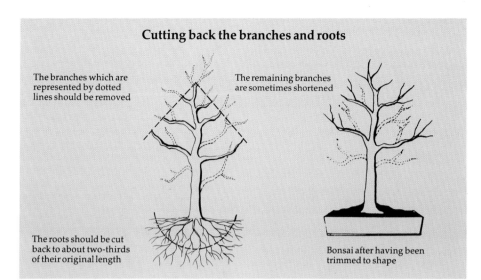

Cutting back the branches and roots

The branches which are represented by dotted lines should be removed

The remaining branches are sometimes shortened

The roots should be cut back to about two-thirds of their original length

Bonsai after having been trimmed to shape

get a fine set of branches. Pruning the branches may be carried out any time between spring and autumn. With a good pair of clippers, you should prune the branches starting at a point above a leaf incept, leaving two or three leaves on each branch.

Structural pruning is the method which allows deciduous trees to achieve a perfect silhouette and prevents them having branches which are too big the next spring. If branches appear which are thought to be undesirable or unattractive in appearance, structural pruning should be carried out in winter on deciduous

trees. This is the season where the structure of the tree becomes clearer with its good and bad points. If a particular branch spoils the general appearance of the tree, cut it back to the level of the trunk, using a good saw, and apply a wound-sealing compound to the stump. On the other hand, if the leaves have not been cut back in summer, you will have to carry out pruning in winter in order to restore its shape to the tree before the wood is too hard. To carry out this pruning, cut the branches which have become too long. It is advisable to buy a deciduous bonsai in winter, for its good and bad points will then be more obvious.

Wiring Wiring consists in winding a copper or brass wire round the trunk and the branches to support the bonsai. Its main aim is to shape the tree. In addition, it slows down growth by making it more difficult for sap to rise. You should wind the trunk and the branches with wire, from the bottom upwards, in the form of a spiral, in the direction of growth. Take care not to wind it too tight; if you do the sap will not be able to flow at all, and the tree would then not receive any nourishment. Make sure that you do not pinch any thorns or leaves between the tree and

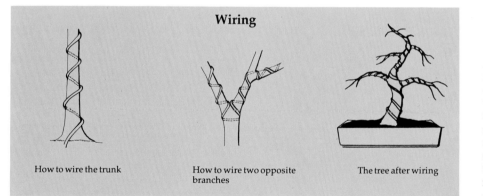

Wiring

How to wire the trunk

How to wire two opposite branches

The tree after wiring

How to create a shape without wiring

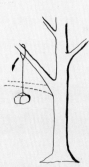

How to shape the growth of a branch by the method of suspension

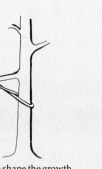

How to shape the growth of a branch by securing it

The branches are secured to the pot or to one another

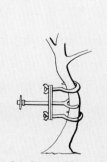

It is also possible to use an implement to twist the trunk

Different types of bracing

the copper wire. Once the wire is wound round the branch, bend it gently so that it goes in the direction you have chosen. To make a bend more firm, you can wedge a piece of wood between the trunk and the branch as a support, or stretch a string between the pot and the branch, taking care that you do not break the branch by tightening the string too much. However, it is necessary for it to be taut and not sagging if it is to do any good.

To increase the curvature of the trunk or the main branches, you could use a clamp, but if you do you should be careful. Protect the bark with some moss or a piece of rag. Place the clamp where you want the curve to be and gently fix it in place by steadily tightening it. Be careful that you do not crack the wood, but at the same time it should be tight enough to be effective. This can be done at the same time as wiring. It is also necessary not to allow the wire to become embedded in the bark. Pull it out with pliers, being careful not to damage the tree. If the bark is damaged, coat it with a wound-sealing compound.

- Conifers should be wired in winter and keep their wire for a period of eight to ten months.
- Deciduous trees are wired in spring and keep their wire from four to six months.
- Fruit trees should be wired in June or July and keep their wire for three to four months.
- Indoor bonsai should be wired when the young shoots have had the benefit of the August sun. Take the wire away after about a month, because the bark is not strong. Start the whole operation again two months later if the shape you are aiming for has not been obtained, because the bark is delicate.

Watering The quantity must be carefully gauged. A bonsai recovers more easily from having too little water than too much. The roots will rot if they have too much water; the sap will not be able to circulate and carry nutrition to each part of the tree. In such cases the leaves dry up and then fall. Before long the tree will die. The quantity of water you give should be gauged according to the climate and the

In the case of heavy rain, tilt the pot to avoid the soil being washed away

volume of the container (the smaller it is the more often you must water the plant). You should take into account the state of health of the tree, for if it is not very healthy it absorbs less water because it has fewer leaves. You should also make allowance for the sun and wind. In the period between watering make sure that the earth is dry but not too dry. If a bonsai has been receiving too little water, first, give it a little amount, wait about half an hour before giving it some more, this time in greater quantity. Never leave a saucer filled with water underneath the pot because this will rot the roots.

In winter you only need water the plant once a day, in the morning, to allow the bonsai to absorb the moisture by nightfall. If you want to get rid of an excess of water, this should be done by tipping the pot. Never water when the weather is frosty. If the tree is receiving rainwater (which is best), make sure that the earth round the roots is not soaked. If that should happen, pour the excess water out by tipping the pot. If you get a frost followed by a thaw, take special care that the earth does not get waterlogged. If, in summer, you must water twice a day, you should not do this in direct sunlight. Never give demineralized water.

You should only water indoor bonsai once or twice a week, according to how hot it is, the brightness of the room and also the size of the pot. The more heat and light there are, the bigger the pot is, the more you will have to water. When you have just trimmed a tree or repotted it, reduce the supply of water. In summer and in winter you should water more frequently than in spring and in autumn.

Spraying Spraying is an essential part of watering. It is absolutely necessary to mist-spray bonsai; (this is spraying with a very fine rose attached to your watering can). This will refresh the tree, provide it with a humid atmosphere and wash away any dust. It is a good idea, while you are mist-spraying the leaves, to water the surrounding parts, for as the water evaporates it will create a humid atmosphere round the tree. Outdoor bonsai should be

The traditional watering can with a long spout and head, and a heavy base, used for important watering purposes

mist-sprayed in summer. How often you do this depends on the region where you live and the climate. Indoor bonsai will not be harmed by daily spraying. These trees are used to a lot of humidity in the air, and spraying restores the level of humidity which is necessary for them. Never spray flowers, for they will fade.

Feeding Fertilizer is nutritious and it also acts as a tonic. It replaces those chemicals which the bonsai has absorbed from the earth. You should use an organic fertilizer which decomposes slowly (bonemeal, dried blood, fishmeal, roast horn), so that the tree is not harmed. The fertilizer may be in the form of powder, pellets or a liquid. Fertilizer in the form of pellets or powder may be kept in place with the help of a little plastic basket which can be turned upside down and inserted in the earth. Liquid mineral fertilizer may be applied in diluted form when you are watering the plant if you think it needs a stimulus. It does not matter whether you give the fertilizer in the form of powder or as pellets. Fertilizer should be given at the beginning of spring and the end of autumn, but not in mid-summer. There are three things that you must not do:

- never give any during the winter;
- never give any to unhealthy trees;
- never give any to trees that have just been repotted.

Since no fertilizer is given in the winter, you should increase the dose given in the autumn. The fertilizer turns moss yellow: you should therefore rub the yellow moss away before applying the fertilizer. The less soil you have, the more frequently you must apply fertilizer. Too much fertilizer is worse than too little. Fertilizer should be applied at the following times:
Conifers from the beginning of April to halfway through October.
Deciduous trees from the beginning of spring (after the buds have opened) to halfway through October.
Fruit trees just before the fruit appears, to halfway through October.
Indoor bonsai very varied treatment according to the individual species: see Part 2.

Fertilizer should be applied as follows:
Powdered fertilizer One or two teaspoons of powder sprinkled on the soil where the bonsai is gowing, once a month for outdoor bonsai, once a fortnight for indoor bonsai.
Fertilizer pellets You should place a solid pellet of fertilizer (two in the case of large pots) on the earth, a fair distance away from the trunk, and allow it to sink in as the plant is watered. Alternatively, the pellets may be placed either in the open air, or in a see-through plastic basket.
Liquid fertilizer It can be diluted in the watering can. Another possibility is to place the bottle of fertilizer in the soil and leave the contents to drip out slowly.

'Jin' practised on almost all of the trunk of a very old juniper. The appearance of dead wood is striking

5 SPECIAL TECHNIQUES

'Jin'

This technique is a means of giving an artificial appearance of age to the large branch of a mature bonsai. Strip back the bark of the bonsai branch, using a knife, then rub it with very fine glasspaper. Trim the end of the branch and apply a product which will clean the wood, bleaching it and protecting it at the same time. By treating the tip of the tree, using this 'Jin' method, the tree will be made to look smaller. The 'Jin' technique also makes it possible to reduce the size of trees.

'Shari'

A technique similar to 'Jin' which can be applied to older bonsai. Simply peel back a single strip of bark and not a whole branch; the strip will be chosen from the trunk or from one of the major branches; you should then continue as for 'Jin'. You should also make sure that the product you are using to clean the wood does not penetrate beneath the bark. These two techniques may only be used with very fine mature trees. Apply the cleaning fluid every two or three years to bleach the branch again and provide it with protection against pests.

Planting on rocks

Bonsai rooted in a rock Choose a stone having the same scale as the tree, which will therefore be small in size. The same piece of rock can quite easily support several trees of different sizes and different species. You will have selected a porous stone which has a number of cavities and the bonsai can be placed firmly in these, once you have chosen which part will be the back and which the front. The tree must be attached to the rock, preferably with a copper wire. Fill the hollow with a suitable mixture of soil, press down firmly on top and keep everything in place by securing it with a silk stocking which should remain on the tree for a year. This should all be done in the spring. Your planting can be completed by adding grass and ferns. Protect it from the wind, from direct sunlight and the cold, just as you would a bonsai which has been re-potted. Once the bonsai have taken root in the rock, you must not try to remove their support. Repotting them is out of the question. But from time to time you will have to renew the surface layer of soil. The plants can dry out quickly, so you must water them using a fine spray. They are particularly susceptible to frost, which is capable of detaching the roots from their support.

Root-over-rock bonsai It is necessary to choose a fine piece of rock to support the tree and keep it in place. Some of the roots will penetrate the rock. You should plant the roots in the soil mixture which is suitable for the species, having first spread out the roots symmetrically round the rock. Keep everything in place with the aid of a stocking wound round the tree which should be slipped right down to the roots. The stocking will keep the soil and the roots tight against the stone. You should apply damp sphagnum moss to the earth and this will keep the roots in a state of freshness which will assist their growth. Protect from the wind and sun, as you would a bonsai which has just been repotted. Wait two months before giving it any fertilizer. Choose a fairly flat container to wedge the rock into and in which you will then bed the roots. The repotting and the soil mixture depend on the species. These plantings should be created in the spring.

Forests

Forests occupy a special place in the affections of enthusiasts. They can be created, using young plants, or trees of different ages, which must always be planted in odd numbers. The style may vary (Formal Upright style, Informal Upright style, Windswept style, those grown on rocks etc). The bonsai will be of the same species. Forests should be planted in the spring. Choose a long flat container and healthy trees, whose roots and branches you will trim. Plant the bigger trees at the back, the medium sized at the side, and the smallest in front, to create perspective. If you want to give a more life-like impression, place a dead tree in the composition, possibly, but not necessarily, treated with the 'Jin' technique.

The longest branches should be turned outwards; be careful that the trees do not get in each other's light. The spacing between the trees should vary. To create the illusion of unplanned growth, the distance between the trees can vary. It is very important to place the main tree first. It may be attached to the container with wire, just like the others. The roots of each tree should be wrapped round with a ball of moist earth. When all the trees are in place, heap up the soil mixture. As you are gently building up this mass of earth, you must be careful to leave sufficient space for the air and the water to circulate. Water well. Treat your forest as if it were a newly potted bonsai.

Chinese juniper (*Juniperus sinensis*) about seventy years old, style 'sekijoju'. Here you can see the roots gripping the rock, and 'pouring down' like a waterfall to spread out in a harmonious way over the ground

6 PESTS AND DISEASES

Bonsai may fall victim to the same pests and diseases that attack normal trees. To prevent or arrest such attacks, the trees must be checked at regular intervals. Hygiene is very important. Use only clean tools and containers. Wounds should always be well sealed with wound-sealing compound or tar. When looking after your trees (repotting, pruning, wiring), beware of damaging them.

Pests and diseases can attack the roots, the trunk, the branches or the leaves. The attack must therefore be localized. Certain pests, such as scale insects, aphids and spider mites, reappear regularly. Diseases are very uncommon, owing to the fact that the roots, branches and leaves are frequently pruned. Ants are not pests. They indicate the presence of aphids. The latter excrete a sticky substance called honeydew which attracts the ants. However, it is best to get rid of ants by rinsing the soil. Earthworms are not harmful but it is best to remove them, as they make tunnels in the soil; fungicides and pesticides are available on the market. Some are multi-purpose, others are formulated to treat a particular condition only. Before buying a product, make sure that you know exactly what pest or disease you have got to deal with.

Before treating a sick tree, you must give it plenty of water, either the preceding day or else several hours beforehand. If the bonsai is thirsty, the fungicides or insecticides will have no effect. It is advisable to protect the soil with plastic when spraying with chemicals or sprinkling with a solution. The products used are often harmful to humans. You are therefore advised to wash your hands, and do not let the leaves get near your face.

We will see which pests and diseases can attack each kind of tree and how to treat them. If you have any doubts about diagnosis or treatment, do not hesitate to seek expert advice.

If you care for a bonsai properly, by recreating the conditions of its natural habitat, there is no reason why it should fall victim to disease. If the leaves turn yellow, then wither and drop, before focusing on pests and diseases, you should first check to see whether the tree is being properly cared for. Giving the plant too much water often causes the leaves to turn yellow, wither and drop: the roots stagnate in the water and rot, the sap no longer circulates and the tree dies through lack of nourishment. Lack of light causes etiolation: the tree loses its compact shape and grows long stems with small pale leaves. Too much strong or direct sunshine burns the leaves. The amount of light the tree receives must be carefully controlled; likewise the amount of sunshine, which provides warmth, reduces growth and helps the sap to circulate properly. There must be a correct balance between the amount of water given to the soil and the amount lost through transpiration. So, before focusing your attention on pests and diseases, it is important to check that the tree is being properly cared for. We will now take a look at the most common pests and diseases and how to treat them to keep your bonsai healthy.

Pests

WEB-FORMING TETRANYCHUS OR GLASSHOUSE RED SPIDER MITE

Symptoms Glasshouse red spider mites

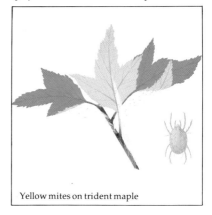

Yellow mites on trident maple

are found on the underside of the leaves and pierce the foliage. The leaves usually develop a yellow mottled appearance. It may turn silver-grey if the attack is severe. There is a danger that the tree may wither. The mites weave webs to protect themselves (hence the name).
Treatment The foliage should be well sprayed, particularly the underside. As soon as the first symptoms appear use specific acaricides. Use a variety of products so that the mites do not develop tolerance to any chemical. If necessary, carry out preventive treatment at the beginning of spring.

RED SPIDER MITE

Symptoms **Conifers** The needles become discoloured. They turn yellow, reddish-

Red mites on the bougainvillea

brown, then brown and eventually drop. A matted webbing is produced between the branches, which hinders photosynthesis. Eggs are laid at the base of the needles and in cracks in the bark.
Deciduous trees Eggs hibernate on the branches and red patches may develop on the bark. In spring, holes appear in the leaves. The mites are found mainly on the underside of the leaves, where small discoloured blotches may appear. The leaves turn silver-grey and later, if the attack is severe, brown. They eventually drop. The spiders weaken the tree by sucking at the sap.
Treatment When the air is warm and dry you should leave the conifers well alone. Cut away and destroy the infested branches. At the end of winter, the new growth appears, spray with tar oil (handle with caution) to destroy the eggs. In spring, spray with systemic acaricides. In summer, if necessary, use specific acaricides. In some cases, treatment should be applied with caution or else damage may be done to the host plant. Remember that the mites thrive in hot, dry conditions but do not like humidity. It is therefore important to mist the foliage thoroughly. In summer, the tree should be generously watered.

CATERPILLARS

Caterpillars are butterfly or moth larvae. They weaken a tree by feeding on the tissue. They may sometimes cause fatal damage. They can be divided into several groups.

Bombycoid moths

Symptoms Silken threads are produced between the needles or the leaves. A spongy looking nest appears in the foli-

age, which is why these creatures are known as 'spongy caterpillars'. They eat away at the needles or leaves.
Treatment As soon as symptoms appear, spray with contact insecticides.

Goat moth, Leopard moth

Symptoms Nocturnal moths which eat away at the bark of the trunk and branches, perforating it and then tunnelling upwards. A small heap of sawdust accumulates at the mouth of the tunnel. The caterpillars are red or yellow.
Treatment Cut away the infested parts of the tree. Insert a length of iron wire into the tunnels. This can be wrapped round with cottonwool soaked in carbon disulphide. Block up the hole with wood-sealing compound.

Leaf-rollers

Symptoms Leaf-rollers nibble away at young shoots, flowers, buds and leaves. Silken threads wrap around the leaves and roll them into a cigar shape. The damage is done at night. The caterpillars can sometimes be seen.
Treatment In spring, spray with parathion-based insecticides.

Leaf miners

Symptoms Tunnels in the leaf tissue, holes in the leaves. The cavities are surrounded by black specks. Photosynthesis is reduced.
Treatment Spray with organophosphate insecticides.

Leafroller on lilac leaves

Geometer moths

Symptoms The caterpillars eat away at the foliage and there are holes in the buds. Silken threads are produced between the foliage and the soil, allowing the caterpillars to climb down.
Treatment At the end of winter, treat with oil-based products to destroy the eggs. In spring, use lindane or parathion-based synthetic insecticides.

Small ermine moths

Symptoms Webs wrap around the foliage. Silken threads are produced between the leaves. A cocoon can be seen on the tree. The leaves fall off. The caterpillars can sometimes be seen on the underside of the leaves.

Treatment Cut away the infested branches. Before the damage becomes really serious, use tar oil. Halfway through spring, when the caterpillars shed their skins, use organophosphate contact insecticides.

There are other kinds of caterpillars which cause damage to bonsai but they are uncommon. We will discuss them in Part 2 for the species concerned.

SCALE INSECTS, HARD SHELLED AND SOFT

Hard-shelled scale insects are sedentary insects which colonize the leaves, the fruit and the branches. They are protected by grey-brown or dark-brown waxy shells, which measure about 3 mm (1/8 in). Soft scale insects are protected by a shell which forms part of the insect. They are round and convex in shape.
Symptoms Clusters of waxy shells appear on the leaves, the trunk and the branches. Inside each shell is a scale insect. They excrete honeydew, which damages the leaf blade and often breeds the black fungus known as sooty mould. The trunk becomes distorted, the branches die and the leaves (or needles) turn yellow and drop. The tree withers, photosynthesis is reduced.
Treatment Clean the stem and leaves with a sponge soaked in water and alcohol. Cut away and destroy the infested branches. Encourage ladybirds to feed on the scale insects. At the end of winter and beginning of spring destroy the insects with petroleum-based oils and organophosphate insecticides. At the end of spring and beginning of summer spray with organophosphate insecticides to destroy active larvae. However, scale insects are not easy to get rid of, as they are protected by their shells. Be careful not to damage the leaves. Isolate the infested tree so that other bonsai or other plants are not affected. Beware when treating fragile varieties: treatment applied in too large doses could be fatal.

MEALY-BUGS

Symptoms These insects excrete honeydew, which breeds sooty mould. Photosynthesis is reduced and growth slows down. The bugs are active and look like white blobs of cottonwool. The leaves turn yellow and drop.

Beetles on a quince tree

Treatment As soon as the first symptoms appear, spray with organophosphate insecticides.

APHIDS

Greenfly, blackfly, gall aphid

Symptoms Eggs hibernate on the bark. In April, larvae appear on the tips of the shoots. The aphids, visible to the naked eye, colonize the tender young shoots and suck at the sap. If conifers are affected, the needles shrivel: they become distorted and silver blotches appear on them. They wither and eventually drop. The aphids excrete honeydew, which leads to the growth of sooty mould. Growth slows down and cankers appear. If the tree is infested with gall aphids, galls develop on the shoots. The blackfly is a carrier of virus diseases.
Treatment When watering the tree, aim a strong jet of water at the foliage to wash the aphids away. Use insecticides derived from plants (that work either through direct contact or by being ingested or inhaled), organochlorine insecticides (that also work through direct contact or through being ingested or inhaled), organophosphate insecticides (that work through direct contact or being ingested) or systemic organophosphate insecticides. To destroy eggs laid in winter by greenfly, which are attached to the bark of outdoor trees, carry out preventive treatment (tar oil) at the end of winter before the leaves appear. Wet the trunk and branches, then spray thoroughly. While the tree is in leaf, as soon as aphids appear on the shoots spray all areas with insecticide, whether they are infested or not. Repeat ten days later. Spray again if necessary. If the tree is infested with gall aphids, spray at the end of winter with mineral-based tar oils. At the beginning of spring, use organochlorine or organophosphate insecticides.

Mealy bugs on white poplar

WOOLLY APHIDS

Symptoms Woolly aphids attack the woody parts of the tree, both above and below ground. They pierce the surface and this leads to the formation of galls. Fungus may develop. Growth slows down.
Treatment Remove the galls and disinfect the wounds with a copper-based solution. In winter, spray with tar oil. When new

growth appears, spray yet again with another variant of tar oil. When the buds begin to open, use oleoparathion. While the tree is in leaf, spray with insecticides.

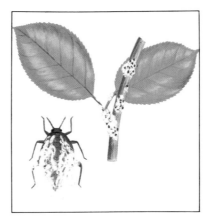

Greenfly on beech

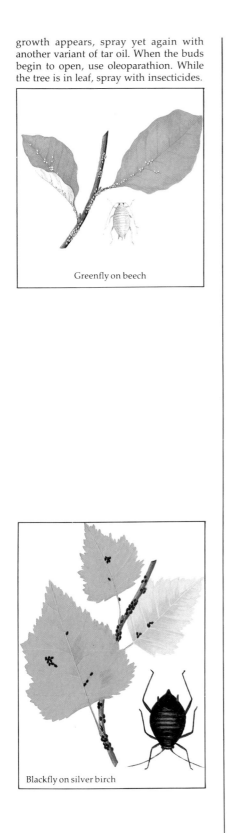

Blackfly on silver birch

BARK BEETLES

These are cylindrical beetles, black or brown, and from 1 to 5 mm long ($\frac{1}{32}$-$\frac{3}{16}$ in). They live in the wood or under the bark of trees, where they have tunnels. They do a great deal of damage. Conifers are the main victims.

Symptoms The eggs are sheltered in longitudinal tunnels between the bark and the sap wood. The larvae extend the tunnels at right-angles to the parent gallery. Fungus develops in the tunnels. There are holes in the bark, made by adults emerging. The bark may fall off. Sap circulation is disrupted, branches die. These insects are carriers of Dutch Elm disease.

Treatment Remove and destroy the affected branches. Enrich the soil with phosphorus and potassium. Halfway through April spray the trunk and branches with parathion and lindane-based insecticides to destroy the adults on the bark and, if necessary, spray again in July. To destroy the larvae, spray at the end of winter with just a thin film of oleoparathion.

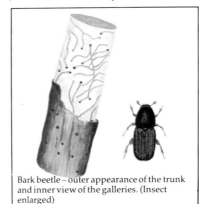

Bark beetle – outer appearance of the trunk and inner view of the galleries. (Insect enlarged)

EELWORMS OR NEMATODES

These are worms which inhibit growth by attacking the roots.

Cyst eelworms cause rot and over-development of rootlets.

Root-knot eelworms pierce the roots and cause strings of galls to develop. The galls protect the worms and distort the roots.

Ectoparasitic eelworms arrest growth. There is a gradual yellowing of the foliage, from the base of the tree to the top. These eelworms may be carriers of viral diseases.

Root-lesion eelworms build nests which cause canker in the roots, thereby destroying them. The foliage turns yellow. Fungus may develop.

Treatment Remove yellow leaves. Mix nematicides into the soil. Wet the tree and then spray with parathion-based washes. Eelworms spread in damp soil with a temperature of between 16 and 20°C (61-68°F). Make sure the soil is not too wet.

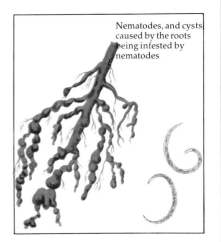

Nematodes, and cysts caused by the roots being infested by nematodes

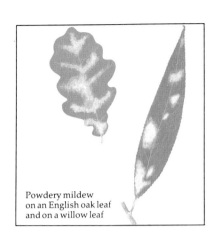

Powdery mildew on an English oak leaf and on a willow leaf

POWDERY MILDEW

A fungal disease.

Symptoms Whitish, powdery patches (mycelium) appear on the upper parts of the tree (leaves, stem, flower buds). The patches grow larger and the powder thickens. The leaf blades become distorted. Small black granules may appear on the leaves, which wither. The tree weakens. The fungus thrives in warm, dry conditions.

Treatment Cut away and burn affected branches. Remove dead leaves. Spray with mineral or synthetic fungicides. If the tree had mildew the year before, preventive treatment must be carried out in spring, before the buds open. Sulphur is particularly useful for this purpose.

Root rot on maple tree; close-up of roots

ROOT ROT (HONEY FUNGUS)

A serious condition caused by fungal mycelium. It can develop if the tree is wounded during pruning or if it is pierced by insects.

Symptoms The roots turn brown and wither. White patches (mycelium) and black threads (rhizomorphs) can be seen under the bark. Shoots are stunted, the leaves (or needles) drop, the branches die and the tree withers. In the autumn, yellow-capped fungi with brown scales and white gills appear at the base. Patches spread over the tree.

Treatment As soon as the first symptoms appear, treat with fungicide. However, this disease is hard to eradicate and the tree may die.

Root rot on a cypress

ROTTING OF ROOTS AND LEAVES

Symptoms Rot and canker develop on the roots and collar of the tree. As a result, the root system may be reduced in size. The rot is brown and spongy. The foliage changes colour, becoming brown and dry. Conifer needles drop. The tree may then wither very quickly.

Treatment Do not let the pot stand in water. Avoid damaging the collar of the tree. If necessary disinfect the soil. Use maneb-based or systemic fungicide.

Brown rot on pine and on magnolia leaves

RUSTS

A fungal disease.

Symptoms Branches: in May long yellow patches appear on the bark of young shoots. Blisters develop and then burst, releasing an orange substance. Resin flows from the wounds. The branch grows in an S shape. The shoot may wither and growth is thereby disrupted.

Leaves: these become covered with yellow or brown patches and then wither.

Conifer needles: red patches develop on the needles. In the second year, in April or May, white vesicles on the needles burst open, releasing an orange powder, and then heal. In the third year new vesicles develop and the needles eventually drop.

Treatment Cut away and burn affected parts and clean the wounds. Spray with special antirust fungicide. This may be repeated 10 to 15 days later. Beware of applying treatment in too large doses: it may damage the tree.

LEAF SPOTS

Symptoms Spots appear on the leaves. They may be white, then brown, and triangular in shape. They may also be grey, with black circles developing on the lesions. Parts of the foliage wither and granules appear in the middle.

Treatment Remove and destroy diseased leaves. Spray with copper-based fungicides. Do not moisten the foliage too much. Avoid misting and watering in direct sunlight.

VERTICILLIOSIS

This disease is caused by a fungus which

Whorls on lime leaves

penetrates damaged areas and attacks the roots and collar of the tree.

Symptoms Leaves sag at the base of the tree. They turn yellow and shrivel up. The tree weakens. The sap cannot feed the upper parts of the tree adequately.

Treatment Avoid using too much nitrogenous fertilizer. Remove weeds. Attend carefully to any damaged parts of the tree. Destroy dead leaves. Disinfect the soil and spray the trunk and neck of the tree with mineral-based fungicides.

7 TOOLS

There is a specific tool for each activity. Nevertheless, it is not absolutely necessary to have one of each unless you are growing several species of tree and you are carrying out all the jobs yourself. Otherwise a good pair of narrow clippers will be quite sufficient for pruning branches, leaves or roots without harming the tree. You must also have some healing compound, to heal any cuts or abrasions that the tree has suffered. You must always clean the tools after you have used them, if possible with alcohol, and then you should put them away tidily. In this way you will prevent the spread of parasites and disease. In addition, this will stop them rusting and so harming the trees.

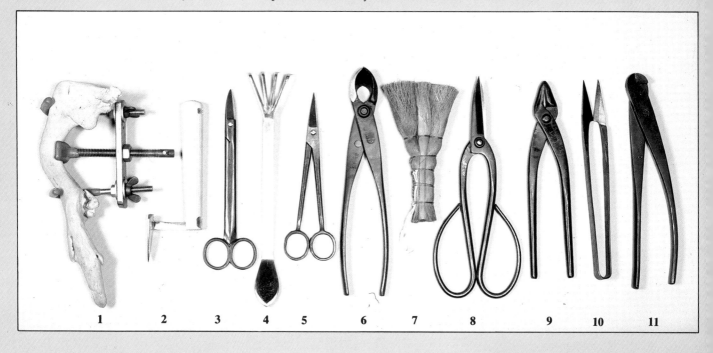

1   2   3   4   5   6   7   8   9   10   11

12   13

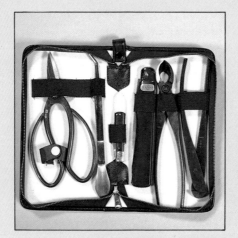

The tools which are necessary are the following:

1 A clamp to direct the growth of trunks and branches.

2 A trowel for repotting.

3 or 5 A pair of very fine clippers to prune young shoots.

4 A 'rake' to turn over the topsoil (surfacing) and moss, and to disentangle the roots when they are being repotted.

6 A pair of secateurs to cut back the large roots or the main branches.

7 A broom to sweep up conifer needles and dead leaves.

8 A pair of clippers to trim branches and roots.

9 Pliers to attach or remove wire.

10 Leaf clippers.

11 A pair of pliers to cut wire.

12 A sprayer.

13 A sieve to sieve soil.

and also:
a pair of pincers to remove dead leaves and parasites,
a saw to cut off large branches when carrying out large-scale winter pruning,
wooden clippers to level out a cut and to round it off,
tools to create 'jin' or 'shari' on trees,
copper or brass wire to wire the bonsai,
a turntable for when you work at your bonsai (it could have drawers to store tools in),
a watering can with a long spout and a rose,
plastic netting to close the drainage holes.

Part 2

A SELECTION OF TREES SUITABLE FOR TRAINING AS BONSAI

Showing indoor bonsai (b.i.) and outdoor bonsai (b.e.). *From left to right upper row:* fig *(Ficus retusa)* b.i. about 8 years old – style 'Ngi Kasi'; temple juniper *(Juniperus rigida)* b.e. about 2 years old – style 'Kengai'; serissa *(Serissa japonica variegata)* b.i. about 25 years old – style 'Hokidachi'; *from left to right lower row:* aleppo pine *(Pinus halepensis)* b.i. about 7 years old – style 'Tachiki'; trident maple *(Acer buergerianum)* b.e. about 3 to 5 years old – style 'Cohon-Jose'.

OUTDOOR BONSAI: CONIFERS

Cedrus
CEDAR

The Pinaceae family. The cedar is a large conifer that can grow to over 50 m (165 ft). The needles are evergreen. The short side branches bear needles that grow in bunches. The egg-shaped cones have a smooth surface, with wide but thin scales that fit tightly over one another. In spring the sharp needles growing on the young shoots are single. The cones produce seed in winter.

Cedrus libani (cedar of Lebanon). Now found mainly in Syria and Turkey. Spreading, horizontal branches, silvery grey or dark-green needles, a thick, scented trunk with dark-grey bark that is scored by close-set cracks.
Cedrus atlantica (Atlantic cedar). Native to the Atlas Mountains. A pyramid-shaped top, and branches that often hang down, either long ones with single needles or short ones with bunches of needles.
Cedrus deodora (Deodar). Native to the western Himalayas. A pyramid-shaped outline, hanging branches, sparse, light-coloured, glaucous foliage, needles more pointed, trunk lighter.
Cedrus brevifolia (Cyprus cedar). Native to Cyprus. Medium sized with small dark-green needles with silvery grey highlights.

Propagation

From seed The seed is gathered in winter from the cones when the lower scales lift, and it is soaked in water for 48 hours to soften it. Then plant in a mixture of peat and clay. Until it is planted it should be kept in the cone. It can also be planted in May when it will germinate more readily. When the seed has germinated, pot up saplings a year later. To get a straight trunk, you can immediately stake the one-year-old sapling.

By layering Layer a low branch. Strip the part to be buried of needles. Make a shallow cut into the bark to encourage rooting. Bury and keep the earth damp. Simple layering is carried out in spring. When roots have sprouted, the layer has taken. Then separate the branch and pot it up. Protect from extremes of weather as you would a bonsai that has just been repotted.

From cuttings Cuttings are taken either in late spring or in autumn; if in autumn, in a greenhouse from short hardwood cuttings. In a warm place, roots will form in winter. Then transplant the following spring into a small pot with a mixture of peat and clay.

By grafting Veneer grafting is practised from September to October.

From young nursery stock

Care

Exposure to sunlight Full sun throughout the year, but protect young specimens from extremes.

Temperature The cedar is very sensitive to extreme cold and can die when there is frost. It is therefore vital to protect it directly it becomes very cold, especially round the container and roots. It adapts perfectly to the climate of the Loire and south-western France as it loves heat.

Ventilation It tolerates wind, but not draughts. Protect young specimens and trees that have just been repotted from strong winds.

Container A medium-deep pot is suitable for a young tree as it is slow growing. A mature tree needs a wide, deep container. It is preferable to use either an unglazed pot, or a glazed brown, brick, or neutral-coloured pot.

Cleaning In autumn pick off any yellow needles. Make sure to prune and remove any dead or damaged material from inside the tree to ensure that it develops well. Clean any dead leaves or twigs away from the soil.

Growth Like most conifers, the cedar is very slow-growing. Its majestic habit develops with age.

Repotting In spring, between March and April, every three to five years. Prune the roots by between a third and a half. Keep a bit of the old soil when you repot. Cedars are hard to re-establish if their roots are uncovered when they are transplanted.

Soil 1/3 leaf mould, 1/3 loam and 1/3 coarse sand. The cedar tolerates a calcareous soil, except for the *C. deodora*. It will thrive in any soil provided it is not too wet, but is happiest in permeable, sandy clay.

Pruning Annually in spring and autumn. *Pinching back* During the spring use the

STYLES

Chokkan

Sekijôju

Sabamiki

Sôkan

Kabudachi

Deodar (*Cedrus deodora glauca*). 15 years old. Height, 40 cm (1 ft 4 in). 'Semi-cascade' style. Photograph taken in May-June.

fingers to pinch back new shoots hard. Do not cut the needles. During the summer remove new shoots.

Leaf pruning The needles of conifers are never cut. Remove a third of the foliage.

Pruning of branches In autumn take off the tips of branches that have grown a lot. In spring prune branches which tend to spread by cutting just above a tuft of needles.

Wiring Cedars have to be wired if you want to train them into a certain outline. This may be already set by pinching back and pruning. Put the wire in position in autumn and remove the copper wires 10 to 12 months later. If the wire has grown into the bark, do not pull it out; carefully remove bits that are accessible using pliers. Repeat this process annually until you have achieved the desired shape. Do not get needles trapped between the wire and the bark.

Watering Copious in spring and summer. Let the cedar have time to absorb all the moisture from the soil before watering again. It does not like wet ground. Water less frequently in autumn. In winter, place the pot at an angle if there is a lot of rain falling on it.

Spraying In summer spray the foliage thoroughly. The cedar likes humidity round its needles. Spraying allows you to clean the trunk and needles of dust and pollution, though it is relatively unaffected by pollution.

Feeding Feed once a month in spring and autumn with an organic fertilizer. Increase the amount given in autumn to set the cedar up for the winter. Do not feed a cedar that has just been repotted for two months, and do not feed one that is in poor condition.

Pests and diseases

Pests
- **Bark beetles** See p. 30.
- **Pine caterpillars**

Symptoms A silky nest attached to the needles in winter. Needles eaten. Defoliation. Branches distorted.

Treatment Remove the nests. Destroy the infested branches. Squirt petroleum oil into the nests. Apply a larvicide in September. May provoke nettlerash.

Diseases
- **Honey fungus** (*Armillaria mellea*) See p. 31.

Sôju

Sambon-Yose

Gohon-Yose

Nanahon-Yose

Kyûhon-Yose

Chamaecyparis
FALSE CYPRESS

The Cupressaceae family. Native to North America, Japan and Taiwan and introduced into Europe more than 100 years ago. The *Chamaecyparis* can live for about 350 years, and in the wild they can grow to a height of 60 m (200 ft), but cultivated specimens are seldom more than 20 to 30 m (65 to 100 ft) in height. Their fan-like branches are flattened, and the leader is curved. They produce small globular cones with a terminal point at the centre. The best-known species in bonsai is *Chamaecyparis obtusa*, the Hinoki cypress. The wood is white and solid, the bark thick and split. The flattened branches are shiny and the bright-green foliage has white lines running along the underside. It is conical in outline and can grow to 35 m (115 ft). Its brown cones are no bigger than a pea.

Propagation

From seed The best method of propagation. In autumn collect the seeds from the cones. To do this, put the cones in a warm place. Stratify the seeds and sow in spring. Plant in a peat-sand mixture, but first soak the seeds in lukewarm water and if necessary make a slit in the outer seed case. Keep in the shade. It takes a long time for the seeds to sprout: sometimes you have to wait a year. As soon as shoots appear, pot the seedlings individually and protect from a drying wind and direct sunlight.

From cuttings Take a cutting from young wood in July or August. Keep in a cool place. Plant the rooted cutting the following spring in a small pot and keep in a shaded place. For best results use lateral shoots. Prune from the first year of cultivating to produce a denser tree. Cuttings taken from the *Chamaecyparis obtusa* are usually successful and produce fine bonsai specimens..

By simple layering In August, using a young *Chamaecyparis*. Strip a low branch of its needles, bury it and hold it in the earth with a hook, first making several shallow cuts to encourage rooting. Leave the tip of the branch sticking out of the ground, with its needles left on it. It should be possible to sever the branch by September if the soil is friable and moist. If necessary add leaf mould to the earth to ensure that it is friable.

By grafting In summer, veneer grafting is used. It is vital that the roots should not dry out during the process. Bind well. Make the graft at a slight slant and be quite sure that the scion is turned towards the light. It is best to use a frame for the graft. Keep the surrounding atmosphere moist. Keep in semishade and spray if it is very hot. As soon as the graft has taken, new shoots will appear.

From young nursery stock Select a tree with an interesting trunk and a lot of branches.

Care

Exposure to sunlight False cypresses prefer slightly shaded sites. They do not like full sun, especially in summer as they quickly become parched.

Temperature The *Chamaecyparis lawsoniana* withstands cold very well. The *Chamaecyparis obtusa* is also resistant to cold. They like a maritime climate.

Ventilation Unhappy in drying winds, but not in humid wind.

Container Choose a deep bowl which can be round, oval, hexagonal or rectangular depending on the style in which the tree is trained. Good drainage is essential.

Cleaning Remove yellow needles in autumn and any dead or damaged foliage or wood. Keep the soil clean to prevent pests and diseases.

STYLES

Chokkan

Sekijōju

Sōkan

Kabudachi

Ikadabuki

Netsunagari

Sōju

Growth False cypresses become majestic as they grow older. They grow slowly and steadily if conditions are right for them.

Repotting Every three to five years between March and April prune between a third and a half off the root hairs, and repot in a deep, well-drained container.

Soil ⅓ leaf mould, ⅓ loam and ⅓ coarse sand. False cypresses like cool, light, calcareous ground open to warmth, and are not fussy about the soil type, provided it is deep.

Pruning Pinch out shoot tips during the growing season. Repeat two or three times. Do not cut the needles. Prune side branches that are becoming over-developed by removing a tuft. They can be pruned with the fingers. If you have to cut a larger branch, use clippers and cut at an axil so that the cut cannot be seen. Remove a third of the foliage.

Wiring Wiring is used to shape the *Chamaecyparis* into the desired style. Put the wire in place at the end of autumn. Do not leave it on the tree for more than 10 months. Do not get needles caught between the bark and the wire. Rewire every year to achieve the shape you are aiming for. If the wire is grown over in some places, leave it there, but remove the pieces of wire you can get at gently with tweezers.

Watering Take care that the roots do not dry out. Keep the earth slightly moist, but never soak it. Water well in summer and check that excess water escapes through drainage holes. Stagnant water rots the roots and the tree will die. Never water during frost.

Spraying The *Chamaecyparis* needs a humid atmosphere. Spray often in summer, making sure both foliage and bark are mist-sprayed. If it is exposed to the wind, spray even in autumn or spring. The needles will be all the greener, denser and shinier.

Feeding If the bonsai is in good condition, feed in spring and autumn. Increase the amount of fertilizer given at the end of autumn to set the tree up for winter. Feed once a month with slow-acting organic fertilizer. Leave for two months after repotting.

Hinoki cypress *(Chamaecyparis obtusa)*. 12-15 years old. Height, 50 cm (1 ft 8 in). 'Yose-Ue' style. Photograph taken in May.

Pests and diseases

Pests
- **Red spider mites** See p. 28.
- **Eelworms** See p. 30.
- **Hard-shelled scale insects** See p. 29.

Diseases
- **Verticillium wilt** See p. 31.
- **Coryneum cardinale**
Symptoms Needles turn red. Presence of black pustules on the bark with resin running from them.
Treatment Guard against wounding the tree. Disinfect the sores using wound-sealing compound. Cut out affected branches. Enrich the soil with potash. Apply a systemic fungicide. As a precaution spray with a mineral fungicide after the spring rains and in autumn.
- **Root and stem rot** See p. 31.

Sambon-Yose

Gohon-Yose

Nanahon-Yose

Kyûhon-Yose

Yose-Ue

Yamayori

Tsukami-Yose

Cryptomeria japonica
CRYPTOMERIA
or
JAPANESE CEDAR

The Taxodiaceae family. Native to China and Japan. The *Cryptomeria japonica* is the only species in its genus, but there are several cultivars.

In Asia cryptomerias can grow to a height of 60 m (200 ft), but are seldom above 25 m (80 ft) in Europe. They are conical in outline with a straight trunk, brick-coloured bark that peels off in narrow strips and hard wood. The tapering, evergreen needles are pointed and bright greeny blue, going russet coloured in winter; they lie against the twigs. Needles tend to fall off readily in dry areas.

In autumn the cryptomeria produces globular, slightly prickly, scaly cones.

Propagation

From seed Seeds are planted as soon as they have been gathered in a peat-sand mixture, under glass. They do not germinate reliably. It is better to propagate by a different method.

By layering Select a low, flexible branch. Strip the part to be buried of its needles, and make two or three cuts into the branch to encourage rooting. Bury the branch, leaving the tip protruding with its needles still on. Keep the soil moist. When you see new growth, the roots have formed. In spring, put a mixture of peat and sand in a growing pot. The cultivar 'Elegans' grows best.

From grafting In March – in a greenhouse if possible. This is more a method for professionals.

From young nursery stock Select a tree with an interesting trunk and a lot of branches.

Care

Exposure to sunlight Put the cryptomeria in a slightly shaded position. It is not happy in full sun in summer.

Temperature The cryptomeria needs heat. The needles turn brown in winter, but revert to their green colour in spring if the tree is protected from the winter cold and frosts. It can be affected by late frost in spring.

Ventilation The cryptomeria needs a humid atmosphere and a change of air, but should be shielded from strong winds (especially young or recently repotted specimens).

Container The cryptomeria grows best in deep, cool, well-drained soil. Select a simple, deep bowl, neutral, brown or willow green in colour, and ensure that drainage is good.

Cleaning In dry areas, the cryptomeria loses more needles. Pick withered needles off the tree and soil. Cut out dead wood. Keep the inside of the tree clean to guard against any problems.

Growth The old needles fall after four or five years, and this is how the branches are formed. The cryptomeria is slow growing, but in the growing season puts out a lot of new shoots.

Repotting Every three to five years repot in the spring when growth is under way (April). You should not repot too early in the spring.

Soil Mixture consisting of ⅓ leaf mould, ⅓ loam and ⅓ coarse sand. Cool, rich, deep, well-drained soil.

Pruning Regularly pinch out new growth from the needles from spring to mid-autumn (until the end of September). Remove shoots coming from the trunk or main branches. With the cryptomeria, pinching back is a long, painstaking task,

Cryptomeria – how to pinch out needles.

STYLES

Chokkan

Sekijóju

Sókan

Kabudachi

Ikadabuki

Netsunagari

but it is essential to keep the foliage compact. If it is carried out properly, it will not be necessary to prune the side branches. Prune out any side branches that have lost too many of their needles and any branches growing in the wrong place in spring exactly at a fork so that the cut cannot be seen.

Wiring Use string to tie up any branches tending to grow away from the trunk (which would spoil its compact appearance). Wire the tree to train it from the end of spring to summer. Do not carry out any work on it in winter.

Watering You can water frequently from spring to autumn; water less in winter. Do not water if there is a frost. Water should never stagnate, so always make sure before you water that the roots have absorbed all the water from the bottom of the pot. Cryptomerias are very thirsty.

Spraying Cryptomerias do not stand up well to dry conditions. Their needles fall early. They like areas with high humidity (Brittany, Limousin, the Pyrenees . . .). In a dry region the foliage should be sprayed often.

Feeding Feed healthy cryptomerias with slow-acting organic fertilizer from spring to autumn with a break in July and August. Wait for two months after repotting before feeding. Increase the last amount of fertilizer given in the autumn slightly to set the tree up for the winter.

Pests and diseases

Pests
- **Red spider mites** See p. 28.
- **Scale insects** See p. 29.

Diseases
- **Die-back**
Symptoms The branches wither and turn brown. The needles drop off.
NB. Weak trees kept in poor conditions are especially vulnerable.
Treatment Cut out diseased branches. Spray with copper-based fungicide.

Cryptomeria (*Cryptomeria japonica*). 30 years old. Height, 45 cm (1 ft 6 in). 'Chokkan' style. Photograph taken in May. You can see the tender young shoots which should be pinched back.

Sôju

Sambon-Yose

Gohon-Yose

Nanahon-Yose

Kyûhon-Yose

Yose-Ue

Bonkei

Kusamono

Ginkgo biloba
MAIDENHAIR TREE

which can grow to a height of 30 m (100 ft), and must be native to Japan; it was planted near Buddhist temples. Its outline is pyramid shaped. The straight, ash-grey trunk has cracks running down the bark. The branches are spreading and horizontal. The top of a male tree is conical while female trees have a wider crown with more deeply incised leaves, which turn yellow a month later than leaves on the male tree. The light-green leaves turn golden yellow in autumn, giving rise to the name 'tree of the forty gold crowns'. A dioecious species. The ginkgo was for a long time classified as a conifer, but is now recognized as a separate though closely allied genus. Its leaves are deciduous. The lamina has a long leaf stalk, and is shaped like a rounded fan, sometimes with a central indentation dividing it into two lobes (*biloba*). The leaves grow in bunches on short side branches. The inflorescences are male. The fruit is like a yellow plum, and is poisonous and foul smelling. When it is old, the ginkgo may grow aerial roots like stalactites.

The Ginkgoaceae family. The name should be spelt Ginkyo, which is the Latin transcription of the Chinese name Yin-Kuo (silver apricot). The present spelling does not make sense from the etymological point of view, and seems to be based on a spelling mistake. It is a very ancient tree, a living fossil,

There are several cultivars:
'Pendula' The tips of the branches turn down, and the crown is rounded.
'Fastigiata' A very narrow pyramid.
'Variegata' The leaves are variegated with yellow.
'Aurea' The leaves are yellow.
'Laciniata' Wide leaves, divided and indented.

Propagation

From seed Collecting seed from an isolated female tree will not yield results as the seed will not have been fertilized, so you need a fertilized tree. Keep the nut stratified for a year after harvesting it. Sowing takes place in the second spring after harvesting: soak the nut in very hot water before sowing it so that the shell will split. Sow the nut. Leave seedlings in the seed tray for a year before transferring to a growing pot. Keep sheltered.

From cuttings It is best to use short lateral shoots. Behead them. Smear the bottom end of the slip with hormone rooting compound, and plant in a peat-sand mixture. Take hardwood cuttings.

By air layering This air layering method produces twisted trees. Strip the bark from the part of the branch to be layered. Wrap sphagnum moss round it and envelop that with polythene, bound at either end with raffia to keep it closed. Spray. When the layer has taken, remove the polythene and moss, and sever the layer from the tree. Pot up and treat as a tree that has just been repotted.

By side grafting In summer, grafting low on to the trunk so that later on the earth will hide the graft union. The incision made into the rootstock is wider deeper down. The following spring the graft should have taken. Then cut off the rootstock above the scion, pot up and treat as a tree that has just been repotted. *'Pendula'* ginkgos are the type most commonly grafted.

From young nursery stock Select a tree with an interesting trunk and a lot of branches.

Care

Exposure to sunlight. The ginkgo likes full sun. However, in summer very young specimens and trees that have just been repotted should be kept in semishade.

Temperature Ginkgos do not like frost. In winter keep protected from severe cold and frost, covering the roots, the container and the stem of the trunk, or keep sheltered in a cold room.

Ventilation The ginkgo is not sensitive to atmospheric pollution and stands up to

STYLES

Tachiki

Hōkidachi

Sōkan

Kabudachi

Ikadabuki

Netsunagari

wind. However, shield trees that have been repotted for six weeks.

Container The ginkgo needs deep soil. Choose a round, hexagonal or square, fairly deep bowl, glazed or unglazed. Cobalt blue or brown go well with this tree.

Cleaning Regularly remove any dead material from the tree and ground to guard against diseases and pests. Mist-spray the leaves to clean them and allow them to respire.

Growth Slow in early years, speeding up later.

Repotting Repot the ginkgo about every three years after new shoots have started to grow. March is a good month for repotting. Prune the roots by a half.

Soil ⅓ leaf mould, ⅓ loam and ⅓ sand. The ginkgo adapts to ordinary soil provided it is deep and contains some red clay and some black loam.

Pruning Pinch out all unwanted growth on the trunk and large branches. Pinch out the tips of shoots and pick off two or three leaves from each branch. When a second set of buds appears, pinch out and pick off again, cutting back to one or two pairs of leaves. After this second pinching back, the new shoots are allowed to develop. Cut the leaves as soon as they have hardened on each branch. The branches are pruned in spring when repotting takes place. Eliminate any superfluous branches. Prune other branches back to about a third of their length. Carry out development pruning in winter, cutting out any branches that detract from the outline of the tree. Apply a wound-sealing compound to the cut.

Wiring The shape is mainly created by pinching back the head and the shoots and pruning the leaves and branches. However, a ginkgo can be lightly wired in autumn, with the copper wire being removed at the end of the summer. But this is unusual and rarely done. As a rule ginkgos are not wired.

Watering Allow the soil to dry out between waterings, and wet it thoroughly each time you water. Never water during frost. Water daily in summer, but not in full sun. In autumn it is best to water the tree in the morning. Protect from heavy rain, but allow the tree to stand in night dew.

Spraying Spray the tree well from mid-spring to early autumn to keep the trunk, branches and leaves free of dust and pollution.

Feeding Feed with an organic fertilizer

Maidenhair tree *(Ginkgo biloba)*. 20 years old. Height, 30 cm (1 ft). 'Sankan' style. Photograph taken in October. In early autumn the leaves take on this golden-yellow hue which gives rise to the maidenhair tree's nickname, the 'tree of the forty gold crowns'.

in spring and in autumn. Do not feed in July and August, or if the bonsai is in poor condition or for two months after repotting. Increase the amount of fertilizer given in the last autumn feed to set the tree up for the winter.

Pests and diseases

Pests
Ginkgos make very hardy bonsai specimens and as far as we know are not attacked by pests.

Diseases
● **Honey fungus** *(Armillaria mellea)*
See p. 31.

Juniperus sinensis
CHINESE JUNIPER

The Cupressaceae family. Native to China. In China the Chinese juniper can grow to a height of 25 m (80 ft) whereas cultivars brought into Europe are not very tall. It is relatively short lived. The Chinese juniper is a conifer which differs in appearance depending on how old it is: young needles are long, light and compact, and old ones are small and form a scale. Both adult and juvenile foliage can be found on the same tree. The trunk is brownish red and the bark peels easily. The Chinese juniper bears a lot of yellow flowers on the male tree, while the flowers on the female are green and discrete, growing in the leaf axil. It produces a lot of berries which are blue-green before they are ripe, and brown on maturity.

Juniperus sinensis 'Aurea' does not differ from the type species in shape, but its foliage is golden yellow and diminishes in winter.
Juniperus sinensis 'Japonica' is more prickly, and its shoots stand up when it is old.
Juniperus sinensis 'Kaizuka' is conical, side branches are bunched and the foliage is bright green.
Juniperus sinensis 'Pyramidalis' is blue and prickly, unlike the 'Stricta' variety which is similar to it.
Juniperus sinensis 'Sargentii' is the variety most often used in bonsai.

Propagation

From seed Seldom grown this way. If you collect the berries yourself, remember they ripen in their second year. They are harvested in winter. Allow the berries to dry in a cool, airy place, and plant in March. But results are very poor.

From cuttings Take a young cutting, and strip it of bark. Remove lateral shoots from the lower part of the stem and pinch out the head of any slip that is too long. A new leader will grow as the roots form. July and August are the best period. Plant the cuttings out in a mixture of coarse sand and peat. A *Juniperus sinensis* raised from a cutting will grow very well. Do not take cuttings after the bark on new wood has turned brown, and if necessary dip the slip into a hormone rooting compound before planting it.

By air layering In spring when the growing season is starting coil some wire round the branch (or trunk) to be layered, allowing the sap to circulate above the layer. Peel off the bark immediately above the wire. Wrap damp sphagnum moss round it and enclose in polythene, sealed at both ends. Does not require much water. Roots will form in three to six months. If the layer is effected early in the season, it can be severed from the tree in September. Plant it out and treat as a tree that has just been repotted; it must be protected fom severe winter weather.

By simple layering Select a low, flexible branch. Strip the part to be buried of bark and remove tufts of needles from it. Make one or two incisions in the wood to encourage rooting. Bury in a compost consisting of coarse sand, peat and loam in equal parts. Water regularly, especially in summer. When new shoots appear, sever the layer and repot.

By side grafting Select a straight, pencil-thick rootstock. Make the graft in February. The scion must be of the same diameter as the stock at the point of union. Bind the graft; grafting wax is not necessary. Keep moist by spraying. Put in a warm place. Protect from wind. In about six months the graft will have bonded, the top of the rootstock is cut off, potted up, and treated as a tree that has just been repotted.

From young nursery stock Select a *Juniperus sinensis* with an interesting trunk and firm, shiny needles.

Care

Exposure to sunlight The *Juniperus sinensis* tolerates full sun. It is not too demanding as regards climate. But it does grow better in the sun than in shady sites. Very young trees should be placed in semishade in summer.

STYLES

Shakan

Kengai

Bankan

Tachiki

Han-Kengai

Bunjingi

Sharimiki

Neagari

Temperature The *Juniperus sinensis* stands up to heat and cold. Even so, its needles tend to be frostbitten in winter, especially if they have snow on them. It stands up well to frost, though the leading shoot may freeze in winter.

Ventilation See Part I.

Container Try to choose a brown, earth-coloured, glazed or unglazed bowl; this should be quite deep, especially for older trees.

Cleaning From spring to the end of autumn regularly pick off any yellow needles from the tree. Spray the foliage and bark to cleanse them of dust and pollution. Keep the soil clean.

Growth Starts quickly, then grows slowly.

Repotting In March, every three to five years, depending on the age of the bonsai.

Soil ⅓ coarse sand, ⅓ loam and ⅓ leaf mould. The Chinese juniper tolerates any soil, but does best in ordinary, permeable, calcareous soil.

Pruning
Pinching back You have to pinch back new shoots from spring to autumn between the thumb and index finger. Never use scissors to cut the needles. Pinch back well inside the foliage to improve the tree's development.
Pruning of new subbranches In March and April, and in September and October, prune quite low to keep the foliage dense.

Wiring Wire in autumn and leave the wire on for about eight months. Repeat every year until the shape you are aiming at has been achieved. Do not trap needles between the wire and the bark.

Chinese juniper *(Juniperus sinensis)*, Sargentii variety. 10 years old. Height, 15 cm (6 in). 'Bankan' style. Photograph taken in May.

Watering The Chinese juniper loves water. Thoroughly moisten the soil, then let it dry out before watering again. Water daily in summer, less frequently in autumn, and increase again in spring. Give specimens that are exposed to the wind more water.

Spraying In summer mist-spray the needles, trunk and branches freely, with extra mist-spraying on the foliage.

Feeding Feed in spring and in autumn. Increase the amount given in the last autumn feed to set up the tree for the winter. Do not feed in July and August or if the tree is sickly or has just been re-potted. Never feed with highly concentrated fertilizer as this might disturb the balance of branch and foliage growth.

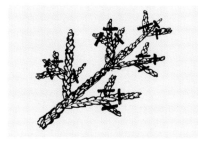

How to prune subbranches.

Pests and diseases

Pests
Same pests as *Juniperus rigida*, see p. 45.

Diseases
● **Coryneum cardinale**
Symptoms The needles turn brown and the branches wither. Black sores on the bark with resin running from them; possibly cankers.

Treatment Guard against wounding the tree. Disinfect the sores using wound-sealing compound. Cut out diseased branches. Add potash to the soil. Apply a systemic fungicide. As a precaution spray with a mineral fungicide after the spring rains and in autumn.
● Other diseases as for *Juniperus rigida*, see p. 45.

Sekijôju

Ishitsuki

Nejikan

Sôkan

Kabudachi

Ikadabuki

Netsunagari

Bonkei

Juniperus rigida
TEMPLE JUNIPER

The Cupressaceae family. The *Juniperus rigida* grows in Japan, Manchuria and Korea. It grows to a height of about 10 m (33 ft). It has a graceful outline, with branches arching at their tips, and side branches curving downwards. The slightly yellowish-green foliage has a light band on its upper face formed by stomata. The foliage is very stiff and needle shaped. The linear needles are narrow, concave and very prickly. The globular berries are green, turning black as they ripen.

Propagation

From seed Collect berries in November. They are picked like bilberries by 'combing' the tree. Dry the berries in a cool, airy place. Soak the cones in water for two days, then grind and sieve them to get the seeds. Stratify these and sow in spring. They germinate the year after. If you buy seed, it may germinate in the second year. So leave the seed bed until shoots appear.

From cuttings Take a heeled or unheeled cutting. Strip it of bark, and remove side shoots from the lower part. If the slip is too long, behead it. When it has rooted, a new leading shoot will develop. Take cuttings in July-August. Plant the cutting in a mixture of coarse sand and sieved peat, using no hormone rooting compound. Put some good compost at the bottom. Take cuttings before the wood has turned brown. When the cutting has rooted, pot it up and keep it protected.

By simple layering Wind some copper wire round the branch (or trunk) to be layered. Pull it tight, but do not prevent the sap from circulating. Cut into the wood where the wire is. This should be done in early spring. Strip the bark off the area above the wire ring. Wrap moist sphagnum moss round the area and enclose in polythene sealed at both ends. Spray to keep damp, but do not overdo it. In six months roots will have formed. If the layering has been carried out early in the season, the layer can be severed in September and potted up. It will be established after a year, but until then protect it from strong wind or sun, severe cold and drought.

From young nursery stock Select a tree with an interesting trunk and shape, with dense, sharp needles. Treat it as a tree to be repotted where pruning, wiring and potting are concerned.

Care

Exposure to sunlight The *Juniperus rigida* likes full sun, but do not expose young specimens and trees that have just been repotted to too much sun.

Temperature Stands up to heat and cold. Very tough. But its needles may turn brown in winter and its leading shoot freeze: protect if it is extremely cold.

Ventilation Is not affected by wind.

Container Choose a bowl of medium depth, deeper when the tree is older. A rectangular container in a shade of brown suits it best.

Cleaning Pick dead needles and twigs and yellow needles off the tree. Always be sure to clean inside the tree to encourage the foliage to develop well. Pick dead leaves and wood off the ground. Spray well in summer to get rid of dust on the needles and trunk.

Growth When the bonsai is young, it grows quickly and its roots develop rapidly. Once it is older its rate of growth slows considerably.

Repotting In spring, towards the beginning of April. Every three to five years. Prune the roots by half.

Soil 1/3 coarse sand, 1/3 leaf mould and 1/3 loam. Grows well in a calcareous, permeable soil. No special requirements.

STYLES

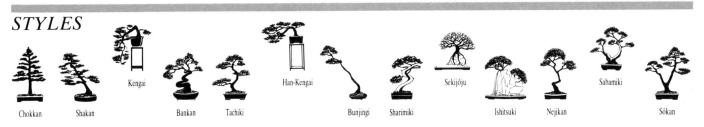

Chokkan   Shakan   Kengai   Bankan   Tachiki   Han-Kengai   Bunjingi   Sharimiki   Sekijôju   Ishitsuki   Nejikan   Sabamiki   Sôkan

Temple juniper (*Juniperus rigida*). 110 years old. Height, 45 cm (1 ft 6 in). 'Saramiki' style. The young, pale green shoots which should be pinched back can be seen clearly.

Pruning
Pinching back Pinch back young shoots from spring to autumn. Do not cut the needles with clippers, which would cause them to yellow and drop off. Even if you get scratched, pinch back well inside the tree. Remove shoots coming out of the trunk.

Pruning of branches In March, shortening them by about a third, taking care not to cut the needles. Cut above a tuft.

Wiring
Coil the wire round the branches, and then train them to achieve the shape wanted. Wrap raffia round the branches before wiring as the bark is very brittle. Be gentle so as not to break the branches. Place the wire in position in autumn and leave for eight to ten months. Repeat every year.

Watering
The *Juniperus rigida* can be allowed to dry out between waterings. It likes water, so drench it thoroughly each time you water as it absorbs a lot. Always check that it has dried out before giving it water.

Spraying
Mist-spray well in summer to give moisture to the atmosphere round the *Juniperus rigida* and to cleanse it of dust and pollution. It likes humidity.

Feeding
Feed with organic fertilizer once a month in spring and in autumn. Increase the amount given in the last autumn feed to set the tree up for the winter.

Pests and diseases

Pests
- **Bark beetles** See p. 30.
- **Red spider mites** See p. 28.
- **Bupestrids**

Symptoms Some branches withered. Galleries hollowed out of the wood. Blue-green beetles in summer.
Treatment Cut out and destroy infested branches. Spray with a systemic insecticide in summer.
- **Leaf miners** (small green caterpillars) See p. 29.
- **Aphids** (*Cupressobium juniperi*) See p. 29.

- **Broad bean blackfly** See p. 29.
- **Hard-shelled scale insects** See p. 29.

Diseases
- **Die-back**

Symptoms Twigs and branches turn brown and then wither.
Treatment Cut out diseased branches and spray with copper-based fungicide. Be careful that the fungicide does not damage the host plant.
- **Rust** See p. 31.

Kabudachi   Korabuki   Ikadabuki   Netsunagari   Sôju   Sambon-Yose   Gohon-Yose   Nanahon-Yose   Kyûhon-Yose   Yose-Ue   Yamayori   Tsukami-Yose   Bonkei

Larix
LARCH
and related species

The Pinaceae family. Larches can live for about 300 years. They are native to the cold and high mountainous areas of the temperate zone in the northern hemisphere, and grow to about 50 m (165 ft) in height. The distinguishing features of the larch are its deciduous, needle-shaped leaves, growing in clusters on short branches and singly on long ones. The small, egg-shaped cones stay on the tree for a long time.

Among some fifteen species of larch we will mention:
Larix decidua (common or European larch). It grows uncultivated in the Alps and central Europe. It sheds its needles in winter; the needles are flat, narrow, soft and green. Cones start off red, turning brown.
Larix leptolepis (Japanese larch). Found in the Japanese archipelago. Needs a damp climate and a light soil. It is conical in habit, with horizontal branches, bluish, thick-growing needles that turn pinkish in autumn, and decorative, globular cones. If it grows on a plain, it rarely lives longer than 50 years.
Pseudolarix kaempferi (Chinese larch). Found mainly in Kiangsi and nowadays in Italy. It is pyramidal in habit with spreading branches; its needles, which are a soft green on the upper face and bluish with two bands of white underneath, turn golden in autumn. Brick-coloured cones.

Propagation

From seed Seeds can be gathered in autumn or winter depending on the climate and the area. They ripen late. Leave the cones you have collected lying in the sun in winter. When they open up, shake them and the seeds will fall out. Take care: the cones close back up again quickly. In March expose the seeds to warmth, turning them over; medium humidity. Sow in late April/early May. They germinate slowly.

From cuttings You will get better results if you take cuttings on a damp, misty day. Always use a hormone rooting compound. Do not take slips from old wood. The best time is August-September, taking slips from leading shoots.

By simple layering Select a low, flexible branch. Strip the part to be buried of foliage and make two or three incisions into the bark to encourage rooting. Bury. Keep the earth moist. Make the layer in spring. When you see new shoots, roots have formed. Then separate the layered branch from the parent plant, pot up and protect from extremes of wind, cold and sun.

By grafting At the end of winter, inlay grafting can be attempted, but it is unlikely to work. Seldom used.

Care

Exposure to sunlight. Tolerates and enjoys full sun. It is still advisable to place it in semishade in summer.

Temperature Larches grow at altitudes of up to 2400 m (8000 ft). They are not affected by cold. They need a mountain climate.

Ventilation Stands up well to wind. Needs to be well aired.

Container It requires a deep container, for the earth it grows in needs water and good drainage, and it grows fast.

Cleaning Make sure you remove any dead material from inside the crown. In autumn, the needles fall: gently shake the tree and sweep the soil.

Growth Fast, especially with the *Larix leptolepis*. The larch grows quickly and steadily.

Repotting In spring, in April. About every three years. Prune the roots by half, and repot in a larger container.

Soil A mixture consisting of ⅓ leaf mould, ⅓ loam and ⅓ coarse sand. The larch thrives in cool, humus-rich, deep, clay soil; it does not like chalky soil.

Pruning
Pinching back Pinch back new shoots from the side branches in spring, and right through the growing period. Remove any shoots coming from the trunk.
Leaf cutting Is not used.
Pruning of branches Cut back side branches that spread too far, taking them off just above a tuft of needles.
Development pruning Carried out on young specimens. You can prune the head of the larch when it has reached the height you want. In winter when the needles have fallen, prune out any branches that spoil the tree's outline, and any branches or side branches that are damaged.

Wiring Usually the larch grows straight. When you want to train it, either stress its erect appearance, or twist it by coiling wire round its trunk and branches in early summer. Remove the wire in autumn. Repeat annually if required.

STYLES

 Chokkan   Shakan   Tachiki   Sharimiki   Sekijôju   Ishitsuki   Sabamiki   Sôkan

Watering If the soil is well drained and permeable, water the larch frequently, especially in summer. The earth should be well wetted, as the larch is native to wet mountains. Even so, take care not to drown it.

Spraying The larch wilts if the air is too moist. So it is not necessary to spray it too often. However, it can be sprayed occasionally in summer to clean it more than to humidify it. It likes a dry atmosphere. The *Larix leptolepis* is better at tolerating humidity.

Feeding Feed with slow-acting organic fertilizer in spring and autumn. Increase the amount given at the last autumn application. Do not feed in July/August, if the larch has just been repotted or if it is sickly.

Pests and diseases

Pests
- **Gall-forming aphids** See p. 29.
- **Woolly aphids** See p. 29.
- **Bark beetles** See p. 30.
- **Caterpillars** See p. 28.
- **Red caterpillars**

Symptoms Needles gnawed. Silky cocoons may be present on the branches.
Treatment Spray with insecticide – in spring to deal with the larvae, and in summer to deal with the adults.
- **Tortrix** (caterpillars)

Diseases
- **Rust** See p. 31.
- **Honey fungus** See p. 31.
- **Die-back**

Symptoms The needles at the base of shoots turn yellow and drop off, and side branches wither.
Treatment Spray with fungicide based on sulphur, maneb, thiram, or zineb.
- **Canker:** larch peziza (*Dasyscypha willkommii*)

Symptoms Appearance of lesions on the branches causing malformations and withering. Only the Japanese larch is not susceptible to this disease.
Treatment There is no cure.

European larch (*Larix decidua*). 15 years old. Height, 55 cm (1 ft 10 in). 'Tachiki' style. Photograph taken in June.

Kabudachi

Sôju

Sambon-Yose

Gohon-Yose

Nanahon-Yose

Kyūhon-Yose

Yose-Ue

Kusamono

Picea
SPRUCE

The Pinaceae family. Spruces were for a long time categorized with pine trees, but for more than a century have been a separate genus. In Latin *Picea* meant tree with resin, and *Pix* resin or pitch. There are about 50 species of *Picea*, native to the northern hemisphere, mainly to mountainous areas. The *Picea* is a conifer, differing from the *Abies* (silver fir) in that it always has a pointed crown, sloping branches and drooping subbranches. The needles form thick, prickly light-green spirals. The cones hang from the tips of the branches; they have thin scales that do not hinge open as they ripen with age.

Picea abies syn. *P. excelsa* (Norway spruce). There is often confusion between this and the fir tree. It is conical in silhouette, and its branches go down almost to the ground. It grows at altitudes of up to 2000 m (6600 ft). Its needles which grow in spirals round the branches are stiff, sharp, shiny, dark green in colour and evergreen. The slender, triangular cones are spindle shaped with red scales, and hang down.

Picea glauca (white spruce). Of restricted size, with a straight, tapering trunk, long spreading branches, and a pyramidal shape. The needles are greeny blue, and the cones are small and green, turning brown as they ripen; strong smell of resin.

Picea mariana syn. *P. nigra* (black spruce). Conical in habit, straight and dense. Dark greeny blue needles, red cones that turn brown.

Picea jezoensis (jezo or Hondo spruce). This spruce can grow to a height of 50 m (165 ft). Its outline is marked by a long leading shoot. The needles are bright green on top and silvery white underneath. The tips of the branches turn back towards the tree. The red cones turn brown.

Picea orientalis (Oriental or Caucasian spruce). It can grow to a height of 50 m (165 ft). The trunk is straight and the tree has a thick, pyramid-shaped crown. The very short, dark-green needles are thick and not spine tipped. The purple cones turn to brown, and have close-fitting scales.

Propagation

From seed The cones are usually picked between September and January; let them dry out. For the *Picea glauca* cones should be picked in late August or September. As soon as seeds appear at the edge of the scales, remove them. Allow the seeds to mature in the cones for as long as possible. Prepare the seeds for germination by leaving in damp sand for about 10 days. You can sprinkle minium over the seeds to protect them. Sow in April when they are beginning to germinate in cool soil. Usually they will have sprouted by the end of three weeks. Keep the seedlings under glass, in shade and in a damp place. Remove the glass in June. Pot up the following spring.

From cuttings Take cuttings from the leaders from the end of June to early August. Rooting is tricky, and it can take up to two years for roots to form (especially for the *ohlendorffii* variety). Using a grafting knife, cut along the base of shoots grown that year. You do not need to remove the needles. Plant cuttings in a warm, shaded place.

By layering Choose low, flexible branches. Strip needles off the part to be buried. Make a slit a couple of centimetres long to encourage root formation. Bury the branch, and keep the soil moist. When new shoots appear at the tip of the branch, roots have formed. Then sever the layer, and replant in a growing pot. Treat as a freshly potted tree, and protect from extreme changes of weather.

By grafting Used particularly for the *Picea glauca*. It can be a summer graft or a winter graft, but it is a tricky procedure of more interest to professional growers than to the amateur because of the special treatments required before and after the graft is made.

From young stock Choose a young nursery plant with the trunk already formed, with thick foliage and a good branch structure. Uncover the base of the trunk. Plant in a pot, taking care to spread out the roots. Remove any branches that cross or overlap one another, or are parallel to each other. Refine the outline of the tree and train into shape.

Care

Exposure to sunlight Spruces like full sun, but they also like shade.

Temperature Many species start growing early in the season and can be affected by night frosts. There is a similar risk with late frosts. These trees like a cool atmosphere.

Ventilation Spruces are happy in the wind, especially the *Picea jezoensis*.

STYLES

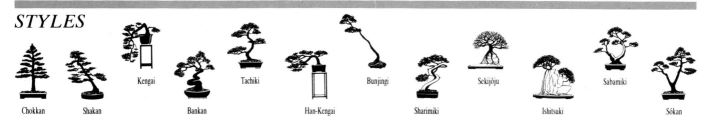

Chokkan   Shakan   Kengai   Bankan   Tachiki   Han-Kengai   Bunjingi   Sharimiki   Sekijōju   Ishitsuki   Sabamiki   Sōkan

Container Choose a shallow bowl as the spruce's roots are not deep.

Cleaning Remember to remove damaged or dead twigs and needles from inside the crown. Keep the soil clear of any dead material.

Growth The *Picea glauca, jezoensis* and *orientalis* species are slow growing. The *Picea abies* grows slowly at a high altitude, but fast if it is lower down. The slower it grows, the more tapering its outline.

Repotting Every third to fifth year, depending on its age, in the spring (April). Prune off a third of the root hairs. Repot in a slightly larger container.

Soil Prepare a mixture consisting of ⅓ leaf mould, ⅓ loam and ⅓ coarse sand. Most species prefer soil that is a mixture of clay, sandy clay and lime-rich clay. Sandy and lime-rich soils are not suitable, nor is clay soil appropriate.

Pruning
Pinching back In April, pinch back the new shoots on the side branches. Pinching back is practised only once a year.
Leaf pruning You do not cut needles.
Pruning of branches In spring cut branches hard back, leaving only a few tufts of needles on each branch. On subsequent occasions, do not cut the branches quite so short.

Wiring Wire the *Picea* at the end of autumn or the beginning of winter. Remove the copper wire about nine or ten months later. Repeat every year until the desired shape has been achieved.

Watering The soil must be well drained. Water copiously, and then allow to dry out. The spruce is used to moist ground, but it should not under any circumstances be waterlogged.

Spraying Wet the foliage as much as possible. Concentrate on wetting in spring and summer. Spruces like a very moist atmosphere.

Feeding Use a slow-acting organic fertilizer in spring and autumn. Increase the dosage at the last autumn dressing (October). Do not feed in July-August, or if the bonsai is in poor condition or has just been repotted.

Jezo or Hondo spruce *(Picea jezoensis)*. 10-40 years old. Height, 60 cm (2 ft). 'Yose-Ue' style. Photograph taken in April. This outstanding group has been planted on a plateau of reconstituted rock.

Pests and diseases

Pests
- **Root eelworms** See p. 30.
- **Red spider mites** See p. 28.
- **Large pine weevils**
Symptoms Bark on the collar and branches gnawed, tissues showing through, resin oozing from the wounds. Galleries hollowed out beneath the bark, needles and buds gnawed.
Treatment Cut out and destroy infested material. At the first sign of attack, use a petroleum emulsion on young trees. Spray with insecticide at the end of March or beginning of April.
- **Bark beetles** See p. 30.
- **Long-horned beetles**
Symptoms Flattened galleries at the base of the trunk. Black beetles may be present.
Treatment Destroy branches affected. Spray with insecticide when the adults emerge.
- **Woodwasps**
Symptoms Cylindrical galleries in the trunk and main branches. Possible presence of wasps indicating white larvae.
Treatment Spray with insecticide when the adults emerge.
- **Bee hawkmoths** (caterpillars)
Symptoms Young shoots are eaten and wither, buds fail to develop. Presence of caterpillars.
Treatment Destroy infested parts.
- **Tortrix** (caterpillars) See p. 29.
- **Sawflies** (larvae)
Symptoms Needles produced that year are completely eaten and the new shoots are distorted.
Treatment Spray with insecticide when the shoots begin to grow.
- **Aphids** See p. 29.
- **Pine gall louse**
Symptoms Formation of spherical or prickly galls at the tips of new branches.
Treatment At the end of winter, spray with mineral-based insecticide. In early spring, spray with organochlorine and organophosphate insecticide.

Diseases
- **Browning of needles**
Symptoms The needles wither and black granulations appear on their underside.
Treatment Use a fungicide. If you are planting a group style, make sure the trees are not too close to one another.
- **Septoria fungus**
Symptoms The needles wither, and the branches grow in the shape of a crook. There are black granulations on the withered parts.
Treatment Cut out and destroy diseased branches. Spray with a copper- or zineb-based fungicide.
- **Rust** See p. 31.
- **Canker**
Symptoms The roots rot, the leaves turn pale, then go yellow and wither. There may be a white dust on the rotted collar.
Treatment Drench soil with a zineb-based fungicide. Make sure that water does not become stagnant, and feed with a well-balanced fertilizer.

Kabudachi   Ikadabuki   Sôju   Gohon-Yose   Kyûhon-Yose   Yamayori   Bonkei

Korabuki   Netsunagari   Sambon-Yose   Nanahon-Yose   Yose-Ue   Tsukami-Yose   Kusamono

The Pinaceae family. More than 80 species. *Pinus* is the largest genus of conifers. Pines prefer mountain areas. Almost all species are native to the northern hemisphere (except for the *Pinus insularis*). A tall tree, usually with a conical top. Its long, scaly branches bear short side branches with circular, evergreen leaves growing in clusters from a scaly sheath. A differentiation is made between pines with two, three, and five needles. The cones are pyramid shaped, with woody scales.

Pinus
PINE

There are more than 26 species found in France: the Scots pine which can live for 600 years, the maritime pine, the *Pinus uncinata*, the Arolla pine and the stone pine are native to France. Most species have a rounded, conical shape when they are old. The shape of the cones varies according to species and is a means of recognizing them.

NB. Pines are also used to form landscapes and group styles based on the seasons.

Propagation

From seed Collect the seeds or pine nuts from the cones. Most of them are winged (except for *Pinus cembra, koraiensis* and *parviflora*). The ripeness and germination of the seeds vary according to the species. Many species have cones that open when the seeds are ripe; others have to be dried to enable the seeds to be released.

Mountain pine *(Pinus uncinata)* Collect the cones in December. Dry them, then keep in a cool shaded place. Pregerminate the seeds and plant them in mid-April. They will germinate in two months.

From cuttings This technique is not used much because roots are very slow to form. It can be done at the end of winter with cuttings taken from young trees: short slips that are two years old. Dip the slips in a hormone rooting compound before planting them.

By layering Strip the part of the branch being layered that will be buried. Make a 3-cm (1¼-in) long slit in the bark to enhance rooting. Bury it, and keep the soil damp. When new shoots appear on the tip of the branch, roots have formed. Separate the layer from the tree and pot up. Air layering is also possible.

By grafting Make a veneer graft or a cleft graft. In winter in greenhouse conditions the Scots pine makes an excellent rootstock for conifers with two needles. The *Pinus nigra* is recommended as a rootstock for strong-growing species.

From young nursery stock You can find a great many species of pine in nurseries. Always look carefully at the trunk and the density of the branch structure before making your selection.

Care

Exposure to sunlight Full sun. As a rule pines need a lot of light and do badly in the shade.

Temperature Pines like warmth and do better in warm areas. They stand up very well to intense winter cold and even to frosts.

Ventilation Pines like the wind and thrive in places with a lot of air movement. Guard against pollution which harms them. The black pine has the best resistance.

Container Pines need deep, well-drained soil, so choose a fairly deep bowl.

Cleaning On the pine, old needles turn yellow in autumn. Use tweezers to remove them. Always prune inside the crown well and remove all damaged or dead material. Clear any dead material from the soil. Brush off moss that travels up from the ground on to the base of the trunk so that it does not become established.

Growth Usually fast: about 10 m (33 ft) in 20 years. The mountain pine stays small, barely exceeding 3 m (10 ft). Some dwarf (rockery) varieties are slow growing.

Repotting Repot in April every three to five years in a larger container. Prune the roots by a third, taking care not to damage the main root.

Soil ⅓ leaf mould, ⅓ loam and ⅓ coarse sand. Pines have no special requirements,

STYLES

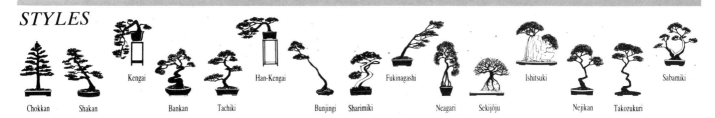

Chokkan   Shakan   Kengai   Bankan   Tachiki   Han-Kengai   Bunjingi   Sharimiki   Fukinagashi   Neagari   Sekijôju   Ishitsuki   Nejikan   Takozukuri   Sabamiki

and adapt to any kind of soil. As a rule mountain species growing on sandy soil are tall and slender, with a straight trunk and a short crown, while those growing on calcareous ground have short, twisted trunks. The soil should be cool and damp for some species, poor and dry for others; the mountain pine likes cold, marshy soil. By and large avoid soil with too much lime (except for the black pine), and provide light soil.

Pruning

Pinching back In April once each year using the thumb and forefinger pinch out

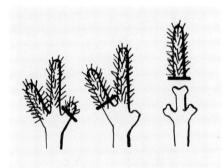

Pruning of branchlets on the two-needle pine.

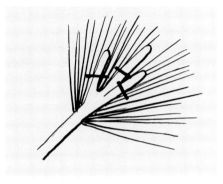

Cut branchlets close to the bottom.

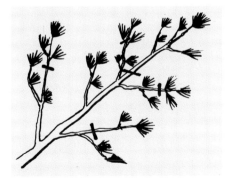

In October, prune branches that are too long.

Japanese black pine *(Pinus thunbergii)*. 70 years old. Height, 60 cm (2 ft). 'Shakan' style. Photograph taken in April.

where the candles are forming. Remove two thirds of them.

Pruning of needles. Once a year in spring remove all new needles after they have appeared but before they harden so as to have dense foliage and small needles.

Pruning of branches Cut the branches in October just above a tuft of needles. Cut back the branch by about a third. Repeat in the autumn if necessary.

Wiring Wire in autumn and in winter. Repeat each year if necessary. Do not squash the needles between the wire and the bark.

Watering Water regularly and copiously if drainage is good. From time to time keep the tree dry. The pine withstands hot, dry summers.

Spraying The pine tolerates a dry atmosphere. It does not have to be mist-sprayed often. Mist-spraying has the primary purpose of cleansing it of the damaging effects of pollution.

Feeding Feed with a slow-acting, organic fertilizer from spring to autumn (October-November). Do not feed in July and August, or if the tree is sick or has just been repotted.

Pests and diseases

Same pests and diseases as the Japanese white pine. See. p. 55.

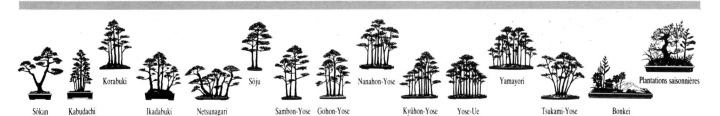

Sôkan Kabudachi Korabuki Ikadabuki Netsunagari Sôju Sambon-Yose Gohon-Yose Nanahon-Yose Kyûhon-Yose Yose-Ue Yamayori Tsukami-Yose Bonkei Plantations saisonnières

Pinus parviflora (var. P. pentaphylla)
JAPANESE WHITE PINE

The Pinaceae family. Native to Japan where it is known as 'Goyo-Matsu'. The *Pinus pentaphylla* is a variety of *Pinus parviflora*, a pine with small flowers. In its natural state it can grow to a height of 25 m (80 ft). When the tree is young, its outline is pyramid shaped and its foliage dense, but, when it is old, the outline alters to an irregular shape, while its wide-spreading branches become horizontal and look very picturesque when the tree is mature. There are not many branches; these curve up at the end, and tend to become bare as they get older. The upper ones form a crown. Resinous knurs appear on the bark of young specimens. The needles are clustered in groups of five, hence the description *pentaphylla*. They are evergreen, can be straight or twisted, bluey green in colour edged with two resin-coloured lines. It is a white pine. The cones go dark brown and stay on the tree for about seven years. The best known of its many cultivars is *Pinus parviflora* var. *P. pentaphylla* 'Kokonoe'.

Propagation

From seed The cones are ripe when they are two years old. Gather them then in September-October. Leave them to dry in a warm place, and they will open up. Then collect the pine seeds and soak them in water. Those that sink can be planted. Apply a fungicide to the seeds. Sow in spring after keeping between layers of sand. They can also be planted at the end of autumn, in which case they are naturally preserved in layers of earth during the winter. The shoot is very delicate after it has germinated. Repot the following spring.

By simple layering Choose a low, pliable branch. Remove needles from the part to be buried. Make a cut in the bark. Bury, and keep moist. Sever the layer from the parent plant as soon as new shoots appear.

By air layering Strip the part of the branch to be layered of its leaves, and make an incision. Hold the slit open with a twist of sphagnum moss. Cover the layer with damp moss, and enclose in a polythene tube that is closed at both ends. As soon as roots appear (in the spring of the following year), sever the layer and pot it, treating it as a bonsai that has just been repotted.

From cuttings Hard to achieve. At the end of winter, take cuttings from young plants. Select short branches, two years old. Dip the cuttings in a hormone rooting compound before planting them.

By grafting Veneer or cleft grafting; in winter, in a greenhouse. It is possible to unite a black pine and a white pine by grafting to accelerate the growth rate of the latter, which is a slow grower.

Care

Exposure to sunlight Full sun. Requires a lot of light to grow well. A few dwarf cultivars need some shade during the summer months. If it is exposed to the sun, the needles will be small and the nodes will be closely spaced.

Temperature Can withstand intense cold and heat. Likes cool places.

Ventilation Tolerates winds, but protect varieties with fine needles from drying winds.

Container Needs soil depth, so select a fairly deep bowl. The needles of the *Pinus parviflora* var. *pentaphylla* give the wind something to catch, and a deep pot holds it in position and prevents it from tipping up. This bonsai is often found in a cobalt-blue container.

STYLES

Chokkan

Shakan

Kengai

Bankan

Tachiki

Han-Kengai

Bunjingi

Japanese white pine *(Pinus parviflora* var. *pentaphylla). 200 years old. Height, 70 cm (2 ft 4 in). 'Shakan' style. Photograph taken in May. Though it is close to the 'Shakan' style, this outstanding tree is in a non-classic style known as the 'Hand of Buddha' – the highly individual shape of the tree (the curve of the trunk and the projecting upper crown) does, in fact, suggest the protective hand of Buddha; placed at the entrance in a garden, a tree in this 'style' is a sign of welcome. There are a few rare specimens in existence.

Sharimiki

Fukinagashi

Neagari

Sekijōju

Ishitsuki

Nejikan

Takozukuri

Sabamiki

Pinus parviflora (var. *P. pentaphylla*)
JAPANESE WHITE PINE

How to pinch out pine buds by hand; here they are cut through with your fingernails.

Cleaning Using the thumb and the index finger, pick off old needles that turn yellow in autumn. Prune the inner foliage, and remove any dead or damaged parts from there or from the soil.

Growth This is especially slow in the case of Japanese white pines.

Repotting Repot every three to five years, in a larger container which must always be fairly deep. In March, prune the roots by a third of their length, and remove old roots. Do not wash and keep some of the old earth on the roots to help the plant to get re-established. Treat with special care for three weeks after repotting.

Soil ⅓ leaf mould, ⅓ loam and ⅓ coarse sand. Good drainage is essential. No special requirements as regards soil.

Pruning
Pinching back In April pinch back the candle or candles by two-thirds before they open, using the thumb and index finger. If the crown is thick completely remove one bud in three. On the other hand, if you want it to thicken up, keep all three buds. First of all pinch out the slowest-growing buds. Pinching back can be carried out over a three-week period. Finish with the fastest-growing buds. This will make the needles more equal.
Pruning of branches In October prune the branches that have grown most. Cut off a third of the branch above a cluster of needles, without cutting the needles.

Wiring Wire in October, and leave until March. Leave the copper wire on the branches until the end of the summer. If the wire seems to be becoming encrusted in the bark, remove it. If the tree is damaged in the course of doing this, treat the wound with a sealing compound.

Watering Do not give too much water for best development. Excessive water is injurious to the *Pinus parviflora*. To get smaller needles, water sparingly in spring. Give more water to trees planted on stone.

Spraying Spray the foliage in summer. This refreshes the bonsai and dislodges any parasites that might be in the foliage.

Feeding From spring to autumn, with a break in July and August, feed with slow-acting organic fertilizer. Little at a time, but often: about once a month. Increase the amount given in the last autumn feed and add a little nitrate which will feed the soil. Do not feed a tree that has just been repotted or one that is sickly.

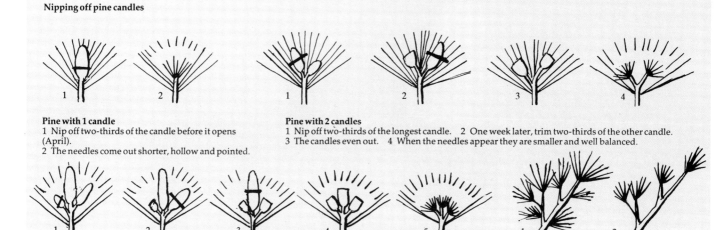

Nipping off pine candles

Pine with 1 candle
1 Nip off two-thirds of the candle before it opens (April).
2 The needles come out shorter, hollow and pointed.

Pine with 2 candles
1 Nip off two-thirds of the longest candle.   2 One week later, trim two-thirds of the other candle.
3 The candles even out.   4 When the needles appear they are smaller and well balanced.

Pines with 3 candles
1 Trim two-thirds of the shortest candle.   2 Trim two-thirds of the middle-sized candle one week later.
3 Finally, trim two-thirds of the biggest candle.   4 The candles are now in line.   5 When the needles appear they are shorter and more regular.

Plucking out pine needles by hand
1 In October remove the old needles by hand.
2 The tree is now clean and ready for winter.

STYLES

Sōkan

Korabuki

Kabudachi

Ikadabuki

Netsunagari

Sōju

Sambon-Yose

Gohon-Yose

Wiring is left on the Japanese pine for about ten months, and must therefore be removed so that it does not mark the bark or, worse still, become embedded in the wood. Removing the wire is a delicate operation; here, you can see the different phases, especially (on the left) the way in which pliers are used to cut the wire.

Pests and diseases

Pests
- **Pine weevils**
Symptoms Nests in the roots. The bark of the collar and the main branches is gnawed; tissues show through; resin oozes from the sores; galleries hollowed out of the wood. Needles gnawed.
Treatment Cut out and destroy infested parts. At the first sign of attack use an oil wash on young trees. Spray with pesticide at the end of March or beginning of April.
- **Bark beetles** See p. 30.
- **Capricorn and bupestrid beetles**
Symptoms The trunk is gnawed, and there are galleries tunnelled in the wood. Beetles may be present.
Treatment Spray with a lindane or parathion-based insecticide in March-April.
- **Pine chafers**
Symptoms The needles and branches are distorted and gnawed. Slowing down of growth. Presence of large brown beetles.
Treatment Spray with insecticide.
- **Chrysomelid or galerucid beetles (leaf beetles)**
Symptoms The needles are gnawed, and the branches misshapen. Growth is slowed down. Presence of yellow beetles.
Treatment Spray with insecticide.
- **Bombyx** (caterpillars) See p. 28.
NB. Rare on Scots pine.
- **Hawkmoth or owlet moth (caterpillars)**
Symptoms The needles are gnawed, and the lamina is holed by caterpillars that come out at night. High temperatures are favourable to their development.
Treatment Use pellets of bran, broken rice or grain mixed with insecticide.
- **Bee hawkmoths** (caterpillars)
Symptoms A hollow in the trunk with resin running from it and sticking on the bark.
Treatment Remove the accumulation of resin. Spray with a lindane-based insecticide.
- **Pine hawkmoth** (caterpillars) See p. 28.
- **Pine sawfly**
Symptoms Presence of a brown cocoon on the trunk, the branches, the needles or in the soil. The needles are gnawed.
Treatment At the first sign of attack, spray with an organophosphate insecticide. Cut out infested branches.
- **Woolly aphids** See p. 29.
- **Scale insects** See p. 29.

Diseases
- **Pine-leaf cast**
Symptoms The needles on the lower branches turn yellow in winter and are covered with black spots in spring. They dry up, turn red and fall. Do not confuse this disease with a tendency for the needles to turn red at the tips if the feeding and transpiration of the tree are not in balance.
Treatment Destroy damaged material, and ensure that the soil is not too wet. As a precaution spray with fungicide in spring. From July to September use combined fungicide.
- **Red band disease** (fungoid)
Symptoms The needles have yellow patches on them in autumn. In spring red bands appear, which are scabs on the wounds.
Treatment During the growing season, spray with a copper-based fungicide.
- **Honey fungus** See p. 31.
- **Rust** See p. 31.

Nanahon-Yose

Kyūhon-Yose

Yose-Ue

Yomayori

Tsukami-Yose

Bonkei

Kusamono

Plantations saisonnières

Taxus
YEW

The Taxaceae family. Native to the northern hemisphere: Europe, America and Asia. Very long lived; the yew can be several hundred years old, sometimes a thousand: in Germany there is a yew known to be 2000 years old. A small conifer, about 20 m (65 ft) tall, with a wide spread. When it is young the trunk is straight and branches, with sparse foliage, rise at an oblique angle, and the top is rounded. As it grows older, the branches rise almost to the point of sometimes forming a parallel trunk. The evergreen, needle-shaped, shiny foliage, dark green on the upper surface, and mid-green underneath, has prominent ribs and is not prickly. The foliage is toxic, especially to horses. The dioecious fruit is at blossom stage in March-April. The *Taxus baccata* is the best-known species. There is also the *Taxus cuspidata*, native to Japan and Korea. Its wider leaves are pointed. The cultivar *T. c. 'Nana'* is better known.

Propagation

From seed The fruit is ripe between August and October. Pick it as soon as it is red, release the seed from the fruit under water, dry, then stratify until the following autumn. Use a hormone rooting compound before you plant the seed. Germination will take place in or around May. Protect the seedlings from the sun and keep them moist. Plant out the saplings the following spring.

From cuttings Take cuttings from lignified shoots in September. Plant them in boxes placed in a greenhouse over winter. Roots form the following spring. If you want a pyramid-shaped tree, take your cutting from a leading shoot; for a spreading tree, take cuttings from lateral shoots.

By layering Choose a low, flexible branch. Strip needles off the part to be buried. Cut through the bark, bury and keep moist. When young shoots appear, the layer is well rooted. Sever, pot up and protect from sun and frost.

By grafting In March-April, using veneer grafting. A few weeks later shorten the leading shoot slightly. As soon as the graft has taken, the top of the rootstock is cut off and the grafted tree is planted.

From young nursery stock Depending on the style you wish to achieve, select a pyramid-shaped or a spreading tree with a well-formed trunk, good branching, hard shiny needles and a good root system.

Care

Exposure to sunlight Adapts to sunlight, and tolerates shade.

Temperature This is a mountain tree found at medium altitudes, and likes mountain temperatures. Stands up well to heat if placed in semishade. Withstands frost.

Ventilation A tree that is used for hedging, it stands up perfectly to wind.

Container The trunk of the yew tends to become big when it is old. Thus, it needs a pot the depth of which is in proportion to the diameter of its trunk. When young it needs a fairly deep pot to help it stand up to wind.

Cleaning Make sure you clean inside the tree, removing all dead or damaged material, and keep the soil clear of any dead material. Pick off dead needles in autumn.

Growth Very slow.

Repotting Repot in spring every third or fourth year in a larger container. Reduce the roots by a third, cutting out any damaged or dead roots. The yew is temperamental about getting re-etablished after repotting.

Soil ⅓ leaf mould, ⅓ loam and ⅓ coarse sand. The yew grows well in any soil, but likes calcareous soil, and really thrives on chalky soil.

Pruning
Pinching back Pinch back the young shoots on the side branches from spring to autumn. If you want to have fruit, do not pinch back until the tree has flowered.*

A female plant cannot fruit without pollen from a male plant.

STYLES

Chokkan   Tachiki   Sabamiki   Fukinagashi   Sōkan   Kabudachi   Yose-Ue

Japanese yew (*Taxus cuspidata*). 70 years old. Height, 40 cm (1 ft 4 in). 'Fukinagashi' style. Photograph taken in May.

Pruning of branches The yew can be pruned either in spring or autumn. Prune side branches that are sticking out, cutting above a tuft of needles. It is possible to train this bonsai quite well by pruning, as it is easy to mould into shape.

Wiring Essential in conjunction with pruning to shape the tree. Wire from September to March. Avoid wiring when the tree has very new shoots.

Watering Water regularly in moderation, not too much, but enough. Do not drown the roots.

Spraying Necessary in hot weather, especially if the tree is in the sun. But do not spray in full sun.

Feeding As growth is slow, feeding is important. In spring and autumn. Never feed in July-August, or if a bonsai has just been repotted or is in poor condition. Increase the amount of fertilizer given in the last autumn application.

Pests and diseases

Pests
- **Galls on buds**

Symptoms The buds turn brown, swell and drop off.
Treatment Spray with insecticide.
- **Weevils**

Symptoms The needles are gnawed, and the bark on shoots withers at the tips. The tree turns yellow, withers and wilts. The roots are attacked and growth comes to a halt.

Treatment Spray with lindane-based insecticide from May to July.
- **Tortrix** (caterpillars) See p. 29.
- **Scale insects** See p. 29.

Diseases
- **Rotting of roots and stem** See p. 31.

DECIDUOUS TREES

Acer palmatum
JAPANESE MAPLE

The Aceraceae family. Native to the cool temperate areas of the northern hemisphere. The Japanese maple is a deciduous tree native to Japan, and particularly attractive because of the variety of colour displayed in its foliage. In winter when it is bare it is still very beautiful because of the way its branches are distributed. Its leaves are opposite and palmatilobate. Its fruit is a double key, made up of two seeds extended by a membranous wing. The foliage is generally green, but it can be variegated green and white or green and pink. It can be purple-pink or purple in spring; in autumn it produces every shade of yellow, orange, red or brown. In summer the Japanese maple tends to turn green again. There are a great many varieties and cultivars.

Acer palmatum rubrum Palmate leaves shaped like a hand. The buds are red. It takes its autumn tints early, with its foliage turning red or yellow. It is rich in sugar, which explains why its leaves are all the more colourful the more sun there is.
Acer palmatum 'Asahi zuru'. Variegated leaves of green and pinkish white.
Acer palmatum deshohjoh Blood-red foliage in spring, turning green from late spring to autumn when it displays brilliant autumn colours.
Acer palmatum seigen Very similar to *A. p. deshohjoh*, but the red is less intense, more pink.
Acer palmatum tamahime Very small light-green leaves that deepen in colour a few weeks after they have broken from the bud.
Acer palmatum dissectum atropurpureum The very finely divided leaves look like lace and are always red.
Acer palmatum aureum The leaves have five lobes. They turn yellow in autumn, but always have a pink edge.
There are so many varieties and cultivars that they cannot all be given by name here.

Propagation

From seed When the fruit has fallen, collect the seeds. Clean them and spread them out to dry. Only seeds with a green embryo are of any use, and you can discover this by cutting into the seed. Remove the seeds from their wings. Keep them in a dry place. Before planting them in March, lay them between layers of damp sand for three days. Plant in a frame, protecting the young shoots from frost. Keep the new shoots dry in the summer. When they are two years old, replant them in the spring.

By simple layering Choose a young branch, and strip leaves from the part to be buried. Lay it lengthwise in a furrow in early spring. Make a notch above the eyes to encourage roots to form. Cover with earth which is kept slightly damp. This method is very slow (you have to wait for two years), and does not always produce results.

By air layering In April make a notch in the bark of the trunk or branch to be layered with sharp, clean knife. Sprinkle hormone rooting powder in the slit and wedge it with a ball of moss or a piece of gravel. Envelop the cut with damp sphagnum moss and wrap this round with a plastic bag and make airtight. Cover the plastic with an opaque piece of canvas or sacking or with aluminium foil to keep protected from direct sunlight and excessive heat. New roots will appear by the following spring. Then cut through the layer, pot carefully and place in the shade.

From cuttings Take maple cuttings in June (from a full-sized or bonsai tree); strip off a thin layer of bark. Insert in a mixture of $\frac{2}{3}$ peat and $\frac{1}{3}$ sand. Take off the soft top. It is advisable to use a hormone rooting compound before inserting the slip. Ensure good drainage to prevent water stagnating. This method gives good results.

By grafting Always choose a rootstock belonging to the same group as the variety to be grafted to avoid incompatibility (the varieties and cultivars actually belong to a number of different groups).
External shield budding A side veneer graft in an unheated greenhouse.
Shield budding on to lignified branches From mid-June. Do not choose a rootstock that is too large or the bark will have covered the eyes; graft on to wood produced that

STYLES

Shakan

Kengai

Tachiki

Han-Kengai

Sekijōju

Sōkan

Kabudachi

Ikadabuki

Netsunagari

Japanese maple (*Acer palmatum*). Deshohjoh variety. 15 years old. Height, 20 cm (8 in). 'Shakan' style. Photograph taken in April. From April to June the leaves are blood red. In summer they tend to become green, then in autumn take on shimmering, fiery orange tints.

year. If a first graft fails, you can try again in August.

Veneer grafting In August. The stock should be pencil thick. The scions are one-year-old lignified side branches. Paint with a sealing compound. Keep in moist conditions in a greenhouse. The graft should have knit within four weeks. Give air. You must wait another year before the top of the rootstock is cut off.

Whip grafting. This can be effected in very early spring if the stock and the scion have an eye drawing the sap on the side opposite the cut to avoid any drying out.

Care

Exposure to sunlight Keep the *Acer palmatum* in semishade. It can tolerate greater exposure to the sun provided the base of its roots is kept moist. Direct sun can scorch the tips of the leaves, But it does need light.

Temperature Protect from frosts below −3°C (27°F). Does not thrive in dry heat.

Ventilation Protect from drying winds.

Good ventilation round the tree prevents powdery mildew fom developing in summer.

Container Plant this bonsai in a flat, elongated bowl to allow the roots to spread and receive summer warmth. The bowl is usually oval, sometimes rectangular. It can be brown, willow green, light blue or beige. Very good drainage is essential.

Cleaning After the leaves have fallen, remove dead leaves from the soil, or from

Sôju

Sambon-Yose

Gohon-Yose

Nanahon-Yose

Kyûhon-Yose

Yose-Ue

Yamayori

Tsukami-Yose

Bonkei

Acer palmatum
JAPANESE MAPLE

the tree. At the onset of winter, remove dead branches.

Growth Slow.

Repotting About every third year in spring; every second year for young specimens. Prune the roots to half their length. If necessary wash them in water. Be very careful to remove dead or damaged rootlets and old roots.

Soil ⅔ loam and ⅓ course sand. An excessively alkaline soil impedes the Japanese maple's development. Dry, even stony, well-compacted, chalky soil suits it.

Pruning
Pinching back Prune terminals leaving only two nodes, and laterals to just one node. Wait for shoots to grow, and pinch back again. Pinching back new shoots

before they become too thin allows the tree to be shaped gently without leaving scars.
Leaf pruning By cutting the leaves you can achieve a tree with thick, bushy, small foliage, tapering at the tips. Do not strip a tree of its leaves the same year as it is repotted, nor if it is weakly. Leaf stripping

Leaves that have become too big have to be reduced by half.

Leaf pruning

is carried out in June; leaf cutting is done during the growing period, usually every second year.
Pruning of branches During the growing period, prune the branches so as to leave

Branches must be cut above a leaf axil.

Pruning of branches

only one or two pairs of leaves on each side branch. When a branch is growing too fast, prune it, and remove the buds and leaves from the part that is left.
Development pruning This is done in winter when the tree is bare. Study its outline. With branch cutters make a concave cut flush with the trunk to remove crossing branches, any growing vertically alongside the trunk or any that are parallel. Leave only every second branch. Good development pruning leads to better branch growth in the spring.

Wiring The shape of the Japanese maple is generally achieved by pruning, but it can be necessary to use wire. If so, protect the bark with raffia as it is fragile and can be damaged by copper wire. Wire the tree when it is in full leaf and remove the wire after six months.

Watering Water sparingly. The maple can be allowed to become dry between waterings. But it does need constant humidity on the surface of its roots. Be careful, though, as excessive water will immediately cause the roots to rot.

Spraying The foliage needs a damp atmosphere, so it should be mist-sprayed frequently, especially if it is exposed to a drying wind or to the sun.

Feeding In spring and autumn give a slow-acting organic fertilizer. Wait for two months after repotting, and do not feed a weakened tree.

a The leaves of this Japanese maple *(Acer palmatum)* should be pinched right out.

b To get rid of the major part of the leaves, first use scissors.

c You complete the process of pinching back all the leaves with scissors.

Pests and diseases

Pests

● **Erineum** (gall mites)
Symptoms Red and green graining on the upper surface of the foliage, while the undersides are felted with beige, grey or brown. A thick down crinkles up the leaves which become distorted. Appearance of galls.
Treatment Spray with a parathion or lindane-based insecticide or with lime sulphur if the attack is severe.
● **Bark beetles** See p. 30.
● **Cossus and leopard moths** (caterpillars) See p. 29.
● **Geometers** (caterpillars) See p. 29.
● **Bombyx and owlet moths** (caterpillars) See p. 29.
● **Leafhoppers**
Symptoms Flecks of white on the foliage caused by stings. The lamina becomes discoloured, stem growth slows and the leaves may drop off. Green insects present on the undersides of leaves.
Treatment Cut out infested branches. Spray with a contact insecticide or a systemic organophosphate insecticide.
● **Scale insects** See p. 29.
● **Aphids** See p. 29.

Diseases

● **Powdery mildew** See p. 31.
● **Canker**
Symptoms Where there are scars or clefts between branches sores develop, deepening, cracking and swelling and causing the branch to die. Adjacent branches form excrescences as a defence mechanism. The canker eats through to the wood and red spots show up on it.
Treatment Cut out and destroy diseased branches. Scrape out the cankers. Apply a fungicide to them, and cover with grafting wax. At leaf fall spray with a fungicidal wash.

● **Coral spot**
Symptoms Branches and laterals suddenly wither. Fungus forms in the ligneous tissues. Red spots and cankerous lesions appear on the dead wood.
Treatment Cut out and destroy diseased material. Dab a copper fungicide on to the wounds.
● **Witches' brooms**
Symptoms Buds develop so vigorously that the branches look bushy.
Treatment Cut out diseased branches.
● **Tar spot or ink disease**
Symptoms Discoloured patches on the lamina. A black scab ringed with yellow forms in the centre.
Treatment Destroy dead leaves. Add nitrogen to the fertilizer. Guard against the disease by spraying with a mineral copper-based fungicide. Repeat when the buds are opening.
● **Die-back**
Symptoms Shoots and young branches wither. Cankers form on branches.
Treatment Cut out and destroy diseased or dead branches.
● **Cercospora fungus**
Symptoms Brown patches on the shoots of young trees. The tree gradually wilts.
Treatment Spray with a fungicide based on copper and zineb.
● **Verticillium wilt** See p. 31.
● **Leaf spot** (fungoid)
● **Anthracnose**
Symptoms Brick-coloured blotches on the leaves and sometimes on the lamina. Foliage withers.
Treatment Pick off dead leaves. Spray with a copper-based fungicide.
● **Honey fungus** See p. 31.

Japanese maple (*Acer palmatum*). 12 years old. Height, 15 cm (6 in). 'Tachiki' style. Photograph taken in April. You can see the pale green colour, edged with brown, of the young leaves. The bonsai is not yet in full leaf.

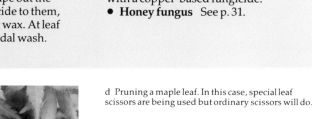

d Pruning a maple leaf. In this case, special leaf scissors are being used but ordinary scissors will do.

e A few weeks later a new crop of leaves appear, that are smaller than the previous ones.

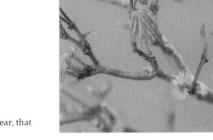

Acer buergerianum (syn. A. trifidum)
TRIDENT MAPLE

The Aceraceae family. Native to the cool temperate areas of the northern hemisphere. *Acer buergerianum* is native to eastern China and can grow to a height of 12 m (40 ft). Its straight, light-beige trunk loses its bark in patches as it grows old. The trident-shaped leaves are green in spring and summer, and yellow-orange, even red, in autumn. Its fruit is a winged key.

Propagation

From seed Collect the seeds, clean them, dry them, and sow them at the end of autumn. They can also be stored between layers straight away and kept in a cool place. Plant in a warm place. Protect the young shoots from possible frost. Replant seedlings in the spring of their second year.

From cuttings Take the cuttings in June, strip off a thin layer of bark and plant in a ⅔ peat, ⅓ sand mixture after treating with hormone rooting compound. Remove the soft tip. Make sure that drainage is very good, as stagnant water is fatal to them. The *Acer trifidum* roots easily.

By air layering In April make a cut through the bark in the part to be layered with a clean, sharp knife. Sprinkle the layer with hormone rooting powder, and wedge the slit open with a twist of moss or a pebble. Pack moist sphagnum moss round the layer and wrap polythene round the whole area, making airtight seals at either end. New roots will appear the following spring. Carefully cut through the layer and pot it up. The new tree will remain delicate for a year.

By simple layering A slower method, not giving as good results. Follow the usual procedure.

Care

Exposure to sunlight. Tolerates full sun. Nonetheless, in areas with a great deal of sunshine, it should be placed in semi-shade in summer.

Temperature Must be shielded from frost. Can withstand heat.

Ventilation Can be exposed to wind. Needs to have plenty of air circulating round it. In Japan where it is planted along avenues as an ornamental tree, it withstands pollution well.

Container Needs a fairly deep pot except when it is planted over stone or in a group. The pot can be rectangular or oval, and is often earth coloured.

Cleaning Ensure that all leaves fall at the end of the autumn, and clear the soil of leaves and dead wood to prevent any attack by parasites or diseases. Brush the trunk gently.

Growth Young trees grow quickly, but growth becomes slower with age.

The wiring on this trident maple (*Acer buergerianum*), shown here in winter, can be clearly seen.

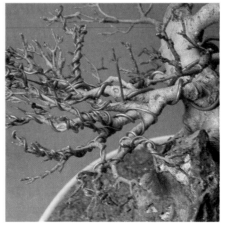

STYLES

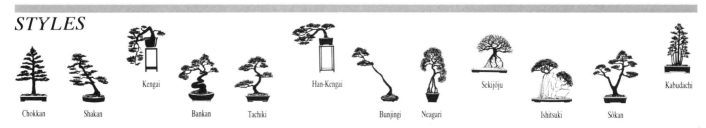

Chokkan   Shakan   Kengai   Bankan   Tachiki   Han-Kengai   Bunjingi   Neagari   Sekijōju   Ishitsuki   Sōkan   Kabudachi

Trident maple (*Acer buergerianum*). 18 years old. Height, 40 cm (1 ft 4 in). 'Yóse-Ue' and 'Sekijôju' styles. Photograph taken in May. It is hard to say which style predominates in this group: a group of maples ('Yóse-Ue') has been planted on a rock so that the roots are displayed on the rock ('Sekijôju').

Repotting Every second or third year repot into a larger container. Cut away between a half and two thirds of the root hairs, and take care to remove all damaged or dead roots.

Soil ⅔ loam and ⅓ coarse sand. Any dry, stony, chalky soil is suitable. Avoid using excessively alkaline compost.

Pruning

Pinching back Pinch back the terminal shoots leaving only two nodes on each side branch. When new shoots appear, repeat the process.

Leaf pruning Prune the leaves which tend to become over large from spring to autumn. This tree is seldom stripped of its leaves.

Pruning of branches Prune the side branches hard, generally reducing them by a third of their length, to preserve the tree's shape.

Development pruning Cut back the branches well before the growing season in February to improve the branch structure. Remove any branches which mar the tree's appearance.

Wiring The trident maple's shape is mainly produced by pruning, but it may be necessary to wire the tree to perfect certain styles. Wiring is then put in place in June-July-August to avoid breaking the branches, and the bark is protected with raffia.

Watering Water freely from spring until autumn, less frequently and less copiously in winter.

Spraying Spray the leaves in spring and summer, but never in full sun. Spraying is a means of ridding the foliage of possible parasites.

Feeding Feed from March to November with a break in July-August, using a slow-acting organic fertilizer. Wait six weeks after repotting, and do not feed a tree that is in poor condition.

Pests and diseases

Same pests and diseases as the *Acer palmatum* See p. 61.

| Korabuki | Ikadabuki | Netsunagari | Sôju | Sambon-Yose | Gohon-Yose | Nanahon-Yose | Kyúhon-Yose | Yose-Ue | Yamayori | Tsukami-Yose | Bonkei |

The Betulaceae family. Native to the temperate and cold areas of the northern hemisphere. It is mainly found in eastern Asia and North America. There are about 40 species. This elegant tree lives about 100 years

Betula
BIRCH

The *Betula pendula* (formerly *verrucosa*) gets its old name from the white warts on its branches. When its branches hang down, which is mainly when it is old, it is called the weeping birch. It has thick foliage, the leaves being small, green and triangular with a double-toothed edge. The underside of the leaves is bright yellow in autumn. Catkins open in April-May. The bark of this species is golden brown when it is young, later becoming silvery white, and it peels off in thin layers.

Propagation

From seed Collect seeds between August and November. They are ripe when the cones are yellow, but they do not all ripen at the same time. Spread the seeds out, and dry them by turning them over and over. Once they are dry, keep them in a bag in a cool airy place. Sow at the end of March on a moist seedbed. Cover with twigs to protect the seeds. Keep the ground damp. Germination gets under way in four weeks. Water the seedlings, which appear within eight weeks, as necessary. Remove the twigs and ensure that the bed does not dry out. The following spring, repot.

By grafting Very seldom used as the graft union can be seen for a very long time. Only used when a new variety is being propagated or when you can obtain a bonsai by no other means.
Approach grafting In June, using old wood.
Shield budding Either in August-September using two shields, or late May-early June when the rootstock is in full growth.

From young nursery stock

Care

Exposure to sunlight Likes sunny positions, needs a lot of light.

Temperature The birch flourishes in warm, dry places and stands up very well to the cold.

Ventilation Is happier in open, but sheltered positions than in windy ones, but does not mind wind.

Container Choose a shallow or flat pot, reddish brown or blue.

Cleaning Remove any dead material. Take care that moss does not climb up the trunk. Remove any shoots coming out of the trunk.

Growth Fast.

Repotting Repot every second year into a larger container. Prune the roots by between a half and two thirds. Leave some of the old earth on the roots when repotting to help the tree to get re-established.

Soil ½ loam, ¼ course sand, and ¼ leaf mould. Likes light, cool, friable earth and will also grow on soil that is acid, poor, sandy or stony.

Pruning
Pruning of shoots From March to November throughout the growing season. After each side branch has produced three to five nodes, use scissors to cut back to one or two.
Pruning of branches During the growing season when the birch starts to lose its basic shape, prune the branches back quite short. Cut above the point where a leaf breaks.
Development pruning Only done early on when the tree is being created. Subsequently to be avoided as the birch does not like being pruned.

Wiring The shape is mainly produced by pruning new shoots. When it is essential to wire it to achieve certain styles, protect the bark with raffia. Wire in spring and in summer.

Watering Generally birches need light but frequent watering. The *pubescens*, *japonica* and *tauschii* varieties need more water than the *Betula pendula*.

Spraying Prefers a dry atmosphere. It

STYLES

Shakan

Tachiki

Sōkan

Kabudachi

Ikadabuki

Netsunagari

Sōju

does not need to be sprayed except in extreme heat.

Feeding From spring to autumn feed with slow-acting organic fertilizer with a break in July-August. Do not feed for two months after repotting or if the tree is in poor condition.

Pests and diseases
Pests
● **Ornamental tree leaf-rolling insect**
Symptoms Leaves and shoots gnawed. Presence of eggs in veins. Lamina curled up in cigar shape.
Treatment Pick off and destroy the rolled up leaves. Spray with organophosphate or organochlorine insecticide when adults appear.
● **Bark beetles** See p. 30.
● **Wasp moths** (caterpillars)
Symptoms The bark on the trunk and branches is gnawed, holed, and galleries run from the holes. Heaps of sawdust lying on the holes. Presence of caterpillars.
Treatment Push a wire through the galleries to destroy the caterpillars.
● **Geometers** (moth caterpillars: range of varieties) See p. 29.
● **Woolly bombyx** (caterpillars) See p. 28.

Diseases
● **Powdery mildew** See p. 31.
● **Blight**
Symptoms White swellings on the leaves which tear and shrivel.
Treatment Destroy dead leaves. Spray with a copper- or thiram-based wash in spring and autumn.
● **Witches' brooms**
Symptoms The buds swell abnormally, and branches and twigs look bushy.
Treatment Cut out and destroy diseased branches.
● **Leaf spot** See p. 31.
● **Canker** (fungoid)
Symptoms Where there are scars or clefts beween branches, sores form, swell and crack, causing the branches to die. Adjacent branches form excresences as a defensive measure. There are dots of red on the wood.
Treatment Cut out and destroy the diseased branches. Scrape out the cankers. Apply a fungicide to the wounds, and cover with a wound-sealing compound. Spray with a fungicidal wash at leaf fall.
● **Honey fungus** See p. 31.

River birch *(Betula nigra)*. 10 years old. Height, 25 cm (10 in). 'Kabudachi' style. Photograph taken in May.

Sambon-Yose

Gohon-Yose

Nanahon-Yose

Kyūhon-Yose

Yose-Ue

Yamayori

Tsukami-Yose

The Corylaceae family. Native to the temperate areas of the northern hemisphere: Europe, central and eastern Asia, the northern Himalayas. It lives for about 200 years and is 20 m (65 ft) tall. It is a tree with a straight, grooved trunk, bark that forms a meandering pattern, a great many long, slender branches and a narrow oval top. The alternate, oval leaves are double toothed, corrugated and do not form branches. Catkins in April-May, ripe fruit in October. There are a great many varieties.

Carpinus
HORNBEAM

Carpinus japonica Elongated, markedly corrugated leaves, dark green on top, browny red underneath. Fruit in clusters.
Carpinus laxiflora Small, glossy, slightly leathery leaves, a smooth, grey-beige trunk, gnarled and rough at the base on 'Yamodori' specimens from Korea.

Propagation

From seed Collect the seeds when they are ripe and sow immediately. If they cannot be sown, stratify the seeds and plant them the following February. Germination will take place in mid-May. When you sow dried-out seeds (in February), they can take a year to germinate. Protect seedlings from late frosts.

From cuttings In spring when pruning. Take a cutting, and lightly strip it of bark. Dip in a hormone rooting compound, behead, and plant in a sand-peat mixture. Protect from cold.

By air layering In spring, using a fairly slender branch.

By grafting When the hornbeam cannot be propagated by any other method, whip grafting or inlay grafting can be practised in January in a greenhouse, using two-year-old wood.

From young nursery stock Produces excellent results: the hornbeam submits well to being pruned and cut back.

Care

Exposure to sunlight Young specimens need shade. It is a copsewood tree and does not like full summer sun very much, but tolerates sun in other seasons.

Japanese hornbeam (*Carpinus japonica*). 50 years old. Height, 60 cm (2 ft). 'Tachiki' style. Photograph taken in October. This remarkable Japanese hornbeam offers a symphony of colours.

Temperature Stands up equally well to frost and heat.

Ventilation Withstands wind (it is often used in hedging).

Container No special requirements, adapts to a very flat container when it is grown in a group style.

Cleaning Remove dead leaves from the branches and soil in autumn. Do not let moss form on the base of the trunk.

Growth Very slow.

Repotting In early spring, every second or third year repot into a larger container. Prune the roots by a good half. Remove any dead or damaged roots.

Soil ⅔ loam and ⅓ coarse sand. The hornbeam is happiest in cool, damp, clayey soil; it tolerates lime and can grow in poor soil.

Pruning
Pruning of branches Use clippers to cut back side branches, leaving one or two pairs of leaves on each lateral, as soon as

STYLES

Shakan

Tachiki

Han-Kengai

Sekijõju

Nejikan

Sõkan

Hornbeam *(Carpinus betulus carpinizza)*. 40 years old. Height, 60 cm (2 ft). 'Tachiki' style. Photograph taken in March. Inflorescences appeared very shortly before the leaves. The polished grey-white colour of the trunk is specific to this variety.

four or five have been produced.

Development pruning   At the end of winter, prune well for neatness and maintenance, so as to train the branches and achieve a well-ordered branch structure. Hornbeams submit well to pruning.

Wiring   The shape is produced mainly by pruning. If necessary, wire in spring and summer.

Watering   Copious, especially from mid-spring to mid-autumn, but there must be good drainage to guard against water stagnating. The ground should be moist, but not sodden.

Spraying   Spray the foliage in summer to cleanse the tree of pollution and possible infestation.

Feeding   Feed in spring and in autumn with a slow-acting organic fertilizer. Do not feed in July-August. Leave for two months after repotting. Give no fertilizer to a tree that is in poor condition.

Pests and diseases

Pests
- **Red spider mites**   See p. 28.
- **Geometers** (moth caterpillars: range of varieties)   See p. 29.
- **Bombyx** (caterpillars)   See p. 28.

Diseases
- **Powdery mildew**   See p. 31.
- **Leaf spot**   See p. 31.

Kabudachi

Sôju

Sambon-Yose

Gohon-Yose

Nanahon-Yose

Kyûhon-Yose

Yose-Ue

The Ulmaceae family. Most species are native to tropical or subtropical zones: about 15 species are native to the temperate zones of the northern hemisphere. About 70 species have been categorized.

Celtis
NETTLE TREE

Celtis bangeana sinensis Large deciduous leaves that are oval, shiny and dark green. Produces red decorative and edible fruit. Of spreading habit, can grow to about 20 m (65 ft).

Celtis australis (southern nettle tree). Grows around the Mediterranean basin, reaches a height of about 25 m (80 ft), has a short, grooved trunk and a rounded, bushy top. Its lower branches are horizontal. It can live for up to 600 years. The long, pointed, deciduous leaves are asymmetric, oblique and smooth at the base, sometimes dentate, a dark-green upper surface and grey and soft underneath. Purple fruit, ripe in October.

Propagation

From seed Collect the seeds when they are ripe, and stratify for a year. Plant in the spring. Germination is very patchy. Keep the soil moist until they have germinated.

From cuttings In summer, using young slips that have been beheaded and dipped in a hormone rooting compound.

By air layering Strip the bark off the part to be layered. Make a slit in it to encourage rooting, and keep partly open. Wrap damp sphagnum moss round the cut. Cover with polythene and make airtight. Keep damp. Sever when roots have formed. Pot up and protect from frost.

Care

Exposure to sunlight Full sun.

Temperature Will not stand up to frost (except for *Celtis occidentalis*). Likes heat.

Ventilation Likes a position with good air circulation, but not exposed to a strong or prevailing wind.

Container A fairly deep pot – the nettle tree needs deep earth.

Cleaning Take care to remove all dead leaves in autumn. Remove any moss that forms on the trunk.

Growth Very slow: it grows 3 m (10 ft) in 20 years.

Repotting In early spring every three years, repot in a larger container. Prune the roots by between a third and a half and remove any dead, damaged or old roots.

Soil ⅔ loam and ⅓ coarse sand. Thrives in light, rich, cool soil, but not if it is wet or clayey. The soil can be calcareous, dry and stony.

Pruning
Pruning of shoots From spring until the end of summer. Wait until new shoots have three or four nodes, then use scissors to cut back to one or two. Take out any shoots that are about to sprout.
Pruning of subbranches Cut back branches that are too long so as to achieve a good branch structure. Prune at the leaf axils, and two new shoots will branch out, which should be left with a single pair of leaves.
Pruning of branches In March-April, before growth gets under way.

Wiring From spring to autumn, protecting the branches with raffia. The shape should be developed mainly by pruning shoots, subbranches and branches.

Watering Water freely in hot weather. Allow the soil to dry out well between waterings. Does not like wet soil.

Spraying You can sprinkle the foliage when you water the tree.

Feeding From spring to autumn feed with slow-acting organic fertilizer preferably in pellets or in liquid form, Do not feed in July-August, or if the tree is weak. A liberal application of fertilizer hardens the branches and makes them stronger.

STYLES

Chokkan

Tachiki

Sôkan

Kabudachi

Sôju

Southern nettle tree *(Celtis australis)*. 20 years old. Height, 18 cm (7 in). An unusual combination here of two styles, 'Chokkan' and 'Hôkidachi'. Photograph taken in May.

Pests and diseases

Pests
- **Mites**   See p. 28.
- **Bark beetles**   See p. 30.
- **Bombyx** (caterpillars)   See p. 28.
- **Greenfly and gall-forming aphids**
  See p. 29.

Diseases
- **Mosaic virus**

Symptoms   The lamina is striated with yellow, and the veins form a mosaic pattern. Old leaves turn yellow and drop off. The disease's virulence varies according to the climate and the area. Not a common virus.

- **Elm disease** (fungoid)

Only the *Celtis australis* is affected.
Symptoms   Leaves turn yellow, veins turn brown, and side branches wither. The leaves fall off and the branches are bent. Buds are dry and brittle.
Treatment   Use a systemic fungicide.

If the nettle tree is badly sited and is given too much or too little water, it can produce yellow leaves and fungi.

Sambon-Yose

Gohon-Yose

Nanahon-Yose

Kyûhon-Yose

Yose-Ue

Fagus
BEECH

The Fagaceae family. Native to the temperate areas of the northern hemisphere. A tree with deciduous leaves. The lifespan of the beech is about 250 years, but can extend to 500 in exceptional circumstances. The beech is a hardy tree. It has smooth, ash-grey bark, long, pointed buds and leaves that are soft green in spring, dark green in summer and russet in autumn. Some of the leaves stay on the tree throughout the winter, not falling until the new shoots burgeon in spring. Such leaves are called marcescent. The nuts or beech mast are edible and occur mainly on old trees. There are about 15 known species, all of which can be developed as bonsai. The best known are:

Fagus sylvatica (common beech). Has oblong, dentate leaves with prominent veins.
Fagus sieboldii Native to japan. Its bole is longer, its trunk whiter and its foliage smaller.
Fagus sylvatica purpurea (purple beech). Has reddish-brown foliage and stands up better to a dry atmosphere. It is a garden species that makes an attractive bonsai.
Fagus sylvatica pendula (weeping beech). Its branches hang down very naturally.

Propagation

From seed The seed is sown in autumn. It does not take long to germinate. If it is impossible to plant the seeds in autumn, keep them stratified in dry sand until spring and sow them then. They are planted at a depth of 2.5 cm (1 in) in a mixture of peat and coarse sand (make sure the compost is not too acid) in a box; do not firm the soil too much to allow air to circulate.

By grafting The method used for the beech is approach grafting. In this method the scion is not severed immediately, but left joined to the parent plant until the union is complete. The scion and the stock can come from the same tree. If the graft is made in early spring, it will have taken by late autumn. The top of the rootstock is cut off, cutting as close as possible to the stock to avoid too large a swelling. The cut is painted with a wound sealing compound so that the scar quickly becomes in-

conspicuous. It also prevents pests and diseases from entering the tree. After grafting the beech is protected from wind and frost and regarded as a tree that has just been repotted.

From young nursery stock You can find young beeches with an interesting trunk in nurseries. In spring you apply bonsai techniques to these specimens, pruning the branches and roots, and putting them in a pot. They will have to be worked on for two or three years before they are real bonsai.

Care

Exposure to sunlight The beech tolerates full sun, but in summer, especially near the Mediterranean, it is better to place it in a slightly shaded position.

Ventilation In its natural state the beech is used for hedging. So it stands up very well to wind. However, very young specimens less than five years old and repotted trees should be protected from a strong wind.

Temperature In the south of France, the beech occurs naturally on high ground where it is cooler. It does not like intense heat. It is mainly found in places with an ocean or mountain climate. It reacts badly to very severe winters and spring frosts. If the temperature falls below −5°C (23°F), the roots and the container must be protected with a covering of wool, straw or dead leaves, or by burying the tree with its container up to the base of the trunk. It can also be brought inside into a cold room, which does not even have to have much light, during very cold weather. However, like all hardy species, the bonsai beech is able to withstand the temperatures encountered in our climate.

STYLES

Chokkan

Shakan

Tachiki

Sôkan

Kabudachi

Korabuki

Netsunagari

Sôju

Yose-Ue

Tsukami-Yose

Siebold's beech *(Fagus sieboldii)*. 150 years old. Height, 55 cm (1 ft 10 in). 'Tachiki' style. Photograph taken in April. On this venerable beech, you can see the previous year's marcescent leaves and the young shoots.

Fagus
BEECH

Siebold's beech *(Fagus sieboldii)*. 50 years old. Height, 65 cm (2 ft 2 in). 'Chokkan' style. Photograph taken in March. We can see:
a – the emergence of the young leaves;
b – all the wiring;
c – how a young tree has been implanted at the foot of the main tree, which is intended to re-establish balance in the rooting base.

Watering Water the beech freely from late spring to late summer. Give less water from late summer and in autumn. Avoid giving too much water in winter.

Spraying The beech particularly likes a damp atmosphere, and has to be sprayed from early spring to late summer. If the tree is small and the weather very dry, it can even be sprayed morning and evening. It is also a good idea to recreate humidity by watering all round the tree; as it evaporates, the water brings necessary moisture to the whole tree.

Beech demonstrates the peculiarity of only shedding its leaves with difficulty.

Growth The foliage of the beech grows very slowly, so you let it grow until the end of spring before cutting it.

Container For aesthetic reasons, the beech is not put in a decorated pot, and the pot should not be too flat; old single specimens need a container aout 4 to 8 cm (1½ to 3 in) deep. A group bonsai, on the other hand can be planted on a flat bowl, or even on a simple tray.

Soil The soil mixture used for beeches consists of equal parts of loam and sand. The beech is happiest in cool, sandy clay soil that drains well, but also it does well in calcareous or stony soil; wet, compressed soil is to be avoided.

Repotting Repotting is always done in the spring just as growth starts and before the new shoots have burst open. Repot every two or three years, depending on the age of the tree. Old trees (over 50 years) are repotted every four or five years. Cut away between a half and two-thirds of the root hairs, and place the tree in the new pot.

Pruning The branches and leaves are pruned at the same time as the beech is repotted and the roots pruned.
Pinching back On the beech new shoots are very vigorous and must be pinched back. The beech does not produce secondary buds. The spacing between the nodes tends to become ever wider and cuts made in pruning are in danger of being visible as a result of this. This is why young shoots should be pinched back while they are still soft, leaving one or two leaves. This process takes place in late spring when the previous year's dead leaves have fallen at the prompting of the new shoots.
Leaf pruning This is a trickier operation carried out in summer on healthy trees. It is done only every second year. It takes it out of the tree, but after leaf cutting the beech will be all the lovelier in autumn, with smaller leaves produced by an artificially created second spring. It is also possible to strip completely the tree of leaves, but not in the same year as it has been repotted.
Pruning of branches They should be lightly pruned, preferably after repotting. The beech is a slow-growing tree, and is only pruned once in the season. Cuts should be made at a slant, leaving two or three leaves on each section of branch, and just above a leaf bud, to encourage a good spread of new branches.
Development pruning This should be done in winter when the tree's outline can be clearly seen. Any main branch that is spoiling the aesthetic effect of the tree should be cut out using a good bonsai saw. Some wound-sealing compound should be applied to each cut to guard against pests and disease.

Wiring The bonsai is mainly sculpted into shape by pruning, but wiring is used too if you want to train the tree into a fixed style. When removing the wire, cut with wire cutters, taking care not to damage the tree; if the bark is cut through, apply a wound-sealing compound. As the beech's bark is easily damaged, it is best to wrap raffia or paper round the wire. The beech is wired between spring and autumn for a maximum period of three months as the new wood is very soft and the pressure exerted by the wire might damage the branches and roots of the tree. Until you achieve the style you are aiming for, repeat this process annually, always taking care not to catch any leaves between the wire and the bark.

Siebold's beech *(Fagus sieboldii)*. Detail showing how the new leaves burst; note the wire wrapped round with paper to prevent damage to the branch.

Feeding Fertilizer can be given in granule, powder or liquid form. Feed from early spring after the buds have opened until the end of autumn when the tree becomes dormant, but not in July-August.

Cleaning The beech has marcescent leaves. Clear away any leaves lying at the foot of the tree, but leave any others that are on the tree. In fact you should remove any dead or damaged material so as to prevent the occurrence of diseases or pests, and keep the tree well aired, including its foliage, and beneath the soil.

Siebold's beech (*Fagus sieboldii*). From 15 to 30 years old. Height, 70 cm (2 ft 4 in). 'Yóse-Ue' style. Photograph taken in December. This group was photographed in winter, and will keep its autumn leaves until spring.

Pests and diseases

Pests
- **Beech-leaf miner** (*Orchestes fagi*)
Symptoms The leaves have round holes in them which get bigger. The weevil appears when the leaves are forming, and is about 2 or 3 mm (⅛ in) long. This pest feeds on leaves.
Treatment Use insecticide in spring when leaves are developing.
- **Gall midges** – pointed galls (*Mikiola fagi*)
Symptoms Red galls about 10 mm (⅜ in) long on the leaves, which ripen and fall to the ground where they can be seen.
Treatment This is not a serious form of infestation, and does not require treatment.
- **Felted beech coccus or scale** (*Cryptococcus fagi*)
Symptoms 'Tufts of wool' fixed on to the bark. If you look closely you can see insects with a white, waxy carapace adhering to the bark.
Treatment Improve the conditions in which the tree is kept.
NB. Only trees that are in poor condition are infested.
- **Gall midges** – hairy galls (*Hartigiola annulipes*)

Symptoms Small, hard, cylindrical, hairy galls turning from white to brown.
Treatment No treatment neessary. (There is no real damage to the tree).
- **Bark beetles**
Symptoms A great many small holes on the bark. Branches gradually die, and the tree falls.
Treatment These brown-black insects, between 1 and 10 mm (1/32 – ⅜ in) in length interfere with the circulation of the sap, and are more inclined to infest trees that are not in physiological equilibrium. Cut out dead branches immediately and burn them. If the beech is heavily infested, use an insecticide.

Diseases
- **Canker** (fungoid)
Symptoms Brownish patches on the trunk and main branches which turn into large sores, causing the upper part of the tree to die.
Treatment If the disease is caught in the early stages, treat it with a fungicide containing a wound-sealing agent. If you act too late, all affected branches must be cut out.

The Fagaceae family. Native to the temperate zones of the northern hemisphere, the tropics, South America (Colombia) and south-eastern Asia. There are 250 known species.

Quercus
OAK

Quercus robur (pedunculate oak or English oak). A white oak 40 m (130 ft) tall. It lives for at least 400 years and can live for 1000. The straight, thick, short trunk divides into big, thick boughs that twist and bend. An irregularly shaped top. The deciduous leaves grow in clusters, with four or five pairs of lobes and two auricles at the leaf base, and are dark green, slightly tinged with blue, and glabrous. The acorns are ripe in autumn.

Quercus petraea syn. *sessiliflora* An oak which grows to a height of 40 m (130 ft). A straight cylindrical trunk with a leading shoot. Branches are less twisted. Leaves are homogeneous with seven or eight pairs of lobes, a round tip and no auricles at the base, they are light green, shiny and go red in autumn. They may stay on the tree in winter. Acorns are ripe in late autumn.

Quercus pubescens (downy oak). Does not grow to above 20 m (65 ft) in height. A short, twisted trunk, an irregularly shaped top; less long lived. Leaves have irregular lobes, are grey underneath and stay on the tree when withered. The globular acorns grow on a stalk.

Propagation

From seed Collect ripe acorns throughout most of October. Dry them out a bit by turning them over occasionally. Then keep in silos (like potatoes) or in barely moist sand. Sow in March-April, once there is no frost, 6 cm (2¼ in) deep. Germination takes place within six weeks. When the seeds have sprouted, protect the seedlings from the birds. Repot the following spring.

From cuttings Choose wood that is one to three years old. Dip the slips in a hormone rooting compound. Keep the cuttings in a warm place until roots have formed.

By air layering Follow the usual procedure (see Part I). Enclose the layer in a double sheath, with polythene inside and foil outside, thus reducing moisture loss and retaining more heat.

From young nursery stock Select specimens with a tap root that is not too deep and with a well-developed root system.

Care

Exposure to sunlight The pedunculate oak needs a lot of light whereas *Quercus petraea* is more of a forest tree and should be placed in semishade in summer. It is best to place the downy oak in a north aspect, but it does need a lot of light. A semishaded site in summer, in the sun for the rest of the year.

Temperature Withstands frost and likes heat. Does not like late frosts. *Quercus petraea* likes a mild, damp climate.

Ventilation Tolerates wind, but may break if the wind is too strong.

Container The main root goes very deep: select a deep container.

Cleaning If there are any old dry leaves left on the tree in spring when the new leaves break, gently pick them off. Do not allow moss to develop on the base of the roots and trunk.

Growth The pedunculate oak is slow growing, as is the downy oak.

Repotting Repot every three years in a larger container. Prune the root hairs by a half. Take care not to damage the tap root, though in young specimens it too must be reduced.

Soil ⅓ loam, ⅓ coarse sand and ⅓ leaf mould. The oak thrives in light, well-drained, relatively dry soil. The downy oak grows in dry calcareous, poor soil. As a rule, deep fertile soil, like the forest floor.

Pruning
Pruning of shoots Allow the buds to burst. Cut with clippers directly they fade and in summer cut before the new shoots are lignified.
Pruning of subbranches Shorten using clippers: leave only one or two pairs of leaves. Cut when the branches have produced about four or five pairs of leaves.
Development pruning Before the growing season starts, cut out any crossing branches. If this is done properly when the tree is young, it should gradually cease to be necessary.

Wiring If necessary, wire the oak from spring to autumn. But shape its outline as far as possible by means of pruning.

STYLES

Shakan

Tachiki

Han-Kengai

Sekijôju

Sôkan

Kabudachi

Watering Water well in spring and summer, letting the earth dry out between waterings. Good drainage is essential. The surface of the soil may be wetter.

Spraying Spray in summer: the water cleanses the leaves of pollution and possible pest attack.

Feeding Feed in spring and in autumn with a slow-acting organic fertilizer. Do not feed in July-August or after repotting or if the tree is in poor condition.

English oak *(Quercus robur)*. 9 years old. Height 20cm (8 in). 'Sekijôju' style. Photograph taken in June.

Pests and diseases

Pests
- **Chafer beetles**
Symptoms Gnawed roots harbouring a nest of chafer beetles. Leaves with holes on edges and eaten.
Treatment Spread insecticide on the soil in autumn to destroy the larvae. In spring spray with insecticide to attack the adult beetles.
- **Buprestid beetles**
Symptoms Holes in the bark with galleries running from them. Withered branches. Presence of silver-grey beetles.
Treatment Cut out and destroy infested branches.
- **Bark beetles** See p. 30.
- **Capricorn beetles**
Symptoms Holes in bark with galleries running from them. Withered branches. Presence of brown beetles.
Treatment Cut out and destroy infested branches.
- **Stag beetles**
Symptoms Trunk is gnawed by big white worms. Brown beetles possibly present. These insects only attack trees that are dying.
- **Orchestres**
Symptoms Leaves gnawed by larvae and the lamina gnawed by weevils.
Treatment Spray with insecticide.

- **Cossus** (Goat moth caterpillars) See p. 29.
- **Geometers** (moth caterpillars: range of varieties) See p. 29.
- **Tortrix** (green oak roller moth caterpillars) See p. 29.
- **Leaf miners** (caterpillars) See p. 29.
- **Aphids** See p. 29.
- **Gall wasps**
Symptoms Hairy green-red galls on the tissues of the tree containing larvae. Round artichoke-shaped galls on the branches.
Treatment Cut out the infested branches. No chemical treatment required.

Diseases
- **Damping off**
Symptoms The buds open with a fungus which causes them to collapse. Damp rot at the neck. The tree seems to fade away and collapse, then dies.
Treatment Do not allow water to stagnate and avoid excessive humidity. Place the tree in the air.
- **Powdery mildew** See p. 31.
- **Blight** (fungoid)
Symptoms Green blisters turning to brown on the foliage. In a bad attack, the leaves fall.
Treatment Spray with copper-based fungicide.
- **Canker** (fungoid)
Symptoms Where there are scars and gaps where the branches separate out, wounds form, swell and crack open; branches die. Neighbouring branches form excrescences as a defence mechanism. There are spots of red on the wood.
Treatment Cut out and destroy affected branches. Scrape out the cankerous areas. Apply fungicide to the wounds, then treat with wound-healing compound. Spray with a copper-based wash when leaves fall.
- **Coral spot**
Symptoms A canker on twigs and branches which wither and die. Red spots appear on dead wood.
Treatment Cut out and destroy affected branches. Chemical treatment not recommended.
- **Leaf spot** See p. 31.
- **Anthracnose**
Symptoms Irregular, grainy, russet spots on the leaves. Young branches wither.
Treatment Spray the leaves with a copper-based wash.
- **Honey fungus** See p. 31.

Salix
WILLOW

The Salicaceae family. Native to the cold and temperate areas of the northern hemisphere. A small tree that can live for 100 years. Catkins (inflorescences) appear in early spring or in summer according to variety.

Salix alba (white willow). The largest species with grey-white leaves. A straight trunk that breaks into a large number of branches. A full top.
Salix nigra (black willow) is a hybrid.
Salix babylonica (weeping willow). The flexible branches can hang down to the ground. Native to China, Japan and Korea. Small, about 10 m (33 ft). Long, lanceolate, slightly dentate leaves, dark green on top, watery green underneath. The catkins come out at the same time as the leaves, and are slender and yellow. There are a great many small-leaved varieties that can be used in bonsai.

Propagation

From seed The seed ripens in May-June and germinates directly it is sown. As soon as you have collected the seed, sow in damp soil, preferably sandy. Keep the seedlings for two years before repotting.

From cuttings Take soft cuttings in June. Plant in a peat-sand mixture and keep moist.

By simple layering Strip the part to be buried, and cut through the bark. Keep the sandy soil damp. Roots will form rapidly. Sever the layer and pot up. In May-June.

From young nursery stock

Care

Exposure to sunlight Likes a sunny position. In summer, place in semishade, but with good light.

Temperature Not fussy, adapts to cool temperatures. Avoid excessive heat.

Ventilation Flourishes in well-aired places. Unworried by wind.

Container Select a fairly flat bowl for an upright style. If it is in a cascade or semi-cascade style, a deep pot is necessary. Always ensure good drainage.

Cleaning Keep the inside of the crown well cleaned in summer. Remove all dead material from the tree and the soil in autumn. Brush the trunk.

Growth Usually fast. Male trees grow less strongly than female ones.

Repotting At the beginning of spring

Development of a willow. 1 Take a cutting. 2 Repot, standing the bottom of the pot in a basin of water. 3 Wire the long shoots in winter; as the branches are very flexible, they can be interwoven so as to train them in an upward position. 4 a Old soil. b Drainage. c Fill the empty space with additional soil. 5 Prune subbranches. 6 In spring, repot into a larger container.

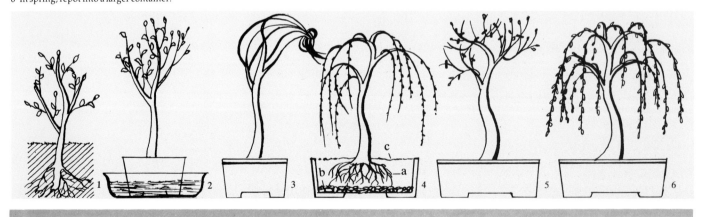

STYLES

Kengai   Tachiki   Han-Kengai   Hôkidachi   Sekijôju   Ishitsuki   Sôkan   Kusamono

and the beginning of summer, twice a year, prune the roots by half and repot in a larger container. Prepare good drainage.

Soil ⅓ loam, ⅓ coarse sand and ⅓ leaf mould. The willow needs moist, marshy, light, cool soil.

Pruning
Pruning of shoots Right at the beginning of spring, prune the shoots before the sap is circulating.
Pruning of subbranches Prune down to one eye. When repotting cut off any new long shoots. Prune again at the end of autumn.

Wiring In spring and in summer. Wrap raffia around the wire to protect the branches. The tree's shape can be created by weighting it. After fixing the wire in place, gently direct the branches into position by hand.

Watering Water freely provided drainage is good. Always keep damp. In summer it may be necessary to stand the tree to soak in a basin of water.

Spraying Wet the tree thoroughly as it needs a high moisture level. This protects it against pests, and cleanses the leaves of pollution. Spray frequently during the growing season.

Feeding In spring and in autumn. Feed with slow-acting organic fertilizer. Do not feed in July-August, for six weeks after repotting, or if the tree is sickly.

Weeping willow *(Salix babylonica)*. 15 years old. Height 35 cm (1 ft 2 in). 'Hôkidachi' style. Photographed in October.

Pests and diseases

Pests
- **Erineum** (gall mites)
Symptoms Down that is white in spring and red in summer on the lamina. Misshapen leaves. The catkins look like green galls.
Treatment Cut out infested branches. Spray with acaricide.
- **Capricorn beetle**
Symptoms Holes in the bark with galleries running from them, trunk and branches gnawed by white grubs. The tree withers. Presence of beetles.
Treatment Cut out infested branches. Push a copper wire through tunnelling to destroy adults.
- **Cossus and leopard moths**
(caterpillars) See p. 29.
- **Weevils**
Symptoms Branches and stems hollowed out by white grubs. Branch ends withered. Possible presence of beetles.
Treatment Spray with lindane-based insecticide.
- **Bombyx, sawflies, gall-forming sawflies, leaf beetles** (larvae)
Symptoms The leaves are eaten by grubs or caterpillars. Beetles may be present.
Treatment Spray with an insecticide

based on parathion or lindane.
- **Rosette-shaped galls**
Symptoms The small leaves at the tips of shoot are shaped like artichokes and have tiny worms inside them.
Treatment Cut off and burn infested branches. Spray with an insecticide based on parathion.
- **Aphids** See p. 29.
- **Scale insects** See p. 29.

Diseases
- **Powdery mildew** See p. 31.
- **Canker** (fungoid)
Symptoms Where there are scars and where branching occurs, wounds open, swell, and crack. Branches die. Neighbouring branches form excrescences as a defence mechanism. Small red spots on wood.
Treatment Cut out and burn affected branches. Scrape out the cankers. Apply copper-based fungicide, and cover with a wound-healing compound. Spray with a copper-based fungicidal wash when the leaves fall.

- **Willow scab**
Symptoms Black spots on the wrong side of the leaves. Branches wither and bend. The spots start from the veins, then spread.
Treatment Cut out and burn diseased material. In early spring spray with a copper-zineb mixture as a precaution against scab.
- **Black spot** (fungoid)
Symptoms Thick black scabs on the leaves.
Treatment Pick off diseased and dead leaves, and spray with a copper-based fungicide.
- **Anthracnose** (fungoid)
Symptoms Round brown spots on the leaves. Lesions on the ribs. Leaves curl up. Spots on the stems turn into cankers.
Treatment Cut out diseased material. Spray with a copper-based fungicide.
- **Black canker** (fungoid)
Symptoms Brown spots on the veins of the leaves. Lesions on the stems. Leaves curl up and drop off.
Treatment Cut out diseased material. Spray with copper-based fungicide in early spring and when leaves fall.
- **Rust** See p. 31.

The Ulmaceae family. Native to the temperate areas of the northern hemisphere. Eighteen species have been recorded. A tree with leaves that are usually deciduous, alternate, asymmetrical at the base, and dentate. Tiny red or yellow flowers. The fruit is ripe in May (winged keys).

Ulmus
ELM

Ulmus parvifolia (Chinese elm). A species with tiny little dark-green shiny leaves, unlike the others, harder and which may, depending on the climate, be evergreen or fall late after turning purple or orange in autumn. It flowers very late (September) and usually has a rounded top.

Some elms that are native to South China and Taiwan may be regarded as indoor bonsai in France, especially in the northern part of the country and in mountain areas. Even so, the tree should be allowed a rest from growing in winter.

Chinese elms (*Ulmus parvifolia*). From left to right: 15, 20 and 10 years old. Height, 15, 22 and 8 cm (6, 9 and 3 in). 'Hôkidachi', 'Nejikan' and 'Hôkidachi' styles. Photograph taken in January.

Propagation

From seed Elm seeds are ripe in June – those of *Ulmus parvifolia* in September-October. The former should be planted as soon as they have been gathered. The latter should be allowed to dry out and kept in a dry place during the winter, and stratified for about three weeks before they are planted.

By air layering In June. See Part I.

From cuttings In June; use a hormone rooting compound and plant in a mixture consisting of ⅔ peat and ⅓ coarse sand. Make sure the atmosphere they are in is very humid.

From young nursery stock You can find species of elm that are not susceptible to elm disease *(U. minor, U. parvifolia)* and which make fine bonsai specimens.

Care

Exposure to sunlight Likes full sun, needs a great deal of light.

Temperature Do not expose to very severe cold. Its frost resistance is limited.

Ventilation Stands up well to wind. Needs plenty of air movement round its crown.

Container Select a relatively deep pot as elms like deep earth. Blue, willow green and ivory go well with elms.

Cleaning Remove dead leaves in autumn. Prune branchlets coming off the main branches neatly. Brush the trunk.

Growth Fast.

Repotting Repot every second or third year between early spring and summer in a larger container. Prune the roots by between a half and two thirds.

Soil ⅔ loam and ⅓ coarse sand. Grows well in cool, moist, deep, fertile soil.

Pruning
Pruning of shoots During the growing period prune new shoots down to one or two pairs of leaves.
Pruning of subbranches Branches will form wherever there is a leaf bud. Allow them to grow and pinch out the tip, then prune again leaving only one pair of leaves. This will encourage delicate branching on the elm.
Leaf pruning The elm can be stripped of its leaves in June when it is well rooted and in perfect health. It will then produce dense small foliage, a good network of branches and will look well in autumn.
Development pruning At the end of winter when you can get a good view of the tree's

STYLES

Chokkan

Shakan

Kengai

Tachiki

Han-Kengai

Hôkidachi

Sekijôju

78

outline, cut side branches back fairly short, and prune out any main branches that might mar the tree's appearance.

Wiring End of June. Remove copper wire in October. Elms are seldom wired except for the main branches when the tree is young, their shape being mainly created by successive prunings.

Watering The elm likes moist soil. Water copiously in summer, cut down in autumn, and still further in winter.

Spraying In summer, mist-spray the foliage well to restore a good moisture balance. Needs a humid atmosphere.

Feeding Feed with a slow-acting organic fertilizer in spring and autumn. Do not feed in July-August, or for six weeks after repotting, or if the tree has been leaf-stripped or is in poor condition.

Chinese elm *(Ulmus parvifolia)*. 18 years old. Height, 22 cm (9 in). 'Tachiki' style. Photograph taken in June. The new pale shoots should be pruned.

Pests and diseases

Pests
- **Red spider mites** See p. 28.
- **Bark beetles** See p. 30.
- **Erineum** (gall mites)
Symptoms A thick down on the leaves that turns red in summer. Appearance of green, red or brick granulation. Leaves misshapen.
Treatment Spray young specimens with sulphur. If the attack is severe, spray with an acaricide.
- **Leaf beetles**
Symptoms The lamina has holes in it, with only the ribs of the leaf left. The tree may turn russet.

Treatment Spray with contact insecticide.
- **Geometers** (caterpillars) See p. 29.
- **Bombyx** (caterpillars) See p. 28.
- **Greenfly and aphids that cause galls** see p. 29.

Diseases
- **Black spot**
Symptoms Brown scabs on the leaves

may cause premature leaf fall.
Treatment Cut off the diseased leaves.
- **Blight** (fungoid)
Symptoms Bluey green blisters on the leaves cause them to wither, blacken and drop off.
Treatment Spray with copper-based fungicide.
NB. As far as we know *Ulmus parvifolia* it not susceptible to Dutch elm disease, and we have never encountered this disease on any *Ulmus* or *Zelkova* grown in bonsai form.

Nejikan

Ishitsuki

Sôkan

Kabudachi

Sôju

Sambon-Yose

Bonkei

Zelkova
JAPANESE ELM

The Ulmaceae family. Native to Crete (*Zelkova abelicea*), the Caucasus (*Zelkova carpinifolia*), China (*Zelkova sinica*) and Japan (*Zelkova serrata*). *Zelkova serrata*, a tree with deciduous leaves that are acuminate at the tip, dentate, green, and orange in autumn, can grow to heights of over 30 m (100 ft). The trunk divides into long upright branches, which in turn divide into a large number of erect, ramified subbranches. Oval topped.

Propagation

From seed Sow the seed during the summer in which it was harvested. Keep the seedbed moist, protect from winter frosts, and prick out seedlings into pots in the spring. If you do not sow in the summer, stratify the seeds and plant them in the spring, and pot them up the following year.

From cuttings In June. Lightly strip the bark off the slip, and dip into a hormone rooting compound. Take off the head, and plant in a sand-peat mixture.

By air layering In June, when the *Zelkova* cannot be propagated from seed or from cuttings.

From young nursery stock It is hard to find *Zelkova serrata* in western Europe.

How to train a sapling into a broom shape.
1 Sapling produced from a seed or cutting.
2 When the trunk is large enough, prune the main root.
3 Lop the trunk.
4 Cut the branches.
5 Prune the roots.
6 Prune the subbranches.
7 One or two months before the sap rises, tie up the branches into a broom shape using raffia.

STYLES

Chokkan   Hōkidachi   Sekijōju   Ishitsuki   Sōkan   Kabudachi   Gohon-Yose   Nanahon-Yose   Kyūhon-Yose   Yose-Ue   Bonkei

Care

Exposure to sunlight Full sun. In summer place in semishade.

Temperature Needs warmth. Protect trees planted in flat containers from the frost.

Ventilation Stands up to wind very well. Needs air movement round its foliage.

Container Most *Zelkova* are developed in the broom style in exceptionally flat containers that are glazed on the outside in blue, willow green or beige, or unglazed and earth colour.

Cleaning Keep the inside of the tree's crown well pruned to allow sun and air to get through to it. Remove dead leaves and twigs from the soil and from the tree.

Growth Fast, especially if it has good soil and lighting.

Repotting Every second or third year in early spring. Prune the roots by half and repot in a larger bowl. Ensure good drainage.

Soil ⅔ loam and ⅓ coarse sand. *Zelkova* likes heavy soils with soft clay, or cool sandy clay soils.

Japanese elm (*Zelkova serrata 'makino'*). 70 years old. Height 45 cm (1 ft 6 in). 'Hôkidachi' style. Photograph taken in June.

Pruning

Pruning of shoots Prune these from spring to autumn so as to keep only two or three leaves on side branches. Remove new shoots.

Pruning of side branches Each time branches form cut back the new branches, leaving only one or two pairs of leaves to achieve a good branch structure.

Leaf pruning A well-rooted healthy *Zelkova* can be stripped of its leaves in June.

Development pruning In winter prune out any main branches that mar the tree and ensure that side branches are balanced.

Opposite This *Zelkova serrata* badly needs pruning as it is becoming overgrown.

Below left Pruning is carried out methodically, with scissors.

Below right After pruning the tree has regained its harmonious proportions. The process may be repeated several times during the growing season.

Wiring *Zelkova* is rarely wired. However this method can be used after leaf burst up until October. Wire the branches and train them by hand in the direction you want. The *Zelkova* shape is mainly produced by pruning.

Watering Water more freely in summer. Allow to dry out between waterings. Give less water in spring and autumn, and very little in winter.

Spraying Spray the foliage in summer to clean off any pollution and prevent parasites.

Feeding In spring and autumn feed with slow-acting organic fertilizer. Do not feed for six weeks after repotting. No fertilizer should be given in July-August, or to a sickly tree.

Pests and diseases

Pests and diseases similar to those of *Ulmus*. See p. 79.

81

FLOWERING AND FRUIT TREES

Berberis
BARBERRY

The Berberidaceae family. Native to Europe, North Africa, America, and central and eastern Asia. A shrub that grows no higher than 3.5 m (11½ ft), with deciduous, partially evergreen or evergreen leaves depending on the species. Evergreen leaves are green, while deciduous leaves can be purple or green with bright autumn colours. In shape leaves are generally oval, and rounded to a greater or lesser extent. They can be prickly or smooth edged. The barberry is thorny. The flowers are yellow and fruit comes in the form of berries in a variety of colours.

Berberis thunbergii Native to Asia. Of compact habit. Deciduous red or purple leaves. The yellow flowers are edged with red in May and orange tinged in autumn. It bears red berries in the winter.

Berberis darwinii South America. The dark-green leaves are evergreen. This species flowers in April-May with hanging bunches of golden yellow blossom tinged with red. It bears purple fruit in autumn.

Berberis verruculosa Of upright habit, with branches covered with warts and thorns. The evergreen leaves are compact and shiny, the flowers golden yellow and the autumn fruit is black.

Propagation

From seed Clean the seeds after harvesting them and stratify. Sow in spring. Germination is very rapid, and the shoots come up quickly. Pot up straight away.

From cuttings Take soft cuttings at the beginning of the summer. Species that have evergreen leaves are grown from cuttings taken in August-September from hard wood so that they do not rot. Remove thorns, cut off leaves, but leave the eyes on the cutting. Evergreen species take longer to form roots. Wait until the following spring before repotting.

By air layering In spring.

From young nursery stock

Care

Exposure to sunlight The barberry likes the sun. It needs light for its leaves to turn to their vivid colours. Evergreen species should be placed in semishade.

Temperature In France *Berberis darwinii* can be grown only near the Mediterranean or along the Atlantic coast.

Ventilation No special requirements.

Container The barberry grows in fairly shallow earth, so it is not necessary to choose a very deep pot, but very shallow bowls do not suit it. Try to choose a colour that will harmonize with the foliage and flowers.

Cleaning Remove the dead leaves from the tree and the ground. Take off some fruit if there is a heavy crop, and remove berries as soon as they shrivel.

Growth Varies according to species. The *Berberis verruculosa* grows very slowly. *Berberis thunbergii* is fairly fast growing, unlike the *Berberis darwinii*.

Repotting Every year or every second year in early spring repot into a larger container. Prune the roots by between a third and a half.

Soil Half-and-half mixture of loam and leaf mould. The barberry will grow in any soil, even if it is dry and shallow, but does not like wet ground.

Pruning

Pruning of subbranches Prune after flowering: the barberry flowers on one-year-old shoots coming off two-year-old wood. If you prune too early, it will not flower.

Pruning of branches Cut back branches that have grown a lot. Keep shortening new shoots until September.

Wiring Can be done throughout the year. Do not leave copper wire in position for more than a few months.

Watering Water more freely in warm weather. Allow the ground to dry out well between waterings. The barberry dislikes damp conditions.

Spraying In summer mist-spray the foliage lightly to humidify the atmosphere around it. Do not wet the barberry when it is in flower.

Feeding Do not feed until flowering is

STYLES

Shakan

Kengai

Bankan

Tachiki

Han-Kengai

Sekijôju

Barberry (*Berberis atropurpureum*). 10 years old.
Height 20 cm (8 in). 'Tachiki' style. Photograph taken
in June.

Pests and diseases

Pests
• **Sawflies**
Symptoms Leaves eaten by white
grubs with yellow spots. There may
be wasps present.
Treatment Spray with a lindane-
based insecticide.
• **Aphids** See p. 29.

Diseases
• **Powdery mildew** See p. 31.
• **Verticillium wilt** See p. 31.

over; they flower in spring and carry on
until October-November. Feed with
slow-acting organic fertilizer. Do not feed
in July-August or for six to eight weeks
after repotting. Do not feed a weak tree.

Ishitsuki

Sōkan

Kabudachi

Ikadabuki

Netsunagari

Bonkei

Kusamono

Camellia
CAMELLIA

The Theaceae family. Native to China, Japan, Burma and the Philippines. This shrub was for a long time thought of as suited to orangery conditions. Grows in the open. The leaves are green, thick and shiny. The flowers may be scented or unscented, white, pink or red.

Camellia japonica (common camellia). Grows to a height of about 10 m (33 ft) in Europe. Shiny, oval, dark-green leaves. In bloom from March to May, with red, white or pink flowers for the varieties with rounded petals (from five to seven), usually single and unscented.

Camellia reticulata Grows to a height of about 5 m (16½ ft) in Europe. Of irregular habit. Only breaks out into branches as a result of pruning. Long, narrow, dark-green, reticulate leaves. Big, funnel-shaped, pink, red or purple unscented flowers with between 15 and 20 petals.

Camellia sasanqua Between 3 and 7 m (10-23 ft) in height. Of drooping habit. Small, oblong, blunt-ended leaves with downy ribs, lighter green than other species. In flower January to February, in mild coastal areas November-December, white or pink scented flowers (with six to eight petals).

Propagation

From seed Immerse the seeds in water. Plant only those that sink after they have been left to soak for 24 hours in warm water to soften the outer casing; this should be removed on the spot where the seed is to be planted. Sow in a heated greenhouse. Germinates fast.

From cuttings In January-February from tip cuttings or stems with three leaves, or in July-August with lignified shoots. Immerse in a hormone rooting compound for 24 hours and plant in a mixture of ⅓ heath mould and ⅔ sand. Keep in a warm place. Roots form within six weeks.

By air layering In spring.

From young nursery stock

Care

Exposure to sunlight Needs light to produce flowers. Choose a semishaded site. Avoid sudden changes in the amount of sunlight it is exposed to.

Temperature Avoid sudden changes from warm to cold. Can withstand frosts down to −12°C (10°F) provided they are of short duration. Remove snow from the foliage which could be frostbitten. Likes mild weather and a steady temperature. Needs warmth to produce flowers. *Camellia sasanqua* has better resistance to cold.

Ventilation Keep sheltered from the wind, but ensure that there is a regular air supply.

Container Match the container to the flowers of the camellia. Choose a bowl of medium size and depth; the camellia will thrive in an unvarying growing medium that conserves mild warmth and steady humidity.

Cleaning Remove withered flowers, especially if they are white as they go brown and detract from the tree's appearance. Remove any dead leaves.

Growth This is a slow-growing shrub.

Repotting Annually in late spring: in May-June when branches have finished growing and buds have formed. In a container that is only a little larger than the previous one. Prune the roots lightly.

Soil ½ heath mould, ¼ leaf mould and ¼ peat. The soil must be acid; it can be clayey. In it there should be lawn turf, topsoil, peat and possibly a very small amount of coarse sand.

Pruning
Pruning of subbranches Prune with clippers when the flowers have faded and before new shoots harden.

Wiring Can be wired at any season except for early spring. Provide good protection for the brittle branches by using raffia, or use wire wrapped in paper. Do not leave wire on the tree for more than a month or two.

Watering Water well in the summer, especially if it is hot and dry. Reduce water given in September. Allow the branches to droop for lack of water to encourage flowering. On the other hand, keep moist when the flowers are in bud to prevent the buds from dropping off.

Spraying Mist-spray the leaves in summer, except in full sun and when the camellia is in bud. Do not spray the flowers, which would wither.

Feeding Reacts badly to chemical fertilizers. Feed with slow-acting organic fertilizer. The best fertilizer is a compost of its own leaves.

STYLES

Shakan

Kengai

Tachiki

Han-Kengai

Bunjingi

Pests and diseases

Pests

● Weevils

Symptoms Roots and collar gnawed by larvae. Edge of leaves jagged; tree turns yellow and withers; no growth.

Treatment At the first sign of attack, take the tree out of its pot, and remove the larvae and contaminated earth; prune the roots and repot in good soil. Spray with contact insecticide from May to July.

● Scale insects See p. 29.

Diseases

● Sooty mould

Symptoms Black scabs on the leaves and stems. A sticky deposit.

Treatment Wipe the leaves with a sponge soaked in water and spirit. Destroy the insects causing the sooty mould with insecticide.

● Leaf spot See p. 31.

● Blight

Symptoms The leaves and new shoots go hard and then wither.

Treatment Spray with fungicide.

● Mosaic virus

Symptoms The lamina turns yellow. Lighter patches start from the veins; the leaves may fall.

Treatment There is none. Check for parasites.

● Chlorosis

Symptoms The leaves turn yellow round the lamina and near the veins. New leaves are discoloured.

Treatment Apply nitrogen, iron, magnesium and zinc to the soil. Do not give too much calcium, sodium or water; do not expose to cold, draughts or poisonous gases. Place in the light.

● Scorching

Symptoms The lamina is first discoloured then withers. The foliage is shrivelled and has holes in it.

Treatment Do not spray the foliage in sunlight. Keep away from direct sun, cold and late frosts; guard against too much nitrogen in fertilizer, chemicals, pollution and animals. Do not let fertilizer touch the leaves – place it at some distance from the trunk. Spray the foliage to clean it and water round the foot of the tree late in the day.

● Blossom wilt

Symptoms Brown patches on the petals causing the flowers to drop off. Formation of globular masses.

Treatment Cut off diseased flowers. Replace the top layer of soil.

Camellia *(Camellia)*. 15 years old. Height, 35 cm (1 ft 2 in). 'Tachiki' style. Photograph taken in July.

Sekijōju

Sōkan

Kabudachi

Korabuki

Ikadabuki

Netsunagari

The Rosaceae family. Native to China and Japan. A shrub with deciduous leaves, striking spring blossom and yellow fruit. Twisted, thorny branches.

Chaenomeles FLOWERING QUINCE

Chaenomeles lagenaria (japonica). A twisted prickly shrub 2 m (6½ ft) tall with shiny green oval leaves that are dentate and glabrous. It flowers in March, with dark-red, pink and sometimes white blossom. Fruit appears in October, yellow, scented and bitter.

Chaenomeles japonica (Maul's flowering quince). A prickly bush as wide as it is tall (approximately 1 m [3¼ ft]). Of compact, spreading habit. Smooth, green, oval leaves. Brilliant red flowers in March. Bears fruit in October, which is round, yellowy green with touches of red, scented but not edible.

Chaenomeles sinensis (Chinese quince). This species can reach 12 m (40 ft) tall – its branches are not prickly, and the bark flakes off. Oblong dentate leaves, downy in spring, turning scarlet in autumn. Salmon pink or white flowers in May. Hard oblong dark-yellow fruit in October.

Chaenomeles×superba Produced by crossing *Chaenomeles lagenaria* with *Chaenomeles japonica*. Not much used for bonsai.

Propagation

From seed Crush the fruit after it has ripened. Clean the seeds. Stratify them. Sow in March. They germinate rapidly.

From cuttings Take cuttings in June-July. Dip the cutting into a hormone rooting compound. Roots form fairly slowly.

By simple layering In May-June-July using wood produced that year. Allow roots to form. Sever from parent plant the following spring and pot up.

Care

Exposure to sunlight Needs sun and light. Place in a southern aspect. At the height of summer may be placed in semishade.

Temperature Loves heat, but dislikes frost.

Ventilation Protect from the wind, but ensure a good supply of air and good air circulation.

Container It can be decorated with a pattern reminiscent of the flowers of the bonsai, and should be fairly shallow to medium deep.

Cleaning After they have ripened, pick some of the fruit as it would exhaust the tree if it was all left on.

Flowering quince (*Chaenomeles speciosa*). 10 to 15 years old. Height, 30cm (1 ft). 'Ishitsuki' style. Photograph taken in April.

Growth Grows all the more slowly for being cut back annually.

Repotting Every second year in early spring after flowering repot in a larger container. It can also be repotted in autumn (October), but it must be protected from extremes of weather and from frost after repotting. Prune the roots by about half.

Soil ½ loam, ¼ leaf mould and ¼ coarse sand. A light nutritious soil without much lime.

Pruning
Pruning of subbranches After flowering cut new shoots down to two eyes. Cut out late shoots.
Pruning of branches. In June cut back old branches and side branches. In September, cut the tree back hard. Be sure to remove all unwanted shoots from the trunk.

Wiring From spring to the end of summer. Leave wire on for about four months, then remove it, taking care not to wound the tree. Repeat every year until the desired shape has been achieved.

Watering Regular. But let the tree dry out

STYLES

Shakan

Kengai

Bankan

Tachiki

Han-Kengai

Bunjingi

Neagari

more before flowering to encourage blossom. Too little water means the buds do not flower, and too much water causes the flowers to wilt.

Spraying Can withstand summer dryness. Do not wet the flowers or the fruit.

Feeding Can manage without if it has to. Feed just a little in the growing season, but never in July-August, after repotting or if the tree is sickly.

Flowering quince *(Chaenomeles speciosa)*. 20 years old. Height, 25 cm (10 in). Style – cannot be defined in accordance with usual classification; two trees that flower differently have been planted in the same pot. Photograph taken in April.

Pests and diseases

Pests
● **Aphids** *(Aphis pomi)* See p. 29.

Diseases
● **Brown rot**
Symptoms Flowers wither. Branches bearing them wither in turn, then die.
Treatment Cut out and destroy diseased branches. Spray with a copper-based fungicide at bud break.
● **Crown gall**
Symptoms Appearance on the collar and upper roots of a caulifower-shaped excrescence, soft and white turning brown, woody and cracked. Rot sets in, endangering the tree. There may be secondary tumours.
Treatment Take care not to wound the tree when caring for it; use clean tools. Cut out tumours, scrape out the wounds, and apply a spirit-based solution to them. Drench the soil with an organomercury fungicide and destroy any parasites.
● **Bacterial fireblight**
Symptoms Flowers and shoots wither and blacken in spring and summer as if burnt. They shrivel and drop off.
Treatment Cut out and burn diseased branches. Disinfect tools. Do not use fertilizer containing nitrogen, and do not let the soil get too wet. Before flowering, use a copper-based fungicide. Repeat during the growing season. If the attack is severe, use a combined fungicide.

Sekijôju — Ishitsuki — Sôkan — Kabudachi — Korabuki — Ikadabuki — Netsunagari — Yamayori — Tsukami-Yose — Bonkei — Plantations saisonnières

The Rosaceae family. Native to the temperate mountain areas of Europe, north Africa and Asia, excluding Japan. These shrubs can be spreading or creeping, or tall and slender, with erect stems. Leaves may be deciduous, evergreen, or semi-evergreen, depending on the species. Small white or pink flowers. Red or black fruit.

Cotoneaster integerrima (common cotoneaster). A pure species. A gnarled tree that grows to 2 m (6½ ft) in height, with spreading brownish-red branches that sometimes creep along the ground, deciduous, oval leaves that are green and glabrous on their upper surface and grey underneath, pink flowers between April and June, and shiny red fruit in August-September.

Cotoneaster horizontalis This species, which is native to China, has horizontal, wide-spreading branches that form a herring-bone pattern, and grows to a height of 1 m (3¼ ft). It has rounded dark-green leaves turning fiery red in autumn, evergreen for part of the winter, pinkish white flowers that bloom in May-June, and coral fruit that appears in September and stays on the branches for a long time.

Cotoneaster microphylla A shrub with a very wide span, with branches that are half bending and half spreading and bright green leaves that curl at the edges, grey on the underside. In May it produces white flowers and in September-October scarlet berries.

Cotoneaster
COTONEASTER

Propagation

From seed Pick the fruit when it is ripe, and leave to rot. Mash the berries down. Stratify in sand until January. Plant in the open. Cover with peat. Germination will take place in April. Propagation from seed produces saplings that do not ripen as well as those obtained by other methods.

Cotoneaster *(Cotoneaster horizontalis)*. Close-up of berries. Titbits for the birds. October.

From cuttings At midsummer in a greenhouse for species with evergreen leaves. End of June to end of July for species with deciduous leaves; roots form within six weeks. Then pot in a mixture consisting of ⅓ garden loam, ⅓ compost and ⅓ sand and peat. Cut back branches the following spring when you repot.

By air layering When the new buds are swelling. Remove the bark from the section to be layered. Wrap sphagnum moss round the stripped stem and enclose in polythene, making it airtight. Keep damp. After three to four weeks, roots appear. After two months, sever the branch and pot it up.

From young nursery stock

Care

Exposure to sunlight Full sun. The cotoneaster likes a sunny position, but can grow in semishade. In full shade it becomes etiolated.

Temperature Protect from frosts below −3°C (27°F). Stands up well to heat.

Ventilation Tolerates wind.

Container Seldom grown in a flat dish. Good drainage is essential. The medium-deep pot may be glazed or unglazed.

Cotoneaster *(Cotoneaster horizontalis)*. 10 years old. Height 20 cm (8 in). 'Nejikan style'. Photograph taken in November/December.

Cleaning Remove dead leaves and withered flowers or fruit. If the tree has a very heavy crop of fruit, remove some berries to prevent exhaustion.

Growth Quite fast in the early years, but slower when it is raised in a pot.

Repotting Annually in spring before the new shoots break. Prune the roots by a third and repot in a larger container.

Soil Mixture consisting of ½ loam, ¼ leaf mould and ¼ coarse sand. It is not fussy about the type of soil, and does well

STYLES

Shakan

Kengai

Tachiki

Han-Kengai

Neagari

Sekijōju

Nejikan

in fertile, sandy clay, humus-bearing soil; it is happiest in dry, light soil. It can be sandy and stony.

Pruning
Pruning of shoots In June. Shorten new shoots to two eyes. In September, prune long stems.

Pruning of branches Prune branches in March before growth restarts. Prune when you repot so as to keep the tree compact.

Development pruning Before the growing season, prune long branches, suckers and any superfluous branches that spoil the outline of the tree.

Wiring
Wire the trunk and branches before the buds come out. Protect the bark with raffia. Wire new stems.

Watering
The cotoneaster likes a dry soil. Do not give much water. Allow to dry out well between waterings, but soak the ground thoroughly each time you do water.

Spraying
Mist the leaves well so as to humidify the surrounding atmosphere. Cotoneaster thrive in a moist atmosphere, and are not too happy in a Mediterranean climate.

Feeding
In spring and autumn apply a slow-acting organic fertilizer. If the need arises, add some phosphate. When it is bearing berries, it is best to give liquid fertilizer.

Cotoneaster *(Cotoneaster horizontalis).* 10 years old. Height 22 cm (9 in). 'Nejikan' style. Photograph taken in May/June.

Pests and diseases

Pests
- Aphids *(Aphis pomi)* See p. 30.
- Woolly aphids See p. 30.
- Hard-shelled and soft scale insects See p. 29.

Diseases
- **Leaf blight**

Symptoms Red patches turning to brown appear on the leaves which go yellow and drop off.

Treatment Remove affected leaves. Spray with a zineb-based fungicide.

- **Bacterial fireblight**

Symptoms New shoots turn black, and leaves wither as if burnt.

Diseased parts shrivel and fall. There may be a seeping beige fungal growth at the base of the diseased area.

Treatment Cut out and burn diseased branches. Disinfect tools. Do not use fertilizers containing nitrogen and keep the soil from getting too wet. In spring, use a copper-based fungicide, and repeat during the growing season. If the attack is severe, use a combined fungicide.

- **Crown-gall**

Symptoms Appearance on the collar and upper roots of cauliflower-shaped excrescences, white and soft at first, turning brown, cracked and woody. Rot that leads to the tree dying. There may be secondary tumours.

Treatment Take care not to wound the tree when dealing with it. Clean tools. Get rid of the tumours, scrape out the wounds and apply a spirit-based solution to them. Drench the soil with an organomercury fungicide. Be careful that the fungicide does not damage the host plant. Get rid of any parasites.

Ishitsuki

Sōkan

Kabudachi

Ikadabuki

Netsunagari

Bonkei

Kusamono

Crataegus

ORNAMENTAL THORN

The Rosaceae family. Native mainly to North America, Asia and western Europe, this tree seldom grows above 7 m (23 ft). There are at least 150 garden species. They are small thorny trees with deciduous, dentate or lobed leaves. White, pink or sometimes red flowers are in bloom in spring and summer. A few species produce edible red, orange, yellow or black fruit.

Crataegus cuneata Native to Japan. A shrub with deciduous, dentate leaves. The flowers are white, pink in the spring. The fruit is red or yellow.

Propagation

From seed Pick the fruit before it is ripe and allow to rot. Store between layers of sand. Sow in the open the following autumn. Germination takes place in May. Some fruit will not germinate the first year, in which case you have to wait for the second and sometimes the third year.

By air layering In spring.

By shield grafting Ensure that the stock and the scion are reasonably homogeneous so that the graft will take. This method is seldom used, as it is difficult and leaves an aesthetically displeasing swelling.

Care

Exposure to sunlight Thorns like sun and light. Even so, they should be placed in semishade at the height of summer.

Temperature The hawthorn does not like intense heat, but is not affected by cold.

Ventilation A hedgerow shrub, the hawthorn stands up to wind well.

Container Choose a bowl of medium depth, glazed or unglazed. It may be decorated in harmony with the blossom of the hawthorn.

Cleaning Remove some fruit from overloaded branches so that the tree does not become exhausted. After flowering and fruit formation, remove any withered flowers or berries. Keep the soil clean.

Growth An average rate of growth.

Repotting Once a year, either in early spring or in early autumn; reduce the roots by a good third before repotting.

Soil ½ loam, ¼ leaf mould and ¼ coarse sand. No special requirements as regards the nature of the growing medium. It can be poor, dry and stony. But avoid very calcareous or very clayey soil, and very damp or light soil.

Pruning
Pinching back Pinch out the tips of new shoots when the leaves on the new growth are beginning to harden.

Pruning of subbranches In June-July cut the branches to keep them very short. In September shorten long branches again, pruning lightly. Main branches may be pruned before flowering, or after the fruit has formed.

Wiring From spring until autumn. Protect the bark with raffia. Begin to wire after new shoots have hardened.

Watering Water copiously and often. Slightly reduce water given during flowering, but make sure that the blossom does not wither.

Spraying Avoid wetting when the tree is in flower. In warm, dry weather, spray the foliage well.

Feeding After the growing spurt in spring, and in autumn. Reduce the supply of fertilizer when the tree is in flower. It is best to use a liquid fertilizer in autumn. Add potash and phosphate when the tree is bearing fruit.

STYLES

Shakan

Kengai

Tachiki

Han-Kengai

Sekijōju

Ornamental thorn *(Crataegus cuneata)*. 5 years old. Height 22 cm (9 in). 'Tachiki' style. Photograph taken in October.

Pests and diseases

Pests
- **Gall-forming aphids** See p. 29.
- **Pierid butterfly**

Symptoms The lamina is eaten, the epidermis destroyed, the leaf surface is reduced. Presence of green and orange caterpillars.

Treatment Destroy the eggs by squeezing them in the leaf. At the first sign of infestation spray with an organophosphate insecticide.
- **Ermine moths** (caterpillars) See p. 29.

Diseases
- **Powdery mildew** See p. 31.
- **Leaf blight** (fungoid)

Symptoms Red patches turning to brown appear in groups on the leaves. Leaves turn yellow and fall.

Treatment Cut off and destroy diseased leaves. At the first sign of infection, spray with a zineb-based fungicide.
- **Scab** (fungoid)

Symptoms Appearance of browny green patches on the fruit which bursts and on the leaves and shoots.

Treatment Destroy the leaves affected in autumn. Spray with a copper-based fungicide.
- **Rust** See p. 31.
- **Bacterial fireblight** (fungoid)

Symptoms The flowers and young shoots wither and blacken as if burnt. The leaves turn orangy brown and fall. At the base there is a seeping beige fungal growth.

Treatment Cut out and burn diseased branches. Do not use fertilizer with nitrogen in it, and ensure that the soil is not too wet. Disinfect tools. Before flowering use a copper-based fungicide. Repeat when growth is under way.

Sôkan

Kabudachi

Ikadabuki

Netsunagari

Bonkei

The Ericaceae family. Native to east Asia and the Himalayas.

Enkianthus
ENKIANTHUS

Enkianthus campanulatus A tree that grows to a height of 10 m (33 ft) in Japan and 3 m (10 ft) in France; it is an upright tree with red branches, and elliptic, acute, dentate leaves that are green on top and red underneath.

Enkianthus perrulatus A species native to Japan, growing to a height of 2 m (6½ ft), with elliptic, acute oval leaves, bright green on top, and with long veins underneath, and hanging white umbellate flowers that come out before the leaves (April-May).

Propagation

From seed Difficult to achieve. Sow in a greenhouse in mid-March in a mixture of heath mould and peat. Cover the seeds lightly with sieved soil. Keep moist in a dark place. Germination occurs within three weeks. As soon as the seeds have germinated put in the light, keeping damp. Take care no fungi develop. Plant out straight away into growing pots with good drainage. Put a layer of finely sieved heath mould on the surface of the compost. Keep in a cool shaded position as long as the shoots are soft. As soon as they harden, expose them to air and light.

From cuttings In August, in a greenhouse. Root development requires heat.

By layering in March-April, using the simple layering technique in cool soil.

Care

Exposure to sunlight The enkianthus likes full sun throughout the year. Needs light. However, it should be placed in semishade in summer.

Temperature Protect from frost. The enkianthus thrives in fairly humid climates.

Ventilation No special requirements, but does not like strong winds.

Container Of medium depth. Often an unglazed pot.

Cleaning Rid the tree of any leaves that do not fall at the end of autumn.

Growth A slow-growing shrub.

Repotting In early spring every year or every second year, after you have pruned the roots by a third.

Soil ½ leaf mould, ¼ loam and ¼ coarse sand. The enkianthus thrives on leaf mould; it cannot tolerate lime. It needs cool soil that is rich in humus: forest soil.

Pruning
Pruning of subbranches At the end of the summer prune subbranches with clippers – once the flower heads have withered and before the new shoots have hardened too much.
Pruning of branches In September, shorten long branches.

Wiring Wire the enkianthus from the spring until autumn. Do not wire it too tightly as this could result in the sap being cut off and the flowers failing.

Watering Water freely as soon as the leaves appear, continuing until autumn; then reduce the amount of water given.

Spraying Do not spray the tree when it is in flower.

Feeding In spring and autumn feed with a slow-acting organic fertilizer. It is best to use a liquid fertilizer when the tree is in flower.

STYLES

Shakan

Tachiki

Han-Kengai

Sekijôju

Sôkan

Kabudachi

Sôju

Sambon-Yose

Enkianthus *(Enkianthus perrulatus)*. 15 years old.
Height, 20 cm (8 in). 'Tachiki' style. Photograph taken
in April.

Pests and diseases

Pests
- **Aphids** See p. 29.
- **Scale insects** See p. 29.

Diseases
- **Sooty mould**

Symptoms Black scabs on the leaves
and stems. Sticky deposits.
Treatment Clean the leaves with a
sponge soaked in water and spirit.
Destroy the insects with insecticide.

- **Chlorosis**

Symptoms The leaves turn yellow
around the lamina and near the veins,
new leaves are discoloured.
Treatment Apply nitrogen, iron,
magnesium and zinc to the soil. Do not
give too much calcium, sodium or water
and do not expose to cold. Keep away
from draughts and poisonous gases.
Place in the light.
NB. This is not much affected by pests or
diseases.

Ilex
HOLLY

The Aquifoliaceae family. Native to the northern hemisphere, South America, Australia and Polynesia, these are very long-lived shrubs and trees:

some holly trees are over 200 years old. In ideal conditions the holly can grow to a height of 15 m (50 ft). It is a conical shrub with a straight trunk, and spreading branches that curve upwards at the tip; it is bushy and produces branches right from its base. Its leaves are evergreen, oval, with lobes divided by spiny tips, dark green and shiny; the lobe disappears with age, and only the spine at the end of the leaf remains. Leaves can be variegated with yellow or edged with white. Small, pinkish white, scented flowers appear in May-June. The fruit which is ripe in September grows in clusters of bright red, shiny berries which last right through the winter, and it appears only on female trees.

Ilex aquifolium (common holly). A bushy, sometimes tree-like shrub 5 m (16½ ft) tall, often with a multiple trunk, pyramidal in shape, with evergreen, spiny leaves that are glabrous in colour, darker green on top. Fruit appears in September.
Ilex crenata (Japanese holly). A shrub 5 m (16½ ft) tall, of upright habit, with a large number of branches, very leafy, with crenate, dark-green leaves without prickles, and black fruit.
Ilex serrata sieboldii A compact shrub that is very ramified and produces a large quantity of red fruit, sometimes coral coloured in the autumn. The fruit stays on the tree throughout the winter. In spring it has small bluish flowers.

Propagation

From seed Pick the fruit in November. Leave in a heap to rot. Wash the seeds, dry them and stratify in sand. Sow the following autumn or spring in a humus-bearing, peaty soil which is kept damp, in semishade. Germination is temperamental and can take up to three years. Prick out seedlings a year later.

From cuttings In July-August take cuttings from trees with evergreen leaves and plant in a mixture consisting of ⅔ peat and ⅓ sand, under glass. The following spring, remove the glass. It is best to take cuttings from wood grown that year which roots better.

By simple layering Layer for two years in cool, peaty soil. After severing from the parent plant, be careful of extremes of weather, for the new layer is very tender. This method works well.

From young nursery stock

Care

Exposure to sunlight The *Ilex crenata* tolerates full sun, even in summer. Place other varieties in semishade in summer, and leave in the sun in others seasons. Place them in semi-shade if they get a lot of light. The holly is a shrub that lives in the undergrowth.

Temperature The holly likes humid warmth. It reacts badly to intense cold. Protect it if the temperature goes below −5°C (23°F).

Ventilation It likes a sheltered position. It should be protected from strong, cold winds.

Container Choose a medium deep pot,

Deciduous holly *(Ilex sieboldii)*. 30 years old. Height 50 cm (1 ft 8 in). 'Kôrabuki' style. Photograph taken in October/November.

STYLES

 Shakan

 Kengai

 Tachiki

 Han-Kengai

 Bunjingi

 Sekijôju

 Ishitsuki

earth colour or cobalt blue; the pot should be glazed or unglazed.

Cleaning Remove all unwanted growth on the trunk. If there is too much fruit or it stays too long on the tree, exhausting it, remove some.

Growth The holly is slow growing, about 6 m (20ft) in 10 years.

Repotting In early spring, before bud burst, annually or every second year, prune between a third and a half off the roots, and repot in a larger container.

Soil Half-and-half mixture of loam and leaf mould. People say that the holly likes an acid soil, but this is not correct. It thrives in soil that is clayey, calcareous, light, cool or even sandy. It needs fertile soil.

Pruning
Pinching back Pinch out some new buds as they form. Also pinch out any superfluous shoots immediately. But leave the remaining shoots to develop well until the leaves have hardened.
Pruning of subbranches Shorten by 3 to 6 cm (1⅛ to 2⅜ in). Prune away unwanted secondary laterals, and allow the others to develop.
Pruning of branches When repotting, prune branches that have grown the previous year to shape the tree.
Development pruning When you prune out a main branch, make sure that the cut is concave. Apply a wound-sealing compound.

Wiring From spring to summer. Shape young branches with raffia, and protect other branches with raffia when coiling wire round them. The branches do in fact break easily.

Watering Water more freely from the start of flowering until the fruit appears so as to obtain good fruit formation. At other times, moisten the soil well and allow it to dry out between waterings.

Spraying Mist-spray the tree thoroughly. Hollies need good atmospheric humidity.

Feeding In spring and autumn feed with slow-acting organic fertilizer. In autumn the holly requires a little less feeding than in spring, so reduce the dosage, while continuing to feed as often as in spring.

Deciduous holly *(Ilex sieboldii)*. 40 years old. Height 60 cm (2 ft). 'Kôrabuki' style. Photograph taken in October/November.

Pests and diseases

Pests
- **Tortrix** (caterpillars) See p. 29.
- **Leaf miners** See p. 29.

Diseases
- **Leaf spot** See p. 31.
NB. If the holly is badly positioned without good light and ventilation or if it has too much water, it may have toadstools growing on it. You would then have to use a fungicide to combat possible rot.

Sabamiki

Sôkan

Kabudachi

Korabuki

Ikadabuki

Netsunagari

Bonkei

The Oleaceae family. Native to tropical and sub-tropical areas: the Mediterranean basin, southern Europe, north Africa and western Asia. Erect shrubs, often creepers, with green, angular branches, alternate or opposite leaves, white, yellow or pink scented flowers, and black fruit.

Jasminum
JASMINE

Jasminum nudiflorum (winter-flowering jasmine). A species native to northern China, with arched green branches that curve back towards the ground; can grow to a height of 5 m (16½ ft); leaves are deciduous, oval, narrow at both ends, and can appear at the same time as the flowers in the south. The bright-yellow flowers are in bloom from November to March, on the previous year's wood.

Propagation

From cuttings Take soft cuttings from branches that have grown that summer, and plant in June-July. They can also be planted in autumn. Put the cuttings in a greenhouse or under glass. Keep the cutting in a growing pot for two years.

By simple layering In spring.

From young nursery stock

Care

Exposure to sunlight. Jasmines like light. They need a sunny position, but should not receive direct sunlight. Place in semishade in summer.

Temperature Stands up quite well to cold, but protect from severe frost.

Ventilation Not fussy, but happiest in a slightly sheltered position.

Container Choose a small pot. The decoration should be selected to harmonize with the flowers.

Cleaning Cut off roots that grow from nodes on branches as soon as they appear, and remove shoots and suckers. Pick off the flowers as soon as they have faded.

Growth Quite a slow-growing shrub.

Repotting In early spring before the flowers open or in autumn after the flowers have gone. Once a year, preferably in spring. Prune the roots by between a third and a half, and repot in a larger container.

Soil ½ loam, ¼ leaf mould and ¼ coarse sand. Not fussy about the type of soil; winter-flowering jasmine thrives in light, slightly moist, friable, nutritious soil.

Pruning
Pinching back Pinch out all superfluous shoots and allow others to develop. Prune faded shoots to one or two pairs of leaves.

Winter-flowering jasmine *(Jasminum nudiflorum)*. Flowering can occur between the beginning of January and the end of March depending upon the region and the severity of the winter. Photograph taken in February.

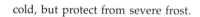

STYLES

Shakan

Kengai

Tachiki

Han-Kengai

Neagari

Repeat in July.

Pruning of subbranches Prune branches you have allowed to grow back to two or three pairs of leaves. Prune again in September leaving three or four pairs of leaves.

Development pruning Prune the main branches: shorten them or cut them out before flowering.

Wiring Wire from spring to summer, protecting the bark with raffia. Train young branches using raffia. The winter-flowering jasmine's branches are brittle.

Watering Water the soil copiously if it is in full sun. The winter-flowering jasmine needs a lot of water, but this must not be allowed to stagnate at root level.

Spraying Sprinkle water on to the leaves during watering, but do not wet during flowering.

Feeding Use a slow-acting organic fertilizer after flowering. Do not feed in July-August. In September, use fertilizer enriched with phosphate.

Pests and diseases

Pests
● **Tortrix** (caterpillars) See p. 29.

Diseases
NB. We have never encountered diseases on jasmines. If the flower buds fail to develop, the flowers fade too quickly, or the leaves turn yellow and fall prematurely, there are problems connected with spraying or watering. Reacts badly to pollution.
● **Phyllosticta blight** (fungoid)
Symptoms There are withered spots on the leaves with tiny black spots on them. Affected leaves drop off.
Treatment Cut off affected leaves; spray with a copper-based fungicide.
● **Jasmine yellow ring mosaic virus**
Symptoms The lamina goes yellow. Yellow patches start from the veins and spread. The lamina may become distorted and the leaves may fall.
Treatment Destroy affected material. Check that there are no parasites.

Winter-flowering jasmine (*Jasminum nudiflorum*). 10 years old. Height 18 cm (7 in). 'Sekijôju' style. Photograph taken in February.

Sekijôju

Ishitsuki

Sôkan

Kabudachi

Ikadabuki

Netsunagari

Lespedeza
LESPEDEZA

The Leguminosaceae family. The *Lespedeza* genus, native to North America, Asia and Australia, should be written *Cespedeza*, in honour of the Spaniard, Cespedez, but there was a spelling mistake.

Lespedeza thunbergii Native to China and Japan; a shrub 2 m (6½ ft) tall and 2 m (6½ ft) across, with arched branches, elliptical, light green leaves which are silky underneath, bright purple, butterfly-shaped flowers growing in clusters that are in bloom in July-August-September, and with fruit that contains a single seed.

Lespedeza bicolor Native to North China, Japan and Manchuria; a shrub about 3 m (10 ft) tall, with angular branches, leaves that are dark green on top and bluey green underneath, and purple and red flowers on the tips of the branches, in bloom in August-September.

Propagation

From seed Only the *Lespedeza bicolor* is grown from seed. Seeds are sown in May in the open, but results are poor.

From cuttings Take cuttings in June. Plant in a half-and-half mixture of peat and sand. Keep well protected during the winter. Pot up the following spring.

By simple layering In spring, remove the leaves from a fair length of a young branch, and bury the whole stripped area in the ground. Roots form easily.

Care

Exposure to sunlight Full sun. The lespedeza likes a sunny position.

Temperature The lespedeza likes warmth, and suffers from frost. But it can grow up again after being frosted if it is pruned right back at the end of the winter. The *Lespedeza bicolor* can withstand cold.

Ventilation No special requirements. Take care with watering if it is in an exposed position.

Container The container should be of medium depth, and is often glazed and blue.

Cleaning Cut off faded flowers as soon as they dry out, and remove any small dead branches.

Growth Fairly slow.

Repotting Annually in spring. Prune the roots by a third, and repot in a larger container.

Soil A half-and-half mixture of loam and leaf mould. The lespedeza likes garden earth which is permeable, sandy, light and dry.

Pruning
Pruning of subbranches Allow to become quite long, then prune by a good third of their length; leave only two or three nodes.
Development pruning At the end of winter when all risk of frost is past, prune the lespedeza very low to encourage new growth. It is important that the stock is not frostbitten.

Wiring Wire from spring until the end of the summer. Protect new branches with raffia.

Watering Do not overwater. The lespedeza likes dry ground. But increase water given when flower buds are forming.

Spraying Mist-spray the foliage in summer to humidify the surrounding atmosphere and provide protection against possible parasite attack.

Feeding Give more fertilizer in spring than in autumn. Always use a slow-acting organic fertilizer. In autumn when the plant is in bloom use a weak solution of liquid fertilizer.

STYLES

Shakan   Kengai   Tachiki   Han-Kengai   Sekijōju   Ishitsuki   Sōkan   Kabudachi

Lespedeza (*Lespedeza bicolor*). 12 years old. Height, 20 cm (8 in). 'Tachiki' style. Photograph taken in July. The purple flowers appear at the beginning of July and continue until the middle of the summer.

Pests and diseases

Pests
- **Aphids** See p. 29.

Diseases
There are no known diseases that destroy the lespedeza. If the bonsai's leaves turn yellow and fall prematurely, check watering: it may be being underwatered or overwatered.

- **Rhizoctonia** (fungal disease)
Symptoms There may be rot on the collar or branches. A cottony white down may follow, and then the tree drops.
Treatment Make sure there is not too much nitrogen in the fertilizer, and do not give too much water. Put in a well-ventilated place. Spray with a benomyl-based fungicide.

Malus
CRAB APPLE
or APPLE

The Rosaceae family. There are at least 25 species of *Malus* in Europe, Asia and North America. The crab apple tree is the best known, as far back as the Neolithic period. Many are ornamental.

Malus baccata mandshurica syn. *cerasifera* (Manchurian crab apple) Native to Japan; this tree is 5-6 m (16½-20 ft) tall, with oval green leaves and white flowers that come out in April-May. The fruit is the size of a cherry, and red or yellow depending on the cultivar involved.

Malus halliana (Hall's apple) Native to China and Japan; a shrub 5 m (16½ ft) tall, of spreading habit, with oval green leaves with purple tints, pink flowers that open in May, and very small edible fruit that ripens late and stays on the tree for a good part of the winter.

Malus sieboldii (Toringo crab) Native to the mountainous areas of Japan; this graceful tree is between 7 and 10 m (23-33 ft) tall, its flower buds are deep pink, the flowers are pale pink, and it produces red or yellow edible fruit of a tiny size.

Malus himekokoh Native to Japan; it bears delicious tasting fruit the size of a small clementine.

Propagation

From seed Pick the ripe fruit and leave in a cool place to rot. Wash the pips, dry them and stratify in sand. Sow in late autumn (November-December) in light soil. Germination varies according to the species. Ornamental crab apples produce heterogeneous seedlings.

By air layering In spring.

By grafting This method is the most widely used. In mid-March shield budding, side grafting, cleft grafting or approach grafting can be practised. All methods produce good results. Seal well to ensure that the point of union is not conspicuous later on. It is possible to graft ornamental crab apples on to the usual fruit tree rootstocks.

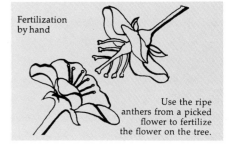

Fertilization by hand

Use the ripe anthers from a picked flower to fertilize the flower on the tree.

Manchurian crab apple *(Malus bacatta mandshurica)*. Detail of flowering (mid-April, mid-May). Flowers and leaves appear at the same time.

Hall's apple *(Malus halliana)*. 25 years old. Height, 35 cm (1 ft 2 in). 'Tachiki' style. Photograph taken in April. Start of flowering. We can see the dark pink colour of the flower buds that have not yet opened, and the pale pink of the open buds. Note the shy emergence of the leaves.

STYLES

Shakan

Kengai

Tachiki

Han-Kengai

Sekijōju

Sōkan

Kabudachi

Bonkei

Malus
CRAB APPLE or APPLE

Crab apple *(Malus himekokoh)*. The fruit is larger than that usually produced by some other species, and tastes excellent.

Care

Exposure to sunlight. The crab apple likes full sun throughout the year.

Temperature The crab apple tolerates frost well, and can withstand very hot weather.

Ventilation Tolerates wind.

Container Crab apples need a fairly deep pot. It can be decorated to harmonize with the flowers, glazed blue colours or willow green, or unglazed earth colour.

Cleaning Remove a few apples so that the tree does not bear too many. If a lot of fruit is produced, remove a third to avoid exhausting the tree. Remove any leaves that have not fallen in autumn as they harbour parasites.

Growth Fairly rapid, even when the tree is grown in a pot.

Repotting Every year in spring, at bud burst. Every second year for old specimens. Repot in a larger container after pruning the roots by between a third and a half.

Soil Mainy loam and leaf mould (half and half) to which some sand and peat can be added.

Pruning
Pinching back Pinch back the tips of new shoots after they have grown.
Pruning of subbranches After flowering, prune subbranches back to two eyes (round about July). Take out late-growing shoots.
Pruning of branches Prune branches when repotting.

Wiring Wire from spring to autumn. Protect the bark with raffia.

Watering Water copiously while the

Pruning when the fruit is setting.
1 Trim the young shoot, leaving from three to five buds.
2 The buds appear, making it possible for twigs to develop.
3 When the apple tree is a little bigger, begin wiring and trimming.
4 Do some more trimming to make it easier for branches to develop.
5 The buds develop.
6 & 7 Each year prevent the trunk from bifurcating and continue to prune.
8 The result will be a tree with a pattern of branches which is both skilfully arranged and aesthetically pleasing.

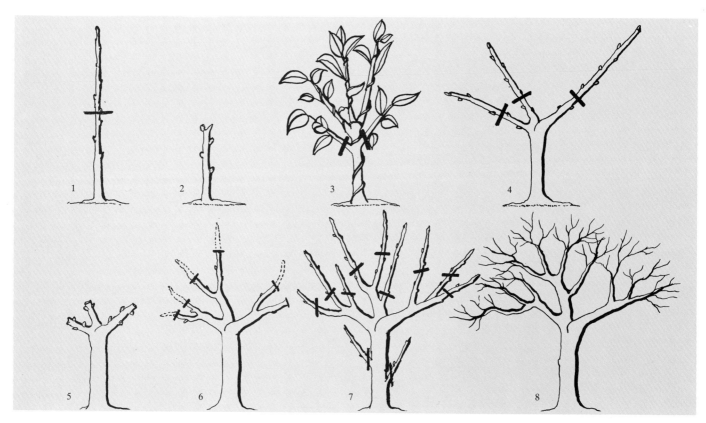

flower buds are forming, give a little less water when the tree is in flower, then resume copious watering.

Spraying Wet the whole tree when watering. Do not get water on to it during flowering. Is seldom sprayed.

Feeding In spring after flowering feed with a slow-acting organic fertilizer, preferably in liquid form, or in a powder form. In autumn, feed less often, but increase the amount given.

Manchurian crab apple (*Malus bacatta mandshurica*). 18 years old. Height, 35 cm (1 ft 2 in). 'Tachiki' style. Photograph taken in October. At the end of autumn, the cherry-sized fruit turn a magnificent blood-red colour; it has a rather acid taste.

Pests and diseases

Pests
- **Red spider mites** See p. 28.
- **Winter moth**

Symptoms Holes in buds, leaves eaten with possibly only the veins of the leaf left. Fruit may be eaten. Presence of caterpillars.
Treatment Spray with tar oil at the end of winter to destroy the eggs. In spring use a lindane or parathion-based insecticide.
- **Ermine moth** (caterpillars) See p. 29.
- **Leaf miners** (caterpillars) See p. 29.
- **Tortrix** (caterpillars) See p. 29.
- **Greenfly** See p. 29.
- **Woolly aphids** See p. 29.
- **Scale insects** See p. 29.

Diseases
- **Powdery mildew** See p. 31.
- **Scab** (fungoid)

Symptoms Irregular greeny brown blotches on leaves. Fruit blotched, discoloured and misshapen.
Treatment Pick off diseased or dead leaves and fruit, and spray with fungicide.
- **Apple canker** (fungoid)

Symptoms Brown crevices appear on wounds or forks of branches. The crevice grows, cracks and girdles the branch which withers and dies at the top. Defensive excrescences appear in the surrounding area. There are red grainings on the canker.
Treatment Cut out and burn diseased branches. Scrape out the canker. Dab the wound with a copper fungicide and seal it. Spray with a copper-based fungicide at leaf-fall.
- **Monilia disease** (brown rot — fungoid)

Symptoms The flowers wither, and the branches wilt.
Treatment Cut out affected branches. At bud burst spray with a copper-based fungicide. Repeat during the growing season.
- **Bacterial fireblight** (fungoid)

Symptoms New shoots and buds turn black and wither as if burnt, and shrivel up. Leaves drop off and the bark is cracked. Presence of a seeping fungal growth.
Treatment Cut out and burn diseased branches. Disinfect tools. Do not use nitrogen in fertilizer and keep the soil relatively dry. In spring, use a copper-based fungicide and repeat during the growing season.
- **Crown-gall** (fungoid)

Symptoms Appearance of cauliflower-shaped excrescences, white and soft to start with, then brown and cracked, on the collar and upper roots. Rot which endangers the tree's survival. There may be secondary tumours.
Treatment Guard against insects. Disinfect tools. Remove the tumours, scraping them out and applying a spirit- and sodium-based solution to the wound. Spray the soil with a wash based on an organomercury fungicide.

Leguminosaceae family. Native to Japan.

Milletia
MILLETIA

Milletia reticulata Like a kind of small wisteria, a climbing shrub that is very long lived, and becomes gnarled as it grows older; very small shiny, leathery dark green leaves. The light- or dark-purple flowers appear in early or mid summer. Branches are flexible, and rise upwards. It produces a good branch structure, but it does not hook itself on to a surface like the wisteria.

Propagation

From seed Collect the ripe seeds in their pods in October. Open the pod. In spring, plant the seed in a warm place. Few seeds germinate, and growth is slow.

From cuttings In spring. Choose a branch that has grown that year, and remove the top of it. Put to root in a peat/sand mixture in a warm place sheltered from cold winds. Beware late night frosts.

By simple layering In spring. In autumn the layer will have put out roots. Pot it after cutting it free, and keep in a warm place until the next spring.

By grafting A whip graft or an inlay graft carried out in a greenhouse in February-March. Bind and seal well with grafting wax.

Care

Exposure to sunlight The milletia likes the sun.

Temperature The milletia likes heat. Protect from frost.

Ventilation The milletia tolerates the wind; it needs a well-aired position.

Container Select a pot that is deep or fairly deep. The milletia cannot develop in a flat container. The pot may be decorated to harmonize with the flowers.

Cleaning In autumn ensure that moss does not cover the base of the trunk; scrape it off and remove it.

Growth Very slow.

Repotting Every year or every second year in spring prune away a third of the roots and repot in a larger container.

Soil An equal mix of loam and leaf mould. Cool, light but substantial soil suits it. Do not use non-porous soil.

Pruning

Pruning of subbranches Prune these with clippers after flowering and before shoots appear, late in the summer. Cut back well leaving only three eyes.
Pruning of branches In autumn cut back the branches quite short.

Wiring In spring and summer. Use fine wire and direct the branches and trunk into the desired shape. Do this every year.

Watering Water well even in winter, except if there is frost. In summer wet well, soak if necessary. Allow to droop between waterings to encourage it to flower again, or you can leave it standing in water for a month at the height of summer.

Spraying Spray the tree and the area round it to humidify the surrounding atmosphere.

Feeding Feed more in spring before flowering. In autumn it is best to use liquid fertilizer in smaller quantities.

STYLES

Shakan

Kengai

Tachiki

Han-Kengai

Sekijôju

Sôkan

Kabudachi

Milletia *(Milletia reticulata).* 11 years old. Height, 25 cm (10 in). 'Shakan' style. Photograph taken in April. The young greeny-yellow leaves have just appeared, and are very fragile.

Pests and diseases

Pests
- **Scale insects** See p. 29.

Diseases
- **Mosaic virus**

Symptoms Yellowing of lamina. Lighter patches start from the veins and spread. The lamina may be distorted and the leaves may fall.

Treatment Destroy diseased material. Check that there are no parasites. No specific treatment.

The Moraceae family. Native to Asia. This is the tree that harbours the famous silkworms which have ben cultivated since 2700 BC. It is about 15 m (50 ft) tall, and is extremely long lived: it can live for 500 years.

Morus
MULBERRY TREE

Morus alba (white mulberry) The shape varies depending on the variety; its leaves are alternate, with deeply indented edges, often lobed, and in colour they are light green with a shiny upper surface and polished underneath, and golden yellow in autumn. The pinkish white, round berries which do not have much flavour are ripe in August-September.

Mulberry (*Morus issai*). 10 years old. Height 20 cm (8 in). 'Sekijôju' style. Notice the aerial roots. Photograph taken in May.

Propagation

From seed Collect the seed in July-August. Crush the fruit. Wash to separate the seeds from the squashed fruit. Dry and store between layers of sand or earth. Sow in April-May. Germination occurs within three weeks. Space the seeds well apart from one another when sowing, and watch out for cockchafer grubs. After they have germinated keep protected in autumn and winter.

From cuttings In spring, select a shoot produced that year. Remove the top, and set it to root in an equal mixture of peat and sand. Protect the cutting from possible frosts and from cold winds.

By air layering In spring.

By grafting Use the bench grafting method in winter when mulberries cannot be propagated by other methods. It is a more professional method of propagation. Shield budding is practised very early in the season when the bark of the rootstock lifts easily.

Care

Exposure to sunlight Mulberries like full sun. They need a lot of light.

Temperature The mulberry dislikes frosts and cold, preferring heat.

Ventilation The mulberry can withstand wind.

Container Choose pots that are fairly flat and preferably glazed, in white, willow green, blue, green, beige etc.

Cleaning Remove withered fruit from the tree if it does not fall of its own accord.

Growth Slow growing: about 3 m (10 ft) in 20 years.

Repotting Repot in spring (April) every year. Prune a good third off the roots, and repot in a larger container. Ensure especially good drainage.

Soil ½ loam, ¼ leaf mould and ¼ coarse sand. Mulberries like light, sandy soil, and dislike damp, heavy soil. If the soil is too fertile, growth finishes late in the autumn, and the tree suffers from frosts.

STYLES

Shakan

Kengai

Tachiki

Han-Kengai

Sekijôju

Sôkan

Kabudachi

Mulberry (*Morus issai*). 10 years old. Height 20 cm (8 in). 'Sekijôju' style. Photograph taken in May.

Pruning

Pinching back Pinch back new shoots directly they have lengthened a little.

Pruning of subbranches After flowering prune subbranches leaving just two eyes. At the end of the autumn, prune long subbranches again, leaving only two or three eyes.

Pruning of branches In early spring before the buds burst prune the branches short.

Wiring In spring and summer. Wind raffia round the copper wire to protect the bark.

Watering The mulberry needs a lot of water. It may be necessary to water twice daily in spring and autumn. Always allow it to dry out between waterings.

Spraying You can sprinkle water on the foliage at the same time as you water. Do not spray when in full flower (a short period).

Feeding Feed more in spring. In autumn when the tree is bearing fruit, a liquid fertilizer is to be preferred. A slow-acting organic fertilizer.

Pests and diseases

Pests
● **Scale insects** See p. 29.
NB. The mulberry *Bombyx* or silkworm does no damage.

Diseases
● **Honey fungus** See p. 31.

The Vitaceae family. Native to North America and Asia, this is a creeping, climbing shrub with clinging tendrils (suckers), inconspicuous flowers and fruit, and bark that does not scale off.

Parthenocissus
CREEPERS

Parthenocissus tricuspidata This is the most widely found creeper (sometimes wrongly called Virginia creeper). This creeping shrub produces a large number of branches, with thin stems, and deciduous leaves that are oval and shiny green in summer, turning yellow-gold and orange in autumn; it bears flowers in July-August and small, round, dark-blue fruit in September-October.

Creeper *(Parthenocissus)*. 8 years old. Height 12 cm (5 in). 'Tachiki' style. Photograph taken in October.

Propagation

From seed Collect the ripe fruit. Allow to rot, and collect the seeds. Keep layered between earth or sand and plant in the spring in a sand-peat mixture. Note: the fruit is barely more than 8 mm (3/10 in) across and the seed is tiny.

From cuttings Take branches that have no leaves, with at least three eyes. Plant deeply in spring, leaving only one eye above ground. The buried eyes grow fast and vigorously. If you plant several cuttings together, take care they do not intertwine. In autumn, cut back the cuttings. Repot the following spring. Keep the soil cool, but shield from frost.

By simple layering In spring, in cool, humus-bearing compost.

By grafting Inlay method in a greenhouse, from January to March. Select one-year-old scions. Remove the eyes from the lower part of the stock. It is not necessary to apply grafting wax. It is better to enclose the graft in a clay mixture to stop it from drying out.

From young nursery stock

STYLES

Shakan

Kengai

Tachiki

Han-Kengai

Sekijōju

Sōkan

Kabudachi

Creeper *(Parthenocissus)*. 10 years old. Height 20 cm (8 in). 'Kengai' style. Photograph taken in October.

Pests and diseases

Pests
● **Scale insects** See p. 29.

Diseases
● **Mildew** (fungoid)
Symptoms Yellow patches on the upper surface of leaves, white dust on the underside. Premature leaf fall.
Treatment Cut off and destroy affected leaves. Spray with a copper-based fungicide.
● **Black rot** (fungoid)
Symptoms Brown-red patches appear on the leaves. Black flecks form on these patches.
Treatment Remove and cut out affected leaves. Spray with a copper-based fungicide.

Care

Exposure to sunlight These creepers like full sun. They need a lot of light if their autumn leaves are to be flamboyant. In very sunny areas, place in semishade in summer.

Temperature Tolerates heat, and is fairly resistant to frost.

Ventilation If exposed to a strong wind, some branches may break.

Container It is preferable to use a fairly deep pot. Glazed blue pots with or without decoration are very attractive.

Cleaning Prevent moss from forming at the bottom of the trunk. These creepers withstand pollution well.

Growth Fast. Large branch structure.

Repotting Repot annually, in early spring, in a larger pot. Prune the roots by a third.

Soil An equal mixture of loam and leaf mould. Likes deep, not too moist soil, and has no special requirements: good garden earth will suit it.

Pruning
Pruning of subbranches After flowering wait for new shoots to have about five eyes, then use scissors to cut back to one or two nodes.
Leaf pruning Cut leaves from healthy trees in late spring or early summer (June), and then give less water.

Wiring In spring and summer. Do not wire if the leaves are still soft – wait for a little while.

Watering Water freely, but allow to dry out from one watering to the next. Requires very good drainage to prevent water stagnating.

Spraying You can sprinkle the foliage and branches when you water the tree. Do not spray after leaf stripping, or when the tree is in flower.

Feeding In spring and autumn feed with slow-acting organic fertilizer on a regular basis.

Prunus communis dulcis
ALMOND

The Rosaceae family. This tree which is native to the mountains of central and western Asia is about 12 m (40 ft) tall, with a thick trunk, gnarled, dividing, angular branches and shiny green oblong leaves with finely serrated edges. The flowers appear before the leaves, sometimes in December-January, more often in February-March. They are white, pale pink or dark pink. The fruit is grey-green and has two seeds: almonds, which are edible on cultivated trees and poisonous on wild trees (*P. communis amara* – the bitter almond).

Almond *(Prunus communis 'Amento')*. This photograph, taken in June, shows young fruit. These small 'vine peaches' are ripe in late August or early September, depending on the area, and the green colour of the skin does not change as they ripen. They taste delicious.

Propagation

From seed Collect the seeds in autumn. Stratify in a dry place and sow in spring. Protect from frost during its first year.

By air layering In May-June-July.

By shield-budding In summer. Leave the graft alone for a whole year. Cut back the one-year-old stem at the end of the winter. The upper eye from which the trunk extends must be on the opposite side from the point at which the graft is made so as to lessen any possible curve and subsequent swelling. Cut back the eye beneath the upper eye which becomes a sucker as it develops.

From young nursery stock

Care

Exposure to sunlight The almond likes full sun and light.

Temperature Almond trees like heat and are affected by cold. They must be protected in winter.

Ventilation Tolerates wind.

Container Choose a fairly deep bowl as the almond likes deep soil.

Cleaning Remove any shoots growing out from the trunk. Remove withered fruit from the tree.

Growth Slow.

Repotting Every year either in very early spring or after flowering prune a good third off the root hairs and repot in a larger container.

Soil Half-and-half mixture of loam and leaf mould. Almond trees thrive in calcareous, deep, dry soil.

Pruning
Pruning of subbranches After the flowers have withered and before the new shoots have hardened, cut back using clippers to two or three eyes.
Pruning of branches Leave slow-growing branches which already have the follow-

Pruning leaves.
Prune the leaves at their point of emergence.

STYLES

 Shakan   Tachiki   Han-Kengai   Sôkan   Kabudachi   Korabuki

ing year's buds on them, and prune long branches at the end of the summer. In October again prune all branches lightly.

Wiring In spring and in summer. Take care when putting the wire in position that you do not wound the tree or knock off developing flower buds.

Watering Water freely just before flowering, and reduce water given while the tree is in flower.

Spraying Do not get the tree wet while it is in flower. After flowering sprinkle water on to it while you are watering.

Feeding In spring and autumn feed with a slow-acting organic fertilizer. A tree that is in flower should not be fed. Increase the amount of fertilizer given a little at the end of autumn to set the tree up for the winter and to encourage good flowering, which is always very early in the season.

Pests and diseases

Pests
- **Scale insects** See p. 29.
- **Tortrix** (caterpillars) See p. 29.
- **Red spider mites** See p. 28.

Diseases
- **Rot** See p. 31.
- **Rust** See p. 31.
- **Scab** (fungoid)
Symptoms Grey patches rimmed with red on the leaves, the fruit and flower buds. Flowers and fruit wither and fail.
Treatment Cut out diseased leaves and branches. Spray with zineb-based fungicide.

Wild spring cherry *(Prunus subhirtella)*. 50 years old. Height, 60 cm (2 ft). 'Kôrabuki' style. Photograph taken in April. A very fine specimen of *Prunus*, covered with small, hanging, white flowers. We wanted to illustrate the *Prunus* genus using a variety other than the one described, for there are a great many varieties of *Prunus*, and very often they are cared for in exactly the same way.

Prunus Mume
JAPANESE APRICOT

The Rosaceae family. This tree, native to China and Korea and widely grown in Japan, is about 12 m (40 ft) tall, and has a rounded top, grey-green bark, an finely serrated, deciduous, oval leaves. The yellow or greenish fruit is barely edible. In February-March-April it has white, pale or dark pink, or red flowers. The 'Rosea-plena' variety flowers in February-March.

Propagation

From cuttings In spring take a one-year-old slip, behead it and plant it in good garden earth lightened with sand. The following year, put the new shoot in a pot and prune it. Repeat this process for two or three years.

By air layering In spring.

By grafting In summer, shield-bud.

Care

Exposure to sunlight The Japanese apricot likes full sun.

Temperature Likes heat. Its branches suffer in frost, but it can withstand cold.

Ventilation This tree needs to be displayed in a well-aired position.

Container Choose a bowl of medium depth with pretty glazing that sets the tree's flowers off to advantage.

Cleaning Pick some fruit if there is too much so as not to exhaust the tree. In autumn after the leaves have fallen carefully remove all dead leaves. Remove any shoots coming from the trunk.

Growth Rapid and vigorous.

Repotting Every year in spring after flowering. Prune a third off the roots and repot in a larger container. Good drainage is essential.

Soil Half-and-half mixture of loam and leaf mould. A little sand may be added to the earth compost. The Japanese apricot likes deep, dry, calcareous soil.

Pruning
Pinching back Pinch out new shoots if there are too many and any unwanted shoots as soon as they appear. Pinch back new growth on side branches to prevent the branches growing too long. Pinching back is carried out just before the leaves harden.
Pruning of subbranches Pinch out the tips of side branches according to a plan so that the branches will grow delicately and will not break in winter and will produce flowers the following spring. Side branches are pruned after flowering; to achieve good results the work has to be done with great attention to detail.
Pruning of branches When repotting study the tree's outline and prune out superfluous branches. Prune once a year leaving only two or three leaves per branch after flowering.

Wiring From the end of spring to autumn. Protect the brittle branches with raffia. It is not always necessary to coil

Japanese apricot *(Prunus Mume)*. 7 years old. Height, 10 cm (4 in). 'Tachiki' style. Photograph taken in June.

STYLES

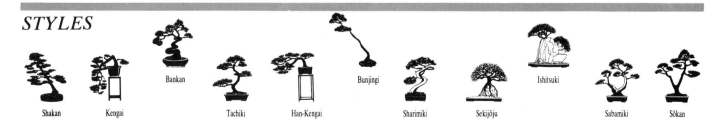

Shakan   Kengai   Bankan   Tachiki   Han-Kengai   Bunjingi   Sharimiki   Sekijōju   Ishitsuki   Sabamiki   Sōkan

Japanese apricot *(Prunus Mume)*. 120 years old. 'Sabamiki' style. Photograph taken in June. A remarkable specimen; the trunk which is partly dead has been sculpted and chiselled to make it appear still older.

wire round the branches. They can be trained by weighting, and the trunk can be shaped by using a clamp, in conjunction with pruning.

Watering As soon as the surface of the soil is dry, water. Water copiously when the tree is in bud and in summer.

Spraying Do not wet the tree when it is in flower. When you are watering in summer, sprinkle the leaves. Never in full sunlight.

Feeding After flowering until autumn, feed with slow-acting organic fertilizer. After flowering until July it is best to use liquid fertilizer. In autumn use fertilizer in a solid or powdered form.

Pests and diseases

Pests
- **Bark beetles** See p. 30.
- **Bombyx** (caterpillars) See p. 28.
- **Tortrix** (caterpillars) See p. 29.
- **Hard-shelled and soft scale insects** See p. 29.
- **Red spider mites** See p. 28.

Diseases
- **Rust** See p. 31.
- **Rot** See p. 31.
- **Crown-gall** (fungoid)
Symptoms A cauliflower-shaped excrescence soft and white to start with, then brown and cracked, on the neck and upper roots. A rot that endangers the tree's survival. There

may be secondary tumours.
Treatment Look out for insects and for damage to the tree when you are caring for it. Disinfect tools. Remove tumours, and scrape out. Apply a solution of spirit and sodium. Apply a wash to the soil based on an organomercury fungicide.
- **Powdery mildew** See p. 31.
- **Bark beetle**
Symptoms Brown patches, red at the edges, on the leaves which wither and fall after developing holes. Branches blotched and distorted.
Treatment Cut out diseased branches. Use a combined fungicide in April-May.

Kabudachi Ikadabuki Netsunagari Sôju Sambon-Yose Gohon-Yose Nanahon-Yose Kyûhon-Yose Yose-Ue Bonkei Plantations saisonnières

Pomegranate *(Punica Granatum).* 20 years old. Height 25 cm (10 in). 'Tachiki' style. Photograph taken in June.

Punica Granatum
POMEGRANATE

The Punicaceae family. Native to eastern and western Asia and the Mediterranean basin, the pomegranate is now grown as far away as the southern United States and South America. The genus consists of just two species: *Punica protopunica* and *Punica granatum*. The *P. granatum* is grown for its flowers and for its fruit. It grows to a height of 7 m (23 ft). It is of irregular habit, with slightly prickly branches, spindly subbranches, and oblong, deciduous leaves that are shiny and glabrous. From June to September it has scarlet flowers with puckered petals. In September-October it bears fruit that is orangy yellow or reddish, with several edible seeds in it.

Propagation

From seed Pick the ripe fruit, and leave to rot. Collect the seeds from inside. Wash them, then dry. Stratify in sand and sow in the spring in a warm place. Can be grown from seed only in the south.

From cuttings In June-July. Make sure the cutting is kept damp and well aired. Pot up the following spring. Protect from cold and frost.

By air layering In spring.

From young nursery stock

Care

Exposure to sunlight The pomegranate likes full sun and needs light. But keep it in semishade at the height of summer.

Temperature The pomegranate reacts badly to cold and frost. Like trees raised in an orangery, it loves warmth.

Ventilation Is not affected by wind. Needs a well-aired position.

Container Pots of medium depth.

Cleaning Remove a few flowers from overloaded branches; if the tree produces fruit, pick them before they fall of their own accord to avoid exhausting the tree.

Growth Quite fast when young.

Repotting Every year or every second year in spring when the leaves are beginning to open. Prune a good third off the roots and repot in a larger container.

Soil Half-and-half mixture of loam and leaf mould. Sand can be added to the compost. Likes clayey soil.

Pruning
Pinching back In early spring and late autumn pinch new growth back to two eyes.
Pruning of subbranches After flowering prune side branches, leaving just two eyes. Leave to grow. When it is about 8 cm (3 in) long, prune branch again leaving only one eye.

Wiring Wire from the end of spring until summer. Protect the brittle branches with raffia. Repeat every year.

Watering Good drainage is essential. Water copiously in summer, lightly in winter. Do not allow the tree to dry out.

Spraying Except during flowering, mist-spray the tree. If possible leave it exposed to the night dew.

Feeding In spring feed with slow-acting organic fertilizer. During flowering in autumn give a little liquid fertilizer.

Pests and diseases

Pests
- **Greenfly** See p. 29.
- **Red spider mites** See p. 28.

Diseases
- **Rust** See p. 31.
- **Powdery mildew** See p. 31
- **Scab**
Symptoms Appearance of brown cankerous lesions on the branches. The leaves are flecked with black and turn yellow and drop off. The fruit has black cankers on it and is cracked.
Treatment Cut off yellow leaves. Pick diseased fruit. Cut out diseased branches. Spray with a copper- or thiram-based wash.

STYLES

Shakan

Kengai

Tachiki

Han-Kengai

Bunjingi

Sekijōju

Nejikan

Sôkan

Kabudachi

Ikadabuki

Netsunagari

Sôju

Sambon-Yose

The Rosaceae family. Five species are native to Asia; the sixth *(Pyracantha coccinea)* is native to Europe and resembles the cotoneaster.

Pyracantha
PYRACANTHA or FIRETHORN

Pyracantha angustifolia Native to China, this shrub is about 4 m (13 ft) tall, spreading in habit, sometimes prostrate. Its oblong, semievergreen leaves can be slightly dentate at the tip, and are shiny and dark green on top, greyish underneath. It flowers in May-June. The fruit, which is present from October, is brick red to orange and stays on the tree throughout the winter until March.

Pyracantha *(Pyracantha angustifolia)*. 12 to 25 years old. Height 60 cm (2 ft). 'Yose-Ue' style. Photograph taken in August/September.

Propagation

From seed Collect the seeds shortly before they are fully ripe and sow in the open. Germination occurs the following spring. Seeds may also be kept for a year between layers of sand or earth and sown the following spring. Germination is temperamental and trees grown from seed take five years to produce flowers and fruit.

From cuttings In early summer remove side branches that bear fruit in the winter. Remove tip of stem, and plant. Roots form rapidly. Repot the following spring.

By layering In spring. Simple layering is to be preferred; keep the soil very moist.

From young nursery stock

Care

Exposure to sunlight The pyracantha likes light and is happy in full sun. But it can be placed in semishade at the height of summer.

STYLES

Shakan

Kengai

Tachiki

Han-Kengai

Hōkidachi

Sekijōju

Temperature The pyracantha likes heat, dislikes frost. It does best in mild southern and south-western areas.

Ventilation Can withstand wind provided it is well watered.

Container Plant in a medium-deep, glazed pot.

Cleaning Remove all yellow leaves to prevent parasites. If there is too much fruit, remove some after it has formed.

Growth It grows faster in open ground. In a pot it grows quite slowly.

Repotting Every second year in spring. Prune the roots and repot in a larger container. Does not like being transplanted. Leave some old soil on the roots to help them to become re-established.

Soil Half-and-half mixture of loam and leaf mould. Pyracanthas like deep, cool, light, loose soil. They need good drainage.

Pruning
Pruning of subbranches After flowering and before the new shoots harden, prune side branches with clippers (in summer). In autumn, prune again dealing with late shoots.
Pruning of branches At the end of the winter, shorten the branches with a view to shaping the tree.

Wiring The pyracantha can be wired at any time during the year. Do not put the wire in place when the new branches are soft. Do not leave wire on the tree for more than six months.

Watering Copious before and after flowering. If it is well drained, the pyracantha needs a lot of water.

Spraying During summer watering, you can sprinkle the foliage, but never wet it when the tree is in flower or carrying fruit.

Feeding Feed with liquid fertilizer in spring before flowering. In autumn feed with slow-acting organic fertilizer once a month.

Pyracantha *(Pyracantha angustifolia)*. 15 years old. Height 25 cm (10 in). 'Néjikan' style. Photograph taken in May.

Pests and diseases

Pests
- **Greenfly** See p. 29.
- **Woolly aphids** See p. 29.
- **Scale insects** See p. 29.
- **Ermine moths** (caterpillars) See p. 29.

Diseases
- **Scab**
Symptoms Appearance of cankerous brown lesions on the branches. The leaves are flecked with black, turn yellow and fall. The fruit has black cankers and is cracked.
Treatment Cut off yellow leaves, and pick diseased fruit. Cut out diseased branches. Spray with a copper- or thiram-based wash.

Bacterial fireblight (fungoid)
Symptoms New shoots and flower buds blacken and wither as if burnt. The affected parts shrivel. Appearance of a seeping, white-beige fungal growth.
Treatment Cut out and burn diseased branches. Do not use a fertilizer containing nitrogen, and make sure the soil is not too damp. Disinfect tools. Use a copper fungicide when flowering starts and during the growing season.

Ishitsuki

Nejikan

Sôkan

Kabudachi

Bonkei

Kusamono

The Ericaceae family. Native to Asia and also found in North America, Europe, Java, the Malay islands, Australia, New Guinea and the Philippines. Some also known by the name azalea. Greenhouse species used to be called azaleas while the name rhododendron was applied to hardy species, but there is no scientific distinction between them, and dwarf rhododendrons are called azaleas.

Rhododendron
RHODODENDRON

Rhododendron impeditum A bushy species with a great many tangled shoots covered with black scales and leaves that are green-grey on top and brown underneath. Slightly scented mauve flowers are in bloom at the end of April.

Rhododendron indicum formerly called *Azalea indica* A shrub 1.5 m (5 ft) tall of dense habit with dark-green evergreen or semievergreen leaves, flowering in June. The flowers are of various colours, but usually salmon red and relatively large.

Propagation

From seed Gather the seeds and keep in a dry place; sow in May. Germination gets under way three weeks after sowing. Keep the soil moist. Leave the seedlings in position for two years before you repot, taking care to avoid mildew.

From cuttings Take cuttings in June. Plant in a greenhouse or under glass in sand and peat. Roots will have formed by October. Leave under glass through the winter. Repot in spring.

Rhododendron impeditum. 8 years old. Height, 12 cm (4¾ in). 'Sôkan' style. Photograph taken in April. The miniaturized flowers and leaves of this variety produce an outstanding result.

By simple layering In July. The following year in September-October, sever the layer and pot up.

From young nursery stock

Care

Exposure to sunlight Place in semishade. Small-leaved varieties can withstand the sun better than others.

Temperature Rhododendrons like warmth and many react badly to frost. Keep in a warm place in winter – but not indoors.

Ventilation The rhododendron stands up well to wind, but needs more copious watering if exposed to it.

Container While the rhododendron is being developed it is best to use an unglazed bowl of medium depth. They are rarely grown in flat bowls.

Cleaning Pick off some flower buds if there are too many. After flowering remove faded blooms. Remove any shoots from the trunk and roots. Keep the soil regularly swept as it is often covered by fallen leaves.

Growth Slow and steady.

Repotting Repot after flowering, every year for young trees, every second year for older trees. Prune the roots by a third, and repot in a larger container.

Soil Mixture consisting of ½ heath mould, ¼ leaf mould and ¼ peat. Rhododendrons need soil that is damp, cool, light, rich in humus and sandy. It can be acid, but must never be calcareous. The rhododendron becomes etiolated in soil consisting only of heath mould.

Pruning
Pruning of subbranches At the end of the summer after the flowers have faded and before the leaves harden, prune side

Pruning a rhododendron.

STYLES

Chokkan   Shakan   Kengai   Tachiki   Han-Kengai   Bunjingi   Neagari   Sekijôju   Ishitsuki

branches with clippers, cutting back to two pairs of leaves.

Pruning of branches When repotting, prune out dead branches or over-crowded branches to let air into the shrub.

Wiring Wire from spring to autumn. Rhododendron branches break easily. To harden them do not water for one day before wiring.

Watering Keep the ground damp. The roots dry out quickly and this is fatal for the tree. Water often throughout the year except when there is frost.

Spraying Mist-spray the foliage morning and evening in the summer. After repotting spray the leaves until the new roots have become established. Do not wet the flowers.

Feeding Give a weak solution of organic fertilizer in spring and autumn. Do not feed during flowering.

Azalea *(Rhododendron Satsuki)*. 15 years old. Height, 45 cm (1 ft 6 in). 'Neagari' style. Photograph taken in June.

Pests and diseases

Pests
- **Eelworms** See p. 30.
- **Weevils**
Symptoms The tree turns yellow and withers, growth is slowed down, there are holes in the leaves and the lamina is gnawed. Damage occurs at night. Presence of larvae in the tissues.
Treatment Spray with contact insecticide from May to July. Incorporate organophosphate insecticide into the soil.
- **Tortrix** (caterpillars) See p. 29.
- **Leaf-hoppers**
Symptoms Leaves yellowed by green insects that puncture the foliage. Lamina discoloured. Leaves may drop off.
Treatment Cut out infested branches. Spray with contact insecticide or systemic organophosphate

insecticide.
- **Rhododendron bug**
Symptoms The underside of the lamina is stained with black spots, and the upper face is yellowed and marbled. Leaves drop off.
Treatment Spray the undersides of the leaves with a wash based on parathion or oleoparathion.

Diseases
- **Root and stem rot** See p. 31.
- **Phyllosticta blight** (fungoid)
Symptoms There are withered patches on the leaves, and small spots of black appear on the dry areas. Affected leaves drop off.
Treatment Cut off affected leaves. Spray with copper-based fungicide.

- **Pestalozzia** (fungoid)
Symptoms Grey patches appear on the lower leaves, which dry out and tear.
Treatment Avoid excess humidity. Remove infected leaves. As a precaution spray with a combined fungicide.
- **Rust** See p. 31.
- **Honey fungus** See p. 31.
- **Chlorosis**
Symptoms Leaves turn yellow around the lamina and near the veins. New leaves are small and discoloured.
Treatment Treat the soil with nitrogen, iron, magnesium and zinc. Do not give too much calcium and sodium, do not expose to excessive cold, and do not give too much water; keep away from draughts and poisonous gases. Place in the light.

Sabamiki

Sōkan

Kabudachi

Korabuki

Ikadabuki

Netsunagari

Yamayori

Bonkei

The Rosaceae family. Native to the temperate regions of the northern hemisphere; a dense, elegant shrub with graceful, deciduous leaves that can be dentate or lobed. From early spring to late summer it has small clusters of white or pink flowers.

Spiraea
SPIRAEA

Spiraea japonica This bush which is native to Asia is not very ramified; it has stiff, erect branches, is 1.5 m (5 ft) tall, and has large, green, oval, dentate leaves; new shoots are red. In June-July it has bright pink or purplish-pink flowers.

Propagation

From seed Seeds are sown in spring under glass. They germinate rapidly. But spiraeas are seldom grown from seed as they do not breed true to type (the characteristics of the plant producing the seed are not completely reproduced).

From cuttings Take cuttings in early summer. Behead and plant in a sand-peat mixture. The slips are very delicate: be careful with spraying and shade. Remove flower buds from the slip.

By plant division In spring.

From young nursery stock

Care

Exposure to sunlight The spiraea needs sun to flower, but tolerates semishade.

Temperature The spiraea stands up well to heat. It should be protected from frost.

Ventilation Stands up to wind. Needs a well-aired position.

Spiraea (*Spiraea japonica*). 5 years old. Height, 10 cm (4 in). The somewhat special shape of this shrub does not belong to any definite style.

Container Select a bowl of medium depth. A glazed or unglazed pot is equally suitable.

Cleaning Cut off flowers as soon as they fade, using scissors.

Growth Slow when the spiraea is grown in a pot.

Repotting Every year or every second year in spring. Prune off a good third of the root hairs and repot in a larger container.

Soil Half-and-half mixture of loam and leaf mould. The spiraea will grow in any soil, even poor or dry soil. But it is happiest in cool, fertile soil that is not damp and stagnating or too rich in lime.

Pruning
Pruning of subbranches After flowering use clippers to prune the side branches leaving only one or two eyes on each. In very early spring and at the end of autumn, prune side branches leaving only two or three eyes. After flowering cut out dry twigs and old branches.

Wiring The spiraea is not wired.

Watering Copious. Keep the ground nice and cool. Ensure that the pot has good drainage. Reduce the amount of water given when the tree is in flower.

Spraying Sprinkle the foliage in summer when you are watering. Do not spray when the tree is in flower.

Feeding In spring before the tree flowers feed with a slow-acting organic fertilizer. Do not feed while the tree is in flower or during July-August. Start feeding again in autumn, slightly increasing the amount given.

STYLES

Shakan | Kengai | Tachiki | Han-Kengai | Sekijōju | Ishitsuki | Kabudachi | Bonkei | Kusamono

Spiraea *(Spiraea japonica)*. 7 years old. Height, 15 cm (6 in). 'Sekijōju' style. Photograph taken in October. The flowers and leaves seem almost to be made of stone; after enjoying these autumn tints, you can cut hard back.

Pests and diseases

Pests
- **Greenfly** See p. 29.
- **Tortrix** (caterpillars) See p. 29.

Diseases
- **Powdery mildew** See p. 31.
- **Rust** See p. 31.

The Oleaceae family. Native to Asia and south-east Europe, this ornamental shrub can live for about 40 years. It reaches 7 m (23 ft) in height and is of upright habit, with stiff branches ending in buds and white, mauve or purple scented flowers.

Syringa
LILAC

Syringa vulgaris (common lilac) Its deciduous leaves are oval, smooth, light green and bright. In April-May it bears mauve or occasionally white flowers, that are highly scented. The fruit is oblong, leathery, smooth and pointed.

Propagation

From seed Collect up the seeds as soon as they are ripe (November-December). Put them in bags and hang in a warm, dry place. They will shed their husks spontaneously. Clean the seeds and stratify in dry material. Plant in the spring.

From cuttings Strip the bark off the slips and plant them in spring in a sand-peat mixture and put in a warm place.

By simple layering This is done in late spring. Roots form quickly. Sever layer in the autumn, pot up and protect from frost.

From young nursery stock

Care

Exposure to sunlight The lilac flowers best if it is in full sun, but will thrive in semishade.

Temperature Lilacs can withstand cold, but do not like excessive frost. They are happier in a warm position.

Ventilation The lilac tolerates wind provided it is not too strong.

Container Select a pot of medium depth, glazed or unglazed. The colour of the container should harmonize with the colour of the flowers.

Cleaning Pick or cut withered flowers. Remove the fruit which takes too much sap and exhausts the tree. Remove shoots growing from the trunk.

Growth Slow.

Repotting Annually in spring before flowering prune the roots by half and repot in a larger container.

Soil Half-and-half mixture of loam and leaf mould. An average soil, preferably cool, firm and clayey. It can be neutral with a little lime. Avoid an acid soil. To combat acidity, add lime.

Pruning
Pruning of subbranches After flowering, prune side branches with clippers, leaving just one or two eyes. At the very beginning of spring and in late autumn, prune the side branches to two or three eyes.
Pruning of branches In winter, prune out old branches and any that are growing untidily.

Wiring In spring and in summer. Coil wire round the branches carefully so as not to break them.

Watering Water freely in summer, more before flowering than during it. Keep the ground slightly damp.

Spraying Sprinkle the tree when you are watering in summer. Do not spray during flowering.

Feeding After flowering and in autumn feed with slow-acting organic fertilizer. The lilac is greedy and needs feeding.

STYLES

Shakan

Kengai

Tachiki

Han-Kengai

Sekijóju

Common lilac *(Syringa vulgaris)*. 8 years old. Height, 15 cm (6 in). 'Shakan' style. Photograph taken in April. The small size of the flowers is typical of the 'dwarfing' of this shrub.

Pests and diseases

Pests

● **Erineum** (gall mites).
Symptoms Formation of a thick beige down turning to brown on the leaves which become distorted. Flower buds drop off.
Treatment Spray with a sulphur-based insecticide or an acaricide.

● **Weevils**
Symptoms The tree turns yellow and withers. Growth slows down, there are holes in the leaves and the lamina is gnawed. Damage at night. Presence of larvae in the tissues.
Treatment Spray the ground with contact insecticides from May to July.

● **Moths**
Symptoms Brown holes on the leaves. Silky threads are coiled round the lamina. Presence of caterpillars.
Treatment Spray with insecticide.

● **Tortrix** (caterpillars) See p. 29.

Diseases

● **Bud rot** See p. 31.
● **Powdery mildew** See p. 31.
● **Leaf spot** See p. 31.
● **Bacteriosis** (fungoid)
Symptoms There are translucent patches on the lamina, turning to black. The shoots wilt then turn brown. The flower buds rot.
Treatment Cut out and destroy affected branches. Spray with a copper-based fungicide.

● **Virus disease**
Symptoms There are wavy lines marking the leaves. The lamina has holes in it, and the leaves are misshapen.
Treatment Cut out and destroy affected branches. Ensure that the tree is getting correct care.

Ishitsuki

Kabudachi

Ikadabuki

Netsunagari

Bonkei

The Leguminosaceae family. Native to eastern Asia and North America. A climbing tree with branches that can grow to lengths of over 30 m (100 ft). The trunk becomes gnarled with age. The deciduous leaves are oval, acuminate at the tip. Flowers are white, mauve or blue and come out in spring and then in summer.

Wisteria
WISTERIA

Wisteria sinensis (Chinese wisteria) It can survive for more than 100 years. It has long twisted branches, leaves that go from golden yellow-green to pale green, and clusters of scented blue-mauve flowers that appear in May-June and then in August.
Wisteria floribunda (Japanese wisteria) It is more rustic in appearance and more scented, with branches about 10 m (33 ft) long and oval leaves, rounded at the base. It flowers in May-June, then again in August-September. The flowers are purple or bluey purple, and grow in long, slender clusters.

Chinese wisteria (*Wisteria sinensis* 'daruma').
Photograph taken in May.

Propagation

From seed Collect the pods in October. Open them. In spring plant the seeds with good bottom heat. Leave the shoots for two years before potting. Not many seeds germinate, and seedlings grow slowly. You will have to wait for about ten years for the wisteria to flower.

By simple layering Choose long stems. Bury them, with just the tip emerging. In autumn roots will have formed round the eyes. Sever and pot up. Keep protected in winter.

By grafting The most commonly used method. Make a whip or an inlay graft in February-March. Select specimens that are four to five years old which are already producing flowers. Make the graft as low as possible to keep the point of union inconspicuous. It is also possible to graft in autumn after leaf fall.

Care

Exposure to sunlight The wisteria likes a sunny position.

Temperature The wisteria likes warmth, but has only moderate resistance to frost. If the temperature falls below −5°C (23°F), it should be protected.

Ventilation The wisteria can withstand wind. Put in a well-ventilated position.

Container Choose a medium-deep, glazed or unglazed pot. If it is decorated, make sure the decoration harmonizes with the flowers or outline of the tree.

Cleaning After flowering, the wisteria produces pods. These are quite attractive, but if there are too many it exhausts the tree. So they should be removed as soon as possible, leaving just a few.

Growth Slow. When its roots are well settled, the wisteria grows faster.

STYLES

Shakan

Kengai

Bankan

Han-Kengai

Sekijōju

Repotting   Repot every year just after flowering. Prune away old or damaged roots, leaving only strong ones. Rearrange the roots and repot in a larger container.

Soil   Half-and-half mixture of loam and leaf mould. Wisterias like cool, light, substantial soil. If it is too hard or impermeable this can cause chlorosis. Good drainage is essential.

Pruning

Pruning of subbranches   After flowering and before the leaves harden, prune side branches with clippers. Do not prune at random, as this would endanger the well-being of the tree and prevent flowering the following year. In autumn after leaf fall cut side branches short, and eliminate unwanted new growth.
Pruning of branches   After flowering prune all superfluous branches.

Wiring   Wire from spring to autumn. Coil wire into position when new buds appear. For bines, use raffia when the leaves are beginning to harden. Always wire well and train in the same direction so that branches do not grow into one another.

Watering   If the pot has good drainage, water copiously after repotting so as to encourage good root development. Watering should be just adequate to keep the soil moist. In early summer water two or three times a day. In midsummer water once every second day – this will strengthen the leaves and help buds to develop. Place the pot in a basin of water and allow it to absorb as much water as it wants. Repeat three times at intervals of five or six days. Bines will stop growing and the buds will produce flowers.

Spraying   When the wisteria is not in flower, it can be sprinkled during watering.

Feeding   After flowering, alternate liquid organic fertilizer with slow-acting fertilizer in powder or solid form. Add phosphate if necessary. In autumn feed first with a generous amount of liquid ferti-

Chinese wisteria (*Wisteria sinensis* 'daruma'). 30 years old. Height 50 cm (1 ft 8 in). 'Shakan' style. Photograph taken in May.

lizer, then of solid fertilizer. Wisterias need two or three times more fertilizer than other bonsai specimens.

How to get a wisteria to repeat flowering every year. Soak it every year during July-August; the rim of the pot should stand slightly above the level of the water in the basin.

Pests and diseases

Pests
● **Scale insects** See p. 29.

Diseases
● **Mosaic virus**
Symptoms The lamina is streaked with yellow. Lighter patches start from the veins and spread. The lamina may be distorted and the leaves may fall.
Treatment Cut out diseased branches.

INDOOR BONSAI

Ampelopsis
AMPELOPSIS

The Vitaceae family. Native to North and Central America and to eastern Asia. These are ornamental creepers with bark that does not scale off. The bines are twining tendrils. The trilobate leaves are bright green, shinier on the underside, and can be variegated green with beige. Fruit forms in September-October, and is not edible.

Propagation

From seed Pick the fruit when it is ripe. Remove the seeds, wash, dry and stratify them. Plant in spring under glass or in a greenhouse.

From cuttings In spring after bud burst but before the new leaves have hardened, take a cutting, behead it and plant it in a warm, well-lit place.

By simple layering In April-May, in a greenhouse or in a light, warm room.

Care

Exposure to sunlight A lot of light, particularly for variegated creepers.

Temperature It is happy indoors in the warm. In winter it tolerates temperatures going down to 12°C (54°F).

Ventilation This creeper cannot withstand draughts. However, it is important for the room it is in to be well ventilated.

Container Choose a pot of medium depth, often a glazed one.

Cleaning Keep the foliage free of dust which blocks its pores. When the leaves fall, remove the dead, withered leaves. Take out any suckers and shoots coming from the base of the trunk.

Growth Slow but regular. The branches are reluctant to ramify.

Repotting Every second year in April, prune the roots by a half and pot into a larger container, if necessary.

Soil ¼ leaf mould, ¼ heath mould, ¼ loam and ¼ coarse sand. The soil must be cool.

Pruning
Pruning of subbranches When the tree is once again in leaf, allow subbranches to grow to three to five eyes, then cut back leaving only one or two eyes. Repeat throughout the growing period. At the final autumn pruning, leave the side branches a little longer.
Leaf pruning You can strip a perfectly healthy tree of its leaves in late spring or early summer so that it will produce denser foliage with smaller leaves.
Development pruning In January when the tree is bare, prune out untidy or damaged bines that are superfluous.

Wiring It is seldom used, but when it is, wire from spring to summer. Start coiling the wire round when the new shoots have hardened.

Watering Water requirements vary according to light and heat. Give more water in summer. Cut down on watering when the tree has no leaves.

Spraying Spray the leaves and trunk daily. Do not spray when the tree is in sunlight.

Feeding In spring and in autumn feed with a slow-acting organic fertilizer.

STYLES

 Shakan

 Kengai

 Bankan

 Tachiki

 Han-Kengai

 Fukinagashi

Ampelopsis (*Ampelopsis brevipedunculata*). 10 years old. Height, 15 cm (6 in). 'Neagari' style. Photograph taken in October. The variegation of the foliage gradually disappears with successive prunings.

Pests and diseases

Pests
● **Scale insects** See p. 29.

Diseases:
● **Mildew** (fungoid)
Symptoms There are yellow patches on the leaves, and white powder on the underside. The leaves drop off.
Treatment Cut out diseased leaves. Spray with a copper-based fungicide.
● **Black rot** (fungoid)
Symptoms There are browny-red patches on the leaves, and black specks appear on these patches.
Treatment Cut out and destroy diseased leaves. Spray with a copper-based fungicide.

Neagari

Sekijōju

Ishitsuki

Nejikan

Takuzakuri

Sōkan

Kabudachi

The Araliaceae family. Native to tropical Asia; this shrub with woody branches is quite tall in its natural environment. The green, evergreen leaves vary according to species.

Polyscias
POLYSCIAS
and related species

Polyscias fruticosa This is also known as *Aralia ming*. Its branches are woody, its bark white and its leaves denticulate.
Dizygotheca elegantissima (syn: Aralia elegantissima) A shrub with digitate leaves that are dark green marbled with white and slightly drooping. The branches are straight and erect.
Dizygotheca castor (syn. *Aralia castor*) A species that is close to *Aralia elegantissima*, but the leaves are smaller.
Aralia blacky A new creation. A shrub of upright habit with quite a large trunk. Thick, dark-green leaves that are fairly smooth edged, scroll shaped and corrugated.

Propagation

From seed In autumn, in a dark, warm room. Keep the soil moist. This method is tricky and the results are uncertain.

From root cuttings The best way to propagate is from a root cutting. Cut off roots that are about 10 cm (4 in) long. Plant these in autumn in a mixture that is half sand and half humus in an unheated greenhouse. Leave in a seed box for a year, then replant the following spring.

From tip cuttings This method is carried out in a greenhouse with a high temperature and a high moisture level in the atmosphere.

By air layering In spring in a warm room; spray the layer daily so that it does not dry out.

Care

Exposure to sunlight As long as it has relatively good light, the polyscia has no special needs. Do not place it in very direct sun.

Temperature In winter the temperature should not fall below 16°C (61°F). The polyscia likes humid heat.

Ventilation Keep the polyscias away from draughts, but it is important to allow air to circulate freely round the tree.

Container Choose a flat dish or one of medium depth, which can be glazed or unglazed.

Cleaning Remove any branches that have turned yellow and any shoots growing out from the trunk.

Growth Growth is slow: it takes four or five years for the trunk to develop.

Repotting Every second year in spring (April), prune the roots by between a third and a half and repot in a larger, well-drained container.

Soil ¼ leaf mould, ¼ heath mould, ¼ coarse sand and ¼ loam. The soil must be fertile, light and cool.

Pruning
Pruning of subbranches Keep cutting the branches back to two pairs of leaves as soon as they have four or five. Leave them a little longer at the final autumn pruning.
Leaf pruning You can use scissors to cut any leaves that are too big off the tree.
Pruning of branches To get a good spread of branches, you can cut back all the branches at the beginning of the growing season. Put the bonsai in a greenhouse or in a plastic bag to encourage bud formation.

Wiring Seldom used. It can be done throughout the year, but it is easier in very warm conditions, as the wood of the branches is more flexible then.

Watering Water freely. Keep the ground damp. Good drainage is essential so that water does not stagnate round the roots.

Spraying Spray the foliage daily to maintain a high level of moisture in the atmosphere which is essential to the polyscia.

Feeding In spring and in autumn feed with a slow-acting organic fertilizer. If the tree is in good condition, you can also give it one application of liquid fertilizer in the winter.

STYLES

Shakan   Tachiki   Han-Kengai   Neagari   Sekijôju   Ishitsuki   Nejikan   Takozukuri   Sabamiki   Sôkan

Polyscias *(Dizygotheca castor)*. 8 years old. Height, 25 cm (10 in). 'Tachiki' style. Photograph taken in June.

Pests and diseases

Pests
- **Gall eelworms** See p. 30.
- **Eelworms** See p. 30.
- **Tarsonemid mites** (prevalent in warm countries)

Symptoms The lamina is curled up and misshapen. There is no further leaf development. Presence of spider mites in the folds of the lamina.

Treatment Take care when repotting. Spray with an acaricide.

- **Glasshouse red spider mites** (web-forming *Tetranychus*) See p. 28.
- **Soft scale insects** See p. 29.

Diseases
- **Verticillium wilt** See p. 31.
- **Root rot** See p. 31.
- **Alternariose of the leaves** (fungoid)

Symptoms There are oily patches on the leaves, sometimes ringed with red. Near the nodes, the branches are discoloured, and the upper part of the branch may wither. Black specks form on the diseased parts.

Treatment Cut out diseased branches. Spray with maneb-based fungicide.

- **Bacterial canker**

Symptoms There are patches on the leaves with uneven holes which may lead to the buds rotting.

NB. Only occurs on the *Polyscias* and related species.

Treatment Cut out and destroy the diseased branches. Feed regularly with organic fertilizer.

Kabudachi

Korabuki

Ikadabuki

Netsunagari

Sòju

Sambon-Yose

Yose-Ue

Tsukami-Yose

Bonkei

Plantations saisonnières

The Araucariaceae family. Native to the southern hemisphere, these are big geometrically shaped trees with straight trunks, and branches at regular intervals; their cones are their characteristic feature. They can grow to a height of 70 m (230 ft). The needle-shaped, tapering leaves curve upwards.

Araucaria
ARAUCARIA

Araucaria excelsa (Norfolk Island pine) This species which is native to Oceania has a pyramid-shaped crown, and overlapping evergreen, needle-shaped green leaves.

Propagation

From seed Sow ripe seeds in April-May in small boxes in a warm place. Germination is slow. Keep the soil moist. Plant out after two years.

From cuttings Take cuttings from terminal shoots, never from laterals. Cut the tip off a branch, and plant in sand. Leave first of all in a cool place, then move to a warm place to allow the new roots to develop.

Norfolk Island pine *(Araucaria excelsa)*. 10 years old. Height, 25 cm (10 in). 'Sôju' style. Photograph taken in June-July. The branches can be cut back taking care that the tips do not turn brown.

Care

Exposure to sunlight Keep away from full sun. The araucaria prefers a shady, but well-lit position.

Temperature This araucaria likes heat. In winter the temperature must not be allowed to drop below 17°C (63°F).

Ventilation This araucaria dislikes draughts. However, the room where it is kept should be regularly aired.

Container A flattish or medium-deep container is suitable. Sometimes it is glazed, but seldom decorated.

Cleaning Remove any yellowing twigs, helping them to drop, and place the leafy part of the tree under the shower to remove any dust that has settled on the needles.

Growth Slow but steady.

Repotting Every second year in spring, prune the roots by a half and repot in a larger container.

Soil ¼ heath mould, ¼ leaf mould, ¼ loam and ¼ coarse sand. The araucaria is happiest in deep, dry, sandy soil.

Pruning
Pinching back Pinch the young shoots between your thumb and index finger in spring (April-May) to shorten them.
Pruning of branches When the growing period starts, reshape the outline of the tree if it is necessary by carefully pruning the branches.

Wiring Can be done at any time of year. Avoid wiring when the shoots are soft. Do not leave wire on the tree for more than four months.

Watering Water regularly. Allow the soil to dry out well between two waterings. The araucaria likes dry ground.

Spraying Spray daily.

Feeding Feed with slow-acting organic fertilizer in spring and autumn.

STYLES

Chokkan   Shakan   Tachiki   Han-Kengai   Bunjingi   Fukinagashi   Sekijôju   Ishitsuki   Sabamiki   Sôkan   Kabudachi

Norfolk Island pine *(Araucaria excelsa)*. 50 years old.
Height, 35 cm (1 ft 2 in). 'Han-Kengai' style.
Photograph taken in October. An outstanding
specimen photographed in Taiwan at an exhibition
organized by a society of bonsai enthusiasts.

Pests and diseases

Pests
- **Glasshouse red spider mites** (web-
forming *Tetranychus*) See p. 28.
- **Red spider mites** See p. 28.
- **Scale insects** See p. 29.
- **Mealy-bugs** See p. 29.

Diseases
- **Chlorosis**
Symptoms The needles turn yellow
round the lamina and near the ribs.
New needles are discoloured.
Treatment Apply nitrogen, iron,
magnesium and zinc to the soil. Do
not give too much calcium, sodium or
water; keep away from cold, draughts
and toxic gases. Place in the light.
Mist-spray the foliage.

| Korabuki | Ikadabuki | Sòju | Sambon-Yose | Gohon-Yose | Nanahon-Yose | Kyûhon-Yose | Yose-Ue | Tsukami-Yose | Bonkei | Plantations saisonnières |

The Gramineae family. Native to temperate zones of Asia. The bamboo is a giant grass. It has lignified haulms and some can grow to a height of over 30 m (100 ft). Some species can live for 100 years. The stems are nodose and grow in bunches, while the sheaths are evergreen and auriculate.

Bambusa
BAMBOO

Bambusa ventricosa Called 'Buddha's belly' because of its ringed, green trunk.
Bambusa multiplex A very fine stem with small, elongated, yellowy green leaves.

Propagation

By division Start with a rhizome. Choose a rhizome (a multiple one if you want a forest) that is growing horizontally, with close growing rings. Dig up a rhizome that is already growing. Leave a healthy shoot on it, and the root hairs growing from the nodes. The shoot left on the rhizome should be two years old. It will be removed a year later when new shoots have appeared. Plant the rhizome in mid-spring before new shoots (clones) have sprouted. Plant in a deep pot, and keep the soil moist. Prune away half of each sheath from the new growth.

Care

Exposure to sunlight The bamboo needs a lot of light, but should not be in direct sun.

Temperature These bamboo need humid heat throughout the year. In winter the temperature should not go below 19°C (66°F).

Ventilation Keep away from draughts, but ensure a regular change of air.

Container Select a fairly deep pot. Some pots are decorated with bamboo leaves, and one of these would be ideal. A brown or reddish-brown unglazed pot is to be preferred. A forest should be planted in a flat bowl.

Cleaning Bamboos continually produce yellow leaves which should be removed. Remove shoots growing from the trunk.

Growth Fast growing in spring. A stem will develop within a few months, or even weeks.

Repotting Every second or third year between May and September repot in new compost, spreading the roots right through the pot. (Make sure that you use the whole surface area of the container.)

Soil A mixture consisting of ½ loam, ¼ leaf mould and ¼ coarse sand. Deep, slightly damp soil.

Pruning If you want a single bamboo, remove all new growth that comes up each year in the spring. Prune with an upward-sloping cut: where each node emerges, prune the sheath by a half. When the shape has been established, use your hands to pull the clone out of its sheath before it develops so as to keep the bonsai compact.

Wiring Bamboos can be wired while they are being given their shape, but when that is established they do not need further wiring.

Watering Water copiously and often. Water should penetrate well to root level, but it must not be allowed to go stagnant (it is essential to provide good drainage). Keep the surface of the compost moist.

Spraying Spray the foliage daily. Bamboos like a humid atmosphere.

Feeding Feed spring and autumn with a slow-acting, organic fertilizer. Lawn fertilizer in granule form can be used and produces good results.

STYLES

Chokkan   Tachiki   Ishitsuki   Sôkan   Kabudachi   Korabuki   Sôju   Sambon-Yose   Gohon-Yose

Bamboo 'Buddha's belly' (*Bambusa ventricosa*). Height, 35 cm (1 ft 2 in). 'Tachiki' style. Photograph taken in November. The age of this bonsai is not stated because its main trunk forms in a year (its height and diameter do not alter after that).

Pests and diseases

Pests
- **Aphids** See p. 29.
- **Mealy-bugs** See p. 29.

Diseases
- **Melancolium culm** (bamboo smut)
Symptoms Canes which have been badly tended turn black at the base and the discoloration climbs between the internodes.
Treatment Cut out the damaged canes and rhizomes until you reach sound material. Disinfect the wound with sulphur.
NB. There is a danger that the bamboo will produce a great many yellow drooping leaves if there is too much water at root level; it must have good drainage, frequent watering and a lot of light to prevent discoloration of the leaves.

Nanahon-Yose

Kyúhon-Yose

Yose-Ue

Yamayori

Tsukami-Yose

Bonkei

Kusamono

Plantations saisonnières

The Nyctaginaceae family. Native to Brazil. A dozen species of shrubs or prickly creepers with smooth-edged, alternate leaves have been classified. The flowers have an involucre (calyx) formed by three pink, mauve or purple bracts.

Bougainvillea
BOUGAINVILLEA

Bougainvillea spectabilis Branches with light bark; evergreen, oval, downy, light-green leaves. In flower from March to June, large pink or mauve bracts. Some varieties are carmine or brick-red. There are also varieties with green-cream variegated leaves.

Propagation

From cuttings In spring, take cuttings from green wood. Lightly strip of bark and insert in a loam-peat mixture with good bottom drainage. Remove the tip. Place in a warm, light position. In winter, put in a cold greenhouse or in a light, unheated room. Repot the following spring.

By air layering Use an older shrub.

Care

Exposure to sunlight A lot of light. Bougainvilleas can be exposed to full sun.

Temperature The bougainvillea likes heat. In the south it can live out of doors in summer. To flower again the following spring, it needs a winter temperature of 12 to 16°C (54-61°F).

Ventilation Keep away from draughts. Outside the bougainvillea can withstand a warm wind.

Container Choose a fairly deep, well-drained bowl. It is a good idea to line the bottom with a bed of pebbles, covered by gravel. You may use a glazed, decorated pot, but make your choice with due regard to the shape and colours of the shrub.

Cleaning Remove flowers as soon as they wither.

Growth Fast to begin with; slower when the tree is grown in a pot.

Repotting Every second year in spring (April-May), prune the roots to half their length, and repot in a larger container.

Soil ¼ heath mould, ¼ leaf mould, ¼ loam and ¼ coarse sand. Bougainvilleas like rich, well-drained soil that is not too heavy.

Pruning
Pinching back Pinch back hard after flowering to keep the bonsai compact and shrubby.
Pruning of subbranches After flowering cut back to two or three eyes.
Pruning of branches In winter when there are not so many leaves on the tree prune overlong branches to keep the tree's shape. Prune dead or damaged branches (February).

Wiring Wire lignified branches. Leave wired for a few (three to five) months only.

Watering Water often and regularly, but not too freely, for bougainvilleas lose their leaves when they are overwatered. In summer, water daily. Just before flowering give no water for at least a week to encourage flower buds. Watering is restricted during flowering, and resumed freely when it is over.

Spraying Spray the foliage daily, but do not spray trees when they are in flower.

Feeding After flowering and in autumn, feed with slow-acting organic fertilizer about once a fortnight. Alternate liquid fertilizer with solid fertilizer.

STYLES

 Shakan

 Kengai

 Bankan

Tachiki

 Han-Kengai

 Bunjingi

 Hōkidachi

 Sharimiki

 Fukinagashi

Bougainvillea *(Bougainvillea spectabilis)*. 20 years old.
Height, 35 cm (1 ft 2 in). 'Hôdikachi' style. Photograph
taken in October.

Pests and diseases

Pests
- **Greenfly** See p. 29.
- **Scale insects** See p. 29.

Diseases
- **Chlorosis**
Symptoms Starting from the lamina and veins the leaves turn gradually yellow.
New leaves are small and discoloured.
Treatment Add iron, nitrogen, magnesium
and zinc to the soil. Do not give too much
sodium, calcium or water; keep away from
cold, draughts and poisonous gases. Place
in the light. Mist-spray the foliage.

Neagari

Ishitsuki

Nejikan

Sabamiki

Sôkan

Kabudachi

Korabuki

Sôju

The Buxaceae family. Native to Asia and the Mediterranean basin; a hardy shrub that can live for several hundred years. It produces a lot of branching and has evergreen dark-green, shiny, leathery leaves. It can be pruned into any style.

Buxus
BOX

Buxus harlandii This shrub which is native to Taiwan is very ramified and can grow to a height of 10 m (33 ft). It has a sturdy trunk, rough but pliable grey bark, and bright-green, evergreen, tiny leaves.
Buxus sinicio This species, native to China, has very hard, beige-coloured wood, and small, shiny, round, leathery leaves.

Propagation

From cuttings In October take cuttings from lignified wood. Plant in a peat-sand mixture in a frame or in the open. It is also possible to take cuttings in early spring before budbreak. Pot up the following spring when they are well rooted.

Care

Exposure to sunlight Place the box near a window in the light. In the south, it can be kept out of doors in summer, when it should be placed in semishade.

Temperature These box like warmth. In winter the temperature should not drop below 12°C (54°F).

Ventilation These box dislike draughts. If kept outside in summer, they should be shielded from the wind.

Container Quite deep so that the tree is really stable.

Cleaning Do not hesitate to knock off any yellowing leaves with your hand.

Growth Slow.

Repotting Every second year in spring (April-May), prune the roots by a half and repot in a larger container.

Soil ¼ heath mould, ¼ leaf mould, ¼ loam and ¼ coarse sand. The soil should not be too dry, but apart from that the *Buxus harlandii* has no special requirements. It tolerates lime.

Pruning
Pruning of subbranches Cut back new growth to two pairs of leaves as soon as shoots have produced five or six throughout the growing season.

Wiring Box can be wired at any time of year. Do not leave wire on the tree for more than two months.

Watering Water fairly copiously. Allow the soil to dry out well before giving more water. If the tree is in a cool room in winter, give slightly less water. Give the soil and roots a good wetting, and then allow to dry out.

Spraying Spray the foliage daily.

Feeding In spring and in autumn feed with slow-acting organic fertilizer, using a liquid and solid form alternately. In winter if the temperature is around 22°C (72°F), feed once.

Box *(Buxus harlandii)*. 12 years old. 'Tachiki' style. Photograph taken in June. As soon as the soft young shoots start to lengthen, they must be regularly cut back.

Pests and diseases

Pests
- **Blackfly and greenfly** See p. 29.
- **Glasshouse red spider mites** (web-forming *Tetranychus*) See p. 28.

Diseases
- **Honey fungus** See p. 31.
- **Rust** See p. 31.

STYLES

Chokkan

Shakan

Tachiki

Nejikan

Sôkan

Sôju

Sambon-Yose

The Leguminosaceae family. Native to central Asia, southern Russia, Manchuria and the Himalayas. The *Caragana* genus contains about 60 species of spinescent shrubs. Most have deciduous, prickly leaves that grow in bunches. Flowers are usually yellow, sometimes white or pink.

Caragana
CARAGANA

Caragana arborescens Native to Siberia and Manchuria; this species is of narrow, upright habit, has bright-green, oblong leaves, and can grow to a height of 6 m (20 ft). Pale-yellow flowers appear in May. The fruit is similar to peas.
Caragana chamlagu This shrub is native to northern China, it is 1.5 m (5 ft) tall, and has upward-growing, spreading branches and prickly subbranches. The glossy, dark-green leaves are more or less evergreen. Orange flowers bloom in June.

Propagation

From seed Collect the seeds, and soak them for 12 hours in lukewarm water before planting them, in May, in a warm place in the open. Germination gets under way three weeks later, and takes a good two months. Pot up the following spring.

From cuttings Take cuttings in July and plant them in a sand-peat mixture.

By air layering Late spring – early summer.

Care

Exposure to sunlight The caragana likes a sunny, well-lit position.

Temperature The caragana stands up equally well to heat and cold.

Ventilation Keep out of draughts.

Container Pots of medium depth, often glazed, seldom decorated.

Cleaning Remove yellow leaves which occur regularly.

Growth Slow; but you can quickly show off the roots at the base of the trunk to advantage.

Repotting Every two years in spring, prune the roots by a half and repot in a larger container.

Soil ¼ heath mould, ¼ leaf mould, ¼ loam and ¼ coarse sand. Caraganas do well in all types of soil, even calcareous, poor, dry soil.

Pruning
Pruning of subbranches After flowering, prune side branches with clippers leaving only two or three eyes. During the growing season, allow side branches to grow to five eyes, then cut back to two. At the end of autumn, cut any late growth hard back.

Wiring This can be done throughout the year. But try not to wire new shoots until they have lignified. Do not leave wire in place for more than six weeks.

Watering Not too much water. The caragana tolerates drought. Let the soil dry out well between waterings. Give a little more water in summer and in winter.

Spraying Mist-spray the leaves daily.

Feeding In spring and autumn, feed once a month with a slow-acting organic fertilizer.

STYLES

Shakan

Kengai

Bankan

Tachiki

Han-Kengai

Fukinagashi

Neagari

Caragana arborescens. 10 years old. Height, 20 cm (8 in). 'Sôkan' style. Photograph taken in June.

Pests and diseases

Pests
- **Greenfly** See p. 29.
- **Red spider mites** See p. 28.

Diseases
- **Mildew** (fungoid)

Symptoms There are yellow patches on the leaves, and a white dust on the underside. The leaves drop off.

Treatment Cut out diseased leaves and destroy them. Spray with a copper-based fungicide.

NB. Mostly, if the leaves turn yellow, wither and fall, it is because of overwatering. If the tree becomes etiolated, it is not getting enough light.

Sekijôju

Ishitsuki

Nejikan

Sôkan

Kabudachi

Korabuki

Sôju

Yose-Ue

The Boraginaceae family. Native to China, Japan, Korea and Taiwan, this tree grows to a height of 10 m (33 ft). The grey bark has a cracked surface, and the leaves are deciduous, oval, pilose on the upper surface, and lighter and reticulate underneath. White scented flowers appear in June. The fruit which is green and acid when flowering is over turns red when it is ripe.

Ehretia
EHRETIA

Ehretia microphylla. This species has very small leaves that are evergreen.

Propagation

From cuttings Cuttings taken from small branches are propagated in a greenhouse, preferably in spring.

Care

Exposure to sunlight The ehretia needs a light sunny position. When it is out of doors in summer, place it in semishade.

Temperature Keep warm. In winter the temperature should not fall below 17°C (63°F). It can be put outside in summer in the south.

Ventilation The ehretia cannot tolerate draughts, but needs to have air circulating round its leaves.

Container Choose a fairly deep pot which can be glazed or unglazed.

Cleaning Remove any yellow leaves from the tree. Also remove any shoots growing out from the trunk and any suckers.

Growth Relatively fast when the tree is young.

Repotting Every second year in spring (April) prune the roots to half their length, and repot in a larger container.

Soil ¼ heath mould, ¼ leaf mould, ¼ loam and ¼ coarse sand. The ehretia likes a fertile soil.

Pruning
Pruning of subbranches Reduce young laterals to two or three leaves as soon as they have produced six or seven. Continue to do this throughout the growing season.
Pruning of branches Can be done in February before growth restarts. Get rid of dead or damaged branches or any that are too long.

Wiring Shaping is mainly achieved through pruning subbranches. However, the ehretia can be wired at any time of year except when the branches have not yet lignified. Do not leave wire in position for more than eight weeks.

Watering Water freely throughout the year. Allow to dry out between waterings. Give less water after pruning or repotting.

Spraying Spray the foliage daily.

Feeding From March to September, feed with slow-acting organic fertilizer. Do not feed in July-August. Perfectly healthy trees can be given one application of fertilizer in winter.

STYLES

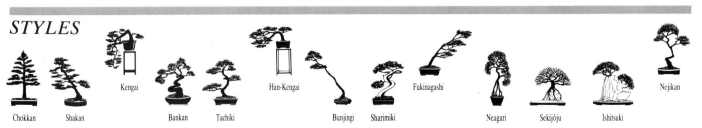

Chokkan   Shakan   Kengai   Bankan   Tachiki   Han-Kengai   Bunjingi   Sharimiki   Fukinagashi   Neagari   Sekijōju   Ishitsuki   Nejikan

Ehretia *(Ehretia microphylla)*. 70 years old. Height, 80 cm (2 ft 8 in). 'Nejikan' style. Photograph taken in March.

Pests and diseases

Pests

- **Hard-shelled and soft scale insects** See p. 29.
- **Mealy-bugs** See p. 29.
- **Aphids** See p. 29.
- **Glasshouse red spider mites** (web-forming *Tetranychus*) See p. 28.
- **Snails**

Symptoms Lamina indented. Leaf surface reduced. Presence of snails.
Treatment Do not let the soil get too wet, remove the snails. Place on the ground snail killer that works by contact or ingestion.

Diseases

- **Chlorosis**

Symptoms Starting with the lamina and the veins, the leaves turn yellow. New leaves are small and discoloured.
Treatment Apply iron, nitrogen, magnesium and zinc to the soil. Do not give too much sodium, calcium or water; keep away from cold, draughts and poisonous gases. Place in the light. Spray the foliage.
NB. If the ehretia's leaves turn yellow and fall, there is too much water in the soil. If it becomes etiolated, it is not getting enough light.

Sabamiki   Sôkan   Kabudachi   Korabuki   Ikadabuki   Netsunagari   Sôju   Sambon-Yose   Gohon-Yose   Nanahon-Yose   Kyûhon-Yose   Yose-Ue   Bonkei

The Crassulaceae family. Native to South Africa. Also known as the jade plant. The genus includes about 130 species. The tree which is bulky in habit grows to a height of about 3 m (10 ft). The branches and leaves are thick and fleshy. Leaves are opposite, often connate, not lobed, smooth and evergreen. Flowers are white, pink or red.

Crassula

CRASSULA

Crassula arborescens Trees with upright, rounded, shrubby trunks, and leaves that are opposite, rounded, fleshy, glaucous and evergreen. Large pink flowers appear in May.

Propagation

From cuttings In mid-spring, take cuttings about 10 cm (4 in) long. Leave these to wilt in the sun or in the light for about three days. Insert in a mixture consisting of half-and-half peat and sand. Do not water. After several days water very lightly. Wait for small roots to form before watering more freely, but do not soak the soil.

Care

Exposure to sunlight Place in a well-lit position. The crassula can be exposed to direct sunlight. But in summer in the south, if it is outside, place in semishade.

Temperature It benefits from even warmth. In winter it can withstand temperatures going down to 10°C (50°F).

Ventilation Beware of draughts, but try to ensure that air can circulate round the crassula.

Container Choose a pot of medium depth. Blues, browns and natural colours look well with this tree.

Cleaning Remove any leaves that turn yellow. Remove all shoots growing out from the trunk and main branches.

Growth Fast to begin with. But three or four years are required for the trunk and branches to take shape.

Repotting Every second year in spring, prune the roots by a third of their length, and repot in a larger container. Leave for a fortnight before watering again.

Soil ¼ heath mould, ¼ loam, ¼ leaf mould and ¼ coarse sand. Likes a very light, sandy soil. To good loam you can add crushed brick, sand, and leaf mould.

Pruning
Pinching back Pinch out the tips of new shoots directly they have reached the desired length.
Leaf pruning Pick the leaves off the old lower branches.
Pruning of subbranches Pinch out or cut off the tips of laterals, leaving only two or three pairs of leaves on each.

Pruning of branches If required, do this between April and October to perfect the structure of the tree.

Wiring Usually the shape is achieved through pruning. But for the 'Han-Kengaï' and 'Kengaï' styles the tree may be wired. Wait until the new shoots have lignified. Do not leave the wire on for more than six weeks. Protect the bark with raffia.

Watering As a rule, keep watering to a minimum. Keep the tree dry in winter. In summer water moderately. Can remain without water for about a fortnight.

Spraying Mist-spray daily with water round the foliage and on to the leaves to restore a high level of humidity. If necessary, place on a container covered with a bed of gravel.

Feeding From May to September, with a break in July-August. Preferably feed once a month with liquid fertilizer (but never feed in winter).

STYLES

Chokkan

Shakan

Kengai

Tachiki

Han-Kengai

Ishitsuki

Crassula *(Crassula arborescens)*. 10 years old. Height, 15 cm (6 in). 'Sôkan' style. Photograph taken in June.

Pests and diseases

Pests
- **Hard-shelled and soft scale insects** See p. 29.
- **Mealy-bugs** See p. 29.
- **Snails**

Symptoms Edge of foliage eaten into, lamina eaten and leaf surface reduced.
Treatment Remove the snails. Make sure the soil is not too wet. Use snail killer that works by contact or ingestion.

Diseases
- **Damping off**

Symptoms The roots are destroyed and the shrub stops growing. There is wet rot at the collar. The branches turn black in places, collapse on to the ground and die. The shrub wilts. There is a down on the stems.
Treatment Keep the plant warm and well aired, and do not give too much water. Apply nitrogen and potash to the soil.
- **Mildew** (fungoid)

Symptoms There are yellow patches on the leaves, and white dust on their undersides. Leaves fall.
Treatment Cut off and destroy diseased leaves. Spray with a copper-based fungicide. Do not let the soil get too wet.
- **Helminthosporium fungus**

Symptoms There are yellow lesions turning to brown on the branches spreading over the shrub.
Treatment As a precaution spray with a captan-based mixture. Make sure that the soil is healthy when you repot.
- **Fusarium wilt** (fungoid)

Symptoms There are brown, cankerous lesions on the upper part of the branches, and these spread.
Treatment Check the condition of the soil. Disinfect if necessary.
- **Anthracnose** (fungoid)

Symptoms Round brown patches with pink spots appearing on them. Soft rot. Diseased parts destroyed.
Treatment Cut out diseased branches. Spray with a copper-based fungicide.
- **Leaf spot** See p. 31.

Nejikan

Sôkan

Sôju

Sambon-Yose

Yose-Ue

Bonkei

Plantations saisonnières

The Cycadaceae family. Native to tropical and subtropical areas. About 15 species of a palm-tree habit. It has a majestic stance; the trunk is subligneous and cylindrical and ends in a bunch of fornicate leaves that are thick, shiny green and leathery. The male and female flowers are dioecious.

Cycas
CYCAD

Cycas revoluta This species which is native to China can grow to 2 m (6½ ft). Its dark-green leaves are long and linear, with spear-shaped, spiky ends, and its trunk is very thick.

Propagation

From seed Collect seeds from a female cycad when they are ripe. Sow. Germination will have occurred within four weeks. Plant out in a peat-sand mixture with good bottom heat, in a light place.

By division In spring, separate the shoots thrown up by the parent plant, and plant out separately, keeping warm and dry.

Care

Exposure to sunlight The cycad likes heat and light, and in the south it can be placed outside between May and September. It can withstand full sun.

Temperature The cycad needs heat. In winter the temperature should not fall below 17 or 18°C (63-64°F).

Ventilation Keep away from draughts. If it is placed outside in summer, it should be in a situation that is sheltered from the wind.

Cycad *(Cycas revoluta)*. These old *Cycas* specimens which were photographed in Taiwan are here grown under a shade.

STYLES

Kabudachi

Korabuki

Tsukami-Yose

Bonkei

Plantations saisonnières

Cycad (*Cycas revoluta*). 90 years old. Height, 70 cm (2 ft 4 in). No definite style. Photograph taken in November. Specimen photographed during a bonsai-lovers' exhibition in Taiwan.

Container Choose a pot of average depth, usually a hexagonal or round one. Blues go well with the cycad. Very good drainage is essential.

Cleaning Brush the trunk, making sure that no moss forms on it. Cut off fronds that have turned yellow at their base.

Growth Very slow. For small, well-proportioned palms, you must expose cycad plants to the sun. It is quite rare for branches to appear along the trunk.

Repotting Every second or third year in spring. Prune the roots by a third, and repot in a well-drained container, larger than the previous one.

Soil ¼ peat, ¼ leaf mould, ¼ loam and ¼ coarse sand. The cycad does well in good-quality loam to which some sand has been added. Good heavy soil suits it.

Pruning As a rule the fronds turn yellow and then fall every year or every second year. At the same time you can see new fronds developing from the centre of the trunk. They all emerge at the same time, and you will not see others appearing later.

Wiring This is not practised.

Watering The cycad has a natural water store in its trunk. It requires very little water. Give it a little water in winter, and a moderate amount in summer.

Spraying Mist-spray the foliage freely in summer. In winter moisten it only if the plant is in a warm, dry place.

Feeding Feed in spring and in autumn with a slow-acting organic fertilizer, applying a liquid and a solid fertilizer alternately.

Pests and diseases

Pests
- **Glasshouse red spider mites** (web-forming *Tetranychus*) See p. 28.
- **Hard-shelled and soft scale insects** See p. 29.

Diseases
- **Damping off**

Symptoms The roots and the collar rot. The stems are spotted with black, rot, and disintegrate on the ground. *Treatment* Maintain a warm temperature and ensure good air circulation. Do not give too much water. Apply nitrogen and potassium to the soil. If necessary, use a fungicide.

145

The Liliaceae family. These trees which are native to the East Indies, Australia, New Zealand and the islands of the South Pacific can grow to a height of 12 m (40 ft). The genus includes about 10 species of an upright habit, shaped like a palm tree. The leaves are long, single, often arched, and oval or elongated. The small single flowers are white. The globular fruit holds a single seed.

Dracaena or Cordyline
DRACAENA or CORDYLINE

Red-edge cordyline Green leaves edged with red.
White-edge cordyline Green leaves edged with white. These are both new varieties which lend themselves well to the art of bonsai.
Dracaena marginata Elongated green leaves edged with red.

Propagation

From cuttings Take cuttings in spring; insert in a peat-sand mixture in a greenhouse. Replant them when the roots are well formed. Cuttings can also be grown in water.

By division In spring. When a cordyline has several trunks growing up together, these can be divided. Repot and keep in a warm, light position.

Care

Exposure to sunlight Cordylines need a lot of light and sun, particularly to get the full benefit of the marvellous colours of the foliage.

Temperature Maintain an even warmth. In winter the temperature should not drop below 17°C (63°F).

Ventilation Protect from draughts.

Container Choose a flattish bowl of medium depth. Any shape will be suitable. A glazed pot is preferable.

Cleaning Clean the foliage by wiping with a damp sponge to remove dust. Remove shoots from the trunk unless you want new growth, and take off lower leaves that are turning yellow. Do not allow to flower as this exhausts the plant and may cause it to die.

Growth Fairly fast.

Repotting Every second year in spring (April-May). Prune the roots to half their length, and repot in a larger container.

Soil ¼ loam, ¼ leaf mould, ¼ heath mould and ¼ coarse sand. Cordylines like a neutral, slightly acid compost with humus in it.

Pruning
Pruning of branches In spring, prune all branches above the point where you want them to start branching out. All branches must be pruned at the same time. Then place the cordyline in a plastic bag to encourage new buds. Do not water for a fortnight, and maintain as high a level of humidity as possible.

Wiring The shape is mainly achieved through pruning. The cordyline can be wired during the summer, but as a rule it is preferable to avoid wiring.

Watering Very little in winter. Water moderately in summer. The cordyline has a store of water in its trunk.

Spraying Moisten the foliage well with spray every day in the growing season.

Feeding In spring and autumn, feed with a little slow-acting organic fertilizer in a liquid form.

STYLES

| Chokkan | Tachiki | Han-Kengai | Neagari | Sekijôju | Ishitsuki | Sôkan | Kabudachi |

Red-edge cordyline. 6 years old. Height, 15 cm (6 in). 'Tsukami-Yose' style. Photograph taken in June. The fiery red colour is at its height in late spring and in summer, the period when the shrub enjoys maximum sunlight.

Pests and diseases

Pests
- **Gall eelworms** See p. 30.
- **Thrips**

Symptoms There are grey, more or less withered patches on the leaves. The lamina is eaten. Presence of insects.

Treatment Spray with combined insecticide on the underside of leaves.
- **Mealy-bugs** See p. 29.

Diseases
- **Leaf spot** See p. 31.
- **Concentric leaf spot** (fungoid)

Symptoms In spring round grey patches ringed with red appear on the leaves parallel to the veins. There are black dots on the patches. The lamina withers.

Treatment Cut off and burn diseased leaves. Spray with a mineral fungicide.
- **Root rot** See p. 31.

| Korabuki | Ikadabuki | Sôju | Sambon-Yose | Gohon-Yose | Nanahon-Yose | Kyûhon-Yose | Yose-Ue | Tsukami-Yose |

The Moraceae family. Native to tropical and sub-tropical areas. There are more than 600 different species with a wide variety of characteristics: evergreen or deciduous foliage, edible or inedible fruit.

Ficus
FIG

Ficus carica (edible fig) This species which has deciduous leaves yields highly prized fruit. The edible fig is found round the Mediterranean basin. In the north of France it is treated as a bonsai for an orangery.

Ficus benjamina (weeping fig) A tree with evergreen leaves, of supple, elegant habit, and with a grey trunk. The oblong leaves are bright green. This tree puts out aerial roots.

Ficus retusa This tree which is very close to the *F. benjamina* is like the banyan. The evergreen leaves are elongated and bright green, and the tree puts out aerial roots. The roots are particularly strong and gnarled.

Ficus retusa formosanum This species has evergreen leaves that are rounder and thicker than the previous species. It is daintier.

Propagation

From seed Only practicable in a greenhouse inside a forcing frame.

From cuttings In July-August, in a frame. Take cuttings that are 5 to 10 cm (2 to 4 in) long. Behead them, and plant in a sand-peat mixture, first removing one or two pairs of leaves from the lower part of the slip. Take the glass away as soon as roots have formed. Repot the next year in spring. Cuttings can also be made by standing slips in water.

By air layering In spring.

Care

Exposure to sunlight This tree loves light. The *Ficus formosanum* needs more light than the other species.

Temperature The *Ficus* tolerates heat. It does not like fluctuations in temperature. The edible fig withstands cold best (a tree for an unheated greenhouse). The other species should be kept in winter in a temperature that does not fall below 13°C (55°F).

Ventilation Keep away from draughts.

Container Choose a medium-deep pot when the tree is young, and the pot must be deep when it is old. It can be glazed or unglazed, decorated or undecorated. Old trees are usually planted in rectangular containers.

Cleaning Do not cut the aerial roots. Remove any shoots growing out of the trunk and any yellow leaves. Wipe the foliage with a sponge soaked in water to remove dust.

Pruning the branches of the *Ficus*.

Growth Fast and steady. You can quite quickly achieve spectacular specimens.

Repotting Every second year (every third year in the case of old trees) in spring

STYLES

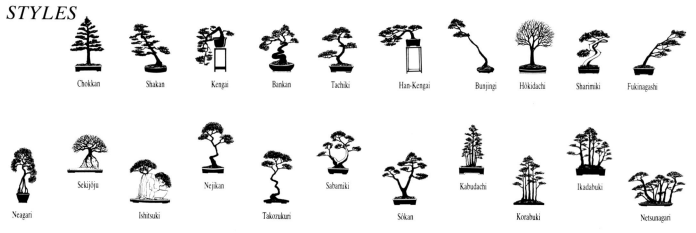

Chokkan   Shakan   Kengai   Bankan   Tachiki   Han-Kengai   Bunjingi   Hōkidachi   Sharimiki   Fukinagashi

Neagari   Sekijōju   Ishitsuki   Nejikan   Takozukuri   Sabamiki   Sōkan   Kabudachi   Korabuki   Ikadabuki   Netsunagari

Fig *(Ficus retusa)*. 150 years old. Height, 1 m 10 cm (3 ft 8 in). 'Tachiki' style. Photograph taken in May. A remarkable specimen with aerial roots that twine round the main trunk.

(April-May), prune the roots by a half and repot in a larger container.

Soil ¼ heath mould, ¼ loam, ¼ coarse sand and ¼ leaf mould. *Ficus* likes warm, medium-damp and slightly calcareous soil, which should be permeable, deep, cool and rich. It is possible to use peat in place of heath mould.

Pruning
Pruning of subbranches During the growing season cut subbranches back to two or three pairs of leaves directly they have produced five or six.
Pruning of branches Prune out branches that are damaged, overlong or broken, in winter (February). Cuts will ooze, and the liquid they produce is rubber. Apply a wound-sealing compound to large cuts.
Leaf pruning It is possible to remove all the leaves from a *Ficus* that is healthy. Give less water after leaf stripping. Or one can cut only large leaves off the tree.

Wiring This can be done at any time of year. Wait until the branches have lignified. Remove copper wire after six to eight weeks.

Watering Keep the roots dry in winter. Give a moderate amount of water during other seasons, a little more in summer.

Spraying Spray the foliage daily as the *Ficus* likes humid heat.

Feeding In spring and in autumn feed with a slow-acting organic fertilizer. If the bonsai is in prime condition, it can be fed once during the winter. Use a liquid and a solid fertilizer alternately.

Pests and diseases

Pests
- **Cyst eelworm** See p. 30.
- **Gall eelworm** See p. 30.
- **Thrips**
Symptoms There are dry, grey patches on the leaves, and spots appear on these. The tree is weakened, the lamina is eaten. There are insects underneath the lamina.
Treatment Spray with a combined insecticide on the undersides of the leaves.
- **Hard-shelled and soft scale insects** See p. 29.

Diseases
- **Anthracnose** (specific to the *Ficus* – fungoid)
Symptoms Yellow patches on the edge of the lamina spreading all over the leaf. Specks of black on these patches. The foliage is discoloured and crumpled. The diseased parts wither and drop off.
Treatment Make sure the soil is not too damp. Keep the temperature steady. Cut out diseased leaves. Spray with a combined fungicide.
- **Scorching**
Symptoms There are discoloured patches on the lamina that shrivel and tear. The foliage is shrivelled, distorted, may have holes in it, and falls.
Treatment Take care not to spray the foliage or to water while the sun is on the tree; keep out of sun that is too direct, and out of cold temperatures, and away from poisonous gases; do not use a fertilizer that is too rich in nitrogen.
- **Leaf-fall**
Symptoms Starting from the base of the branches, the leaves turn yellow and drop off.
Treatment Make sure the soil is not too damp. Place in the light.
- **Grey rot or damping off** (fungoid)
Symptoms There are grey-brown patches on the leaves with grey rot round the lamina, spreading over the whole leaf surface. The leaves wither, then fall. The side branches become cankered.
Treatment Provide good ventilation. Be careful not to give too much water or expose the plant to changes in temperature. Prune out the diseased branches. Spray with a combined fungicide. Take care that the fungicide does not damage the host plant.

Sôju   Sambon-Yose   Gohon-Yose   Nanahon-Yose   Kyûhon-Yose   Yose-Ue   Yomayori   Tsukami-Yose   Bonkei   Kusamono   Plantations saisonnières

The Rubiaceae family. Native to tropical and subtropical areas mainly in Asia. The *Gardenia* genus includes about 70 species of shrubs with evergreen leaves and white, scented flowers.

Gardenia
GARDENIA

Gardenia jasminoides This is native to China and Japan and grows to a height of 1.5 m (5 ft). It is of regular habit, and has evergreen, bright-green leaves and white, highly scented double flowers. It is a fruit-bearing shrub. Most *Gardenia jasminoides* trees grown as bonsai come from natural material collected in Japan and China.

Propagation

From cuttings Choose strong, lateral shoots. Try to take them off with a heel. Cuttings can be grown in a greenhouse virtually at any time of year, but January is a good month. Plant the cuttings in heath mould and keep in a warm place at 22°C (72°F) until they have rooted. Repot in the spring.

By air layering or simple layering This works best in spring in a light, warm room.

Care

Exposure to sunlight Needs a lot of light, but keep out of direct sun. Can be kept outside in summer in the south.

Temperature Very warm during the growing season. During the dormant season, gradually reduce the heat. In winter the temperature should not fall below 12 to 15°C (54 to 59°F).

Ventilation Guard against draughts. Increase ventilation during dormancy.

Container Select a fairly deep bowl. Often grown in unglazed bowls.

Cleaning Remove the flowers as soon as they start to go yellow. The flowers do not last long, but by way of compensation their scent is delightful.

Growth Slow.

Repotting Every second year in late spring when the new buds are appearing, prune the roots by a half and repot in a larger container.

Soil ¼ heath mould, ¼ loam, ¼ leaf mould and ¼ coarse sand. The gardenia likes warm, clayey soil.

Pruning
Pruning of subbranches When flowering is over cut the branches of old trees back hard. On younger trees, cut back side branches to leave just three leaves as soon as they have produced six or seven.

Wiring Wait until new shoots have lignified. Or wire before the buds have hardened. Protect the bark with raffia.

Watering Give very little water in winter, but do not allow the soil to dry out. In summer, water moderately. Just before flowering, slightly increase the amount of water given to encourage blooming.

Spraying Spray the leaves daily except when the tree is in flower. The gardenia needs a lot of moisture in the atmosphere. If necessary, put it on a gravel-covered tray.

Feeding After flowering and in autumn. It is best to use a slow-acting, organic liquid fertilizer. If the leaves turn yellow, add a little nitrogen to the fertilizer.

STYLES

Chokkan

Shakan

Tachiki

Han-Kengai

Sharimiki

Fukinagashi

Neagari

Gardenia *(Gardenia jasminoïdes)*. 15 years old. Height, 14 cm (5½ in). 'Shakan' style. Photograph taken in October. Most specimens of *Gardenia jasminoïdes* are shrubs found growing wild in Asia, and then trained to grow in containers.

Pests and diseases

Pests

- **Hard-shelled and soft scale insects** See p. 29.
- **Mealy-bugs** See p. 29.
- **Greenfly** See p. 29.
- **Greenhouse whitefly**

Symptoms A honeydew with a sooty mould forming on it. Presence of flies on the lamina.

Treatment Spray with organophosphate insecticide and with acaricide, switching from one product to another so that the insects cannot build up immunity.

- **Snails**

Symptoms In winter the snails are protected by a white veil. In spring, stems, leaves, buds and flowers are eaten.

Treatment Collect up the snails, and avoid excessive moisture. Use snail killers acting on contact or by ingestion.

Diseases

- **Chlorosis**

Symptoms Starting with the lamina the leaves turn gradually yellow. Diseased parts wither. The foliage is discoloured.

Treatment Guard against too much calcium and water, and do not let the tree get too cold; keep away from draughts and poisonous gases. Keep in a well-lit position. Apply iron, magnesium, zinc and nitrogen to the soil.

Sabamiki

Sòkan

Kabudachi

Korabuki

Sòju

Bonkei

Plantations saisonnières

The **Rutaceae** family. **Native to tropical areas, especially Asia. The** *Murraya* **genus includes five species of tree, with light-coloured bark, and unlobed, evergreen leaves on stalks of a green that is verging on yellow. Single, white blooms, large and scented. Fruit: an oblong orangy-red berry holding one or two seeds.**

Murraya
MURRAYA

Murraya paniculata (satin-wood or cosmetic bark tree) This tree-like species, native to India, grows to a height of 3 m (10 ft). It has oval, evergreen leaves and scented, white flowers. It bears red fruit in August.

Propagation

From cuttings Take hardwood cuttings, and keep the leaves on. Plant in sand under a cloche with good moist bottom heat. Pot up the following spring.

Care

Exposure to sunlight The murraya needs a lot of light, but does not like direct sunlight.

Temperature The murraya likes heat. In winter the temperature must not fall below 17°C (63°F).

Ventilation Keep away from daughts, but the murraya needs a good air supply: good air circulation round the tree is essential.

Container Select a bowl somewhere between fairly flat and medium deep. It can be glazed or unglazed, oval or rectangular. Beiges and willow-greens go quite well with it.

Cleaning Remove yellow leaves and withered flowers and fruit.

Growth Slow; the trunk takes a long time to develop, and then to expand in diameter.

Repotting Every second year in spring (April-early May). Prune the roots by a half and repot in a larger container.

Soil ¼ peat, ¼ loam, ¼ leaf mould and ¼ coarse sand. The murraya likes loamy, peaty soil, and responds well to a dressing of leaf mould.

Pruning
Pruning of subbranches Cut back side branches to two leaves as soon as they have produced five or six all through the growing season.
Pruning of branches In spring prune branches that are too long, broken, or damaged, or which are growing in an unsightly way.

Wiring The murraya can be wired at any time of the year. Do not leave the wire in position for more than eight weeks.

Watering The murraya needs moisture. Water regularly, keeping the soil slightly damp throughout the year. Do not soak.

Spraying Spray the foliage throughout the year to ensure a good level of humidity and to clean the tree.

Feeding In spring and in autumn feed with a slow-acting organic fertilizer. Alternate between liquid fertilizer and solid fertilizer. You can give a tree that is in perfect conditon one application of fertilizer in winter.

STYLES

 Chokkan

 Shakan

 Tachiki

 Han-Kengai

 Sharimiki

 Fukinagashi

 Sabamiki

Satin-wood tree (*Murraya paniculata*). 150 years old. Height, 80 cm (2 ft 8 in). 'Sabamiki' style. Photograph taken in November.

Pests and diseases

Pests
- **Greenhouse whitefly**

Symptoms Honeydew with sooty mould forming on it. Presence of flies on the lamina.

Treatment Spray with organophosphate insecticide and with acaricide, switching from one product to another so that the insects cannot build up immunity.

- **Aphids** See p. 29.

- **Glasshouse red spider mites** (web-forming *Tetranychus*) See p. 28.
- **Snails**

Symptoms Leaves, shoots and buds are eaten. The leaf surface is reduced. Presence of a white veil that protects the snail.

Treatment Collect up the snails. Do not let the ground get too wet. Use a snail killer that works through contact or ingestion.

Diseases
- **Leaf spot** See p. 31.
- **Mildew** (fungoid)

Symptoms There are yellow patches on the leaves, and white dust on the underside. The leaves drop off.

Treatment Cut off and destroy the affected leaves. Make sure the ground is not too damp. Spray with a copper-based fungicide.

Sôkan

Kabudachi

Korabuki

Sôju

Yose-Ue

Tsukami-Yose

Bonkei

The Berberidaceae family. Native to Japan. The nandina which is the only species of its genus grows to a height of 2 m (6½ ft). Its stiff upright habit and its close-set branches are somewhat reminiscent of the bamboo, and it is sometimes nicknamed 'heavenly bamboo'. The evergreen long, narrow leaves start off red, turn green and take on a purple hue in autumn. The fruit is bright red. Small, white, insignificant flowers appear in July-August. The nandina can live outside, but it does not thrive further north than the Loire.

Nandina

NANDINA

Nandina domestica The leaves are evergreen, unlobed, decompound, acuminate and coriaceous. The flowers are white and very small. The globular fruit is red (white in the case of the cultivar 'Alba').

Propagation

From seed Stratify the berries after they have ripened. In spring sow under glass. Keep the young shoots protected for the first year. Pot the following spring. Protect the roots for the first years.

From cuttings Take lower, semilignified cuttings. Plant in a sand-peat mixture. Keep sheltered in winter.

Care

Exposure to sunlight Nandinas need sunlight and good light, but if they are outside, they should be placed in semi-shade at the height of summer.

Temperature This is a shrub for a cold greenhouse and it likes heat. It sheds its leaves when it gets cold. South of Paris it can be planted out of doors, but you must protect it from frost.

Ventilation Protect from wind outside and from draughts inside. Decide at the beginning whether you want to cultivate it as an outdoor or indoor plant.

Container Of medium depth, often unglazed.

Cleaning Remove berries that form from the flowers as soon as they start to wilt as they exhaust the shrub.

Growth Slow growing.

Repotting Every second or third year in spring. Prune the roots by a half, and repot in a larger container.

Soil Mixture consisting of ½ loam, ¼ leaf mould and ¼ coarse sand. Nandinas are quite happy in good garden earth, and respond well to a leaf mulch. They like light, cool, fertile soil.

Pruning
Pruning of subbranches During the growing period wait until the side branches have grown to four or five nodes. Cut back with clippers, leaving only one or two eyes.

Wiring In spring and in summer, but it is rarely done.

Watering Moderate amounts given regularly.

Spraying Indoors mist-spray foliage daily. Outside mist leaves and branches in summer.

Feeding Feed with a slow-acting organic fertilizer in spring and in autumn.

STYLES

Sōkan

Kabudachi

Korabuki

Yamayori

Nandina *(Nandina domestica)*. 14 years old. Height, 20 cm (8 in). 'Sankan' style. Photograph taken in November.

Pests and diseases

Pests
- **Blackfly** See p. 29.
- **Glasshouse red spider mites** (web-forming *Tetranychus*) See p. 28.

Diseases
- **Mosaic virus**

Symptoms There are lighter yellow patches on the lamina and round the veins of the leaves, forming a mosaic pattern. Old leaves yellow and fall.
Treatment Take steps against possible insect infestation. Cut off leaves affected. Clean tools.
NB. If the nandina does not have enough light, the browny red shades in its foliage will tend to disappear and the internodal spaces will be large.

Tsukami-Yose

Bonkei

Kusamono

Plantations saisonnières

The Podocarpaceae family. This conifer which is native to the tropical and subtropical areas of the southern hemisphere can grow to a height of 12 m (40 ft). It is the 'Buddhists' pine', a tree with needles, large horizontal branches, densely furnished with side branches, and with evergreen foliage. There are about 100 species, but only a few are to be found in western Europe.

Podocarpus
PODOCARPS

Podocarpus macrophyllus Maki (syn. *P. sinensis*) This shrub is native to China; it has erect, almost vertical, extensive branches, and grows to a height of 6 m (20 ft). Its linear, spear-shaped leaves are dark green on top and have an elongated rib running down the middle and are pointed at the tip. The fruit is globular when it ripens.

Podocarpus macrophyllus Native to China, then introduced into Japan. It is very close to the previous species, and can grow to a height of 18 m (60 ft); it has large horizontal branches, long leathery leaves which are red when they first appear, then bright green above and glaucous underneath, and insignificant, pale-yellow flowers. The fruit is green or purple.

Propagation

From seed Collect the seeds when they are ripe. Plant them in July in a warm greenhouse, keeping them stratified until then – or they can be planted in February.

From cuttings Select cuttings from half-ripe wood. Plant the slips in a sandy soil in a frame. Shield from direct sun. After roots have formed, protect from winter frost. Repot the following spring.

Care

Exposure to sunlight The podocarpus likes light and can be stood in full sun.

Temperature The podocarpus needs heat. It can be kept outside in summer in the south. In winter the temperature should not fall below 13°C (55°F).

Ventilation Keep away from draughts.

Container Choose a pot of medium depth. It looks well in glazed, blue ware. The shape of the bowl is chosen to suit the style in which the tree is grown.

Cleaning Take out any shoots growing out of the trunk. Be careful that no insects get in under the bark of the trunk as it may become loose from time to time.

Growth Very slow.

Repotting Every second to third year in late spring. Prune the roots by between a third and a half, and repot in a larger container.

Soil ¼ loam, ¼ leaf mould, ¼ heath mould and ¼ coarse sand. The podocarpus likes light, loamy, well-drained soil.

Pruning
Pinching back Using your thumb and forefinger, pinch back the new shoots (candles) during the growing season.
Pruning of subbranches and branches Taking care not to cut the needles, use clippers to prune excessively long branches above a leaf axil. If necessary you can take off a few needles which are overlarge.

Wiring The podocarpus can be wired at any time of year. Wait until young branches have lignified before you wire them. Remove wire after eight to ten weeks.

Watering Regular and moderate. Keep the soil surface slightly moist. This tree needs good drainage.

Spraying Mist-spray the foliage daily. The podocarpus likes humid heat. If necessary it can be placed on a tray containing water and gravel in winter.

Feeding In spring and in autumn feed with a slow-acting organic fertilizer. A perfectly healthy tree can be given one winter feed.

Pruning the podocarps.

STYLES

Chokkan

Shakan

Kengai

Bankan

Tachiki

Han-Kengai

Bunjingi

Podocarps (*Podocarpus macrophyllus Maki*). 8 years old. Height, 15 cm (6 in). 'Shakan' style. Photograph taken in December.

Pests and diseases

Pests
- **Aphids** See p. 29.
- **Glasshouse red spider mites** (web-forming *Tetranychus*). See p. 28.
- **Hard-shelled and soft scale insects** See p. 29.
- **Mealy-bugs** See p. 29
- **Snails**

Symptoms Shoots and needles eaten. Reduced leaf surface. Presence of a white veil that protects the snails.
Treatment Collect up the snails. Do not let the soil get too wet. Use a snail killer that acts by contact or ingestion.

Diseases
NB. If the podocarps is overwatered, its needles will turn grey, wither and fall. If it does not have enough light, the needles will grow too big, and the tree will become etiolated. A properly tended podocarps should not suffer from any disease.

Sharimiki

Fukinagashi

Neagari

Ishitsuki

Nejikan

Sabamiki

Sôkan

Sôju

Bonkei

The Palmaceae or Arecaceae family. Native to the Tropics. A genus that includes about five species of dwarf palm. There are a lot of erect, slender stems growing in fairly compact clumps, reminiscent of reeds. Shoots come from the base. Pale-yellow flowers with stalks. The fruit is egg shaped, with the narrower end at the base, and carries a single seed. The leaves are alternate, grow on stalks and are divided into three and very veined; a fibrous sheath encircles the trunk, like a net.

Rhapis
RHAPIS

Rhapis humilis Native to Japan. The stems grow to a height of 1 to 1.5 m (3¼ to 5 ft). Of elegant habit. The dark-green, evergreen leaves are in 7 to 10 spreading segments.
Rhapis excelsa (ground rattan cane).

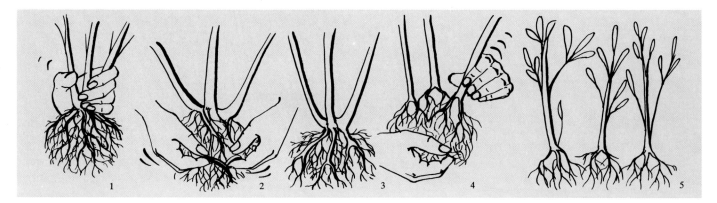

Propagating by division of a clump.
1 Clump of *Rhapis*. Shake off the earth, then wash the roots. 2 Disentangle the root-hairs. 3 Separate the roots belonging to each trunk. 4 Pull at the trunks to separate them; if it proves necessary, you can cut them apart. 5 Each *Rhapis* can be planted in an individual pot.

Propagation

By division of clumps At any time of year in a greenhouse, or in spring.

By separating off side suckers

From seed But it is hard to get hold of seeds.

Care

Exposure to sunlight The rhapis tolerates light, but prefers a darker room and grows well in a poorly lit position.

Temperature The rhapis likes warmth. In winter the temperature should not fall below 17°C (63°F).

Ventilation Keep away from draughts. Air the room regularly.

Container Select a flat container, or one that is between shallow and medium deep. It can be unglazed and brown, or

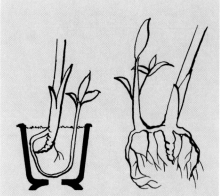
Root development and new trunks.

STYLES

Sekijôju

Ishitsuki

Kabudachi

Sòju

Sambon-Yose

glazed – cobalt blue is the most commonly used colour.

Cleaning Cut the tips off the leaves if they turn yellow, though they will continue to do so. Cut so as to preserve the original shape (do not cut straight across). Remove suckers unless you want a group style. Wipe the leaves with a damp sponge.

Growth Slow throughout its lifespan.

Repotting Every third year in spring (March-April). Prune the roots by a half and repot in a larger container.

Soil ¼ loam, ¼ leaf mould, ¼ heath mould and ¼ coarse sand. The rhapis has no special requirements. The soil should be good loam with sand and leaf mould, or peat, added to it.

Pruning If you want to shorten a rhapis, you can cut the main stem, but only if side shoots have emerged. Other than this the rhapis is not pruned.

Wiring Not done.

Watering Does not need much water. The darker its position, the less water it needs. Keep the soil fairly dry, but it should not dry out completely.

Spraying Spray the foliage daily to humidify the rhapis.

Feeding In spring and in autumn feed with a small amount of slow-acting organic fertilizer.

Rhapis *(Rhapis humilis)*. 10 years old. Height, 25 cm (10 in). 'Kabudachi' style. Photograph taken in December.

Pests and diseases

Pests
- **Glasshouse red spider mites** (web-forming *Tetranychus*) See p. 28.
- **Thrips**
Symptoms There are grey patches on the leaves, which may be withered. The lamina is eaten and dries out. Presence of browny yellow insects.
Treatment Spray with a combined insecticide, on to the undersides of the leaves. If necessary, repeat 10 days later.
- **Hard-shelled and soft scale insects** See p. 29.

Diseases
- **Rotting of buds** See p. 31.
- **Damping off**
Symptoms There is damp rot on the collar, the young roots rot, the plant tissues disintegrate. The leaves droop and wilt.
Treatment Keep in a steady heat, ventilate without exposing to draughts. Do not overwater. Apply nitrogen and potassium to the soil.
- **Fusarium wilt**
Symptoms The leaves turn brown starting from the centre. They may wither and fall. Browning of plant tissues.
Treatment Make sure the soil does not get too wet.

- **Leafspot** See p. 31.
- **Yellow spot** (fungoid)
Symptoms There are black specks on the leaves that tear and emit a yellow powder. The leaves may wither.
Treatment Cut off and burn diseased leaves. Spray with a copper-based fungicide.
- **Disease with black pinpoint spots**
Symptoms There are black spots on the leaves ringed with green, and the leaves gradually wither.
Treatment Cut off and destroy diseased leaves. Keep well aired. Spray with a copper-based fungicide.

Gohon-Yose

Nanahon-Yose

Kyūhon-Yose

Yose-Ue

Kusamono

The Rhameae or Rhamnaceae family. The name sageretia is derived from Sageret, a French agriculturist to whom the Chinese dedicated this tree. It is native to central and southern Asia, the warm regions of North America and Java. Most sageretias that are more than 10 years old come from the People's Republic of China where they were collected as natural material, then grown in bonsai form. The genus includes about 12 species of shrubs with stiff, slender branches, with or without thorns, and evergreen leaves.

Sageretia
SAGERETIA

Sageretia theezans Bark that scales off, rather like that of the plane tree, rough and brown. The branches are stiff, and the short-stalked, opposite leaves are oval and slightly dentate. Small, insignificant, white-green flowers. The fruit consists of blue berries with a seed inside.

Sageretia *(Sageretia theezans)*. 25 years old. Height, 30 cm (2 ft). 'Shakan' style. Photograph taken in June.

Propagation

From seed Collect the seeds when they are ripe, and stratify. Plant it in a greenhouse forcing frame in spring with good bottom heat, and keep the atmosphere moist.

From cuttings Take cuttings from lateral shoots in spring. Behead them. Cut off the bottom pair of leaves. Dip in a hormone rooting compound and plant in a sand-peat mixture in a greenhouse or frame. Very gradually harden off the new shoot by acclimatizing it to a cooler atmosphere. Pot up the following year.

Care

Exposure to sunlight Needs good light. Can be kept outside in the summer in the south. If you do this, place the bonsai in semishade if there is a lot of sun. In winter, keep in a well-lit situation.

Temperature This shrub, similar to trees grown in orangeries, likes warmth. In winter the temperature can go down to 12°C (54°F).

Ventilation It does not tolerate draughts.

Container Of medium depth, often unglazed.

Cleaning Remove shoots growing out of the trunk and yellow leaves.

Growth Very slow as far as trunk formation is concerned. Foliage and branch structure, on the other hand, develop very quickly.

Repotting Every second year in spring (April-May), prune the roots by a half and repot in a larger container.

Soil ¼ heath mould, ¼ leaf mould, ¼ loam and ¼ coarse sand. The sageretia likes a good, cool, loamy soil.

Pruning
Pruning of subbranches During the growing season prune new shoots, leaving two or three pairs of leaves on each branch.

STYLES

Chokkan

Shakan

Kengai

Tachiki

Han-Kengai

Sharimiki

Fukinagashi

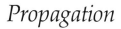

Sageretia *(Sageretia theezans)*. 150 years old. Height, 45 cm (1 ft 6 in). 'Shakan' style. Photograph taken in May. An exceptional specimen produced from a tree collected in the wild in China.

Pruning of branches Before growth starts, prune out any broken, damaged or unsightly branches. If you do not prune the sageretia, soft white flowers appear in the leaf axils and exhaust the tree.

Wiring This shrub can be wired at any time of year. It should not be left with wire on it for more than six to eight weeks. Wait until new shoots have hardened before you wire them.

Watering Give more water in summer than in winter. Make sure that the surface of the soil stays constantly slightly damp. This shrub requires good drainage.

Spraying Spray the leaves daily. In winter grow standing on a tray filled with water and gravel.

Feeding In spring and in autumn feed with a slow-acting, organic fertilizer. Give liquid fertilizer and solid fertilizer alternately.

Pests and diseases

Pests
- **Aphids** See p. 29.
- **Glasshouse red spider mites** (web-forming *Tetranychus*) See p. 28.
- **Snails**
Symptoms Buds, shoots and leaves are eaten. The snails are protected by a white veil.
Treatment Collect up the snails. Make sure the soil is not too moist. Use a snail killer that works by contact or ingestion.

Diseases
- **Chlorosis**
Symptoms The leaves gradually turn yellow starting with the lamina. The diseased parts wither. The new leaves are discoloured.
Treatment Do not give too much calcium or water, and do not expose to cold; keep away from draughts and poisonous gases. Place in the light. Add iron, magnesium, zinc and nitrogen to the soil.
NB. If the sageretia is overwatered, its leaves will wither and fall. It needs light and constant warmth if its leaves are to be really green and well formed. It must be mist-sprayed daily.

Ishitsuki

Nejikan

Sabamiki

Sôkan

Kabudachi

Korabuki

Sôju

Yose-Ue

Tsukami-Yose

The Araliaceae family. Native to Asia. This tree is about 15 m (50 ft) tall, has a slender trunk when it is young, and does not break into branches at its crown, but puts out aerial roots. The evergreen leaves are glossy, green and large, with a long stalk.

Schefflera
SCHEFFLERA

Schefflera arboricola Native to Taiwan. It is also known by the name *Heptapleurum*, and is similar to the *Brassaia*. The branches are fragile, the trunk is flexible and the bright-green, palmate foliage is in groups of seven or eight leaves. The flowers are upright, and orange berries turn black in colour.

Schefflera actinophylla This tree is native to New Guinea and Java and is also known as the *Brassaia*; it can grow to a height of 30 m (100 ft). The branches turn white at the tips. The evergreen, bright-green, oblong foliage forms a kind of sunshade at the crown of the tree. The tip-borne flowers with wine-coloured petals produce purple berries.

Propagation

From seed Collect the seeds from the schefflera's berries when they are ripe. Dry them, then stratify them. Plant them in spring in a greenhouse or frame, in a mixture of peat and clay. Harden off the seedlings and pot up the following spring.

From cuttings In a greenhouse at any time of year. Take cuttings from side branches, and keep protected with a good bottom heat in spring.

Care

Exposure to sunlight The schefflera needs a lot of light. The more light it receives, the smaller its leaves will remain as they develop.

Temperature Good, constant warmth is required. Make sure the temperature is from 16 to 20°C (61 to 68°F) in winter.

Ventilation Keep away from draughts.

Container Of medium depth, often glazed, in shades of blue or willow-green.

Cleaning Remove yellow leaves. Do not cut out the aerial roots which are essential to the tree's survival.

Growth Fairly fast and steady.

Repotting Repot in early spring (March) every second year. Prune the roots by a half and repot in a larger container. Scheffleras that are planted on volcanic rock can have their roots shortened when they are growing rapidly.

Soil ¼ heath mould, ¼ leaf mould, ¼ loam and ¼ coarse sand. The schefflera likes a dry soil.

Pruning
Pruning of subbranches In spring all branches can be reduced in length to encourage branching and keep the tree compact and dense. Eliminate withered or dead branches at the same time.

Wiring The schefflera is not wired. Its shape is produced solely by pruning.

Watering Give very little water. The schefflera will produce smaller leaves if it is kept short of water. If it is planted on a volcanic rock, wet the stone regularly. Do not leave water in the container.

Spraying Mist-spray the foliage occasionally to clean it. When there is too much moisture, the leaves become too big, and are disproportionate in relation to the tree.

Feeding In spring and summer feed with slow-acting, organic fertilizer. Liquid fertilizer is best, but sometimes give solid fertilizer for a change.

STYLES

Shakan

Tachiki

Han-Kengai

Neagari

Sekijóju

Schefflera *(Schefflera arboricola)*. 10 years old. Height, 30 cm (1 ft). 'Kabudachi' style. Photograph taken in June.

Pests and diseases

Pests

- **Glasshouse red spider mite** (web-forming *Tetranychus*) See p. 28.
- **Aphids** See p. 30.
- **Hard-shelled and soft scale insects** See p. 29.
- **Mealy-bugs** See p. 29.

Diseases

- **Rotting of roots and stem** See p. 31.
- **Alternariose of the leaves** (fungoid) *Symptoms* Small oily-looking spots on the leaves, sometimes ringed with red. Discoloured patches at the nodes of side branches which may cause the branch to wither. Black spots on the diseased areas. *Treatment* Cut out diseased wood. Spray with a maneb-based fungicide.

Ishitsuki

Nejikan

Sabamiki

Sōkan

Kabudachi

Sōju

Serissa
SERISSA

The Rubiaceae family. Native to India, China and Japan. A tree with evergreen foliage. *Serissa foetida* is a many-branched shrub; it is glabrous and has foul-smelling bark and roots – whence its name. The best-known species is the *Serissa japonica*, about 60 cm (2 ft) tall. It is called 'June snow' because of its tiny white flowers growing singly or in clusters, that bloom between May and September. But there can be a few flowers all year long. One variety produces double flowers, which is very unusual in the Rubiaceae family. The small oval leaves are opposite and often grow in bunches on short branchlets. One variety produces leaves with golden-yellow edges. The *Serissa japonica variegata* has variegated ivory-green foliage. The grey trunk is rough and slender; it turns white as it grows older.

Propagation

Like all tropical species the serissa is hard to propagate.

From cuttings You can take softwood cuttings from a serissa in spring. They are brought on in a heated place, ie, in a heated forcing frame. Put the cuttings into sand and keep them under a cloche. As soon as new shoots appear on the slips, the cuttings have taken. It is advisable to dip the end of the slip into a hormone rooting compound before planting it in sand.

Care

Exposure to sunlight The serissa is an indoor bonsai and needs a lot of light. This is especially true of the variegated varieties. Keep out of full sun in summer.

Temperature The serissa tolerates being in a hot place. Keep in a cooler temperature in winter, between 15°C and 19°C (59-66°F). Warmer in summer: at least 18°C (64°F).

Ventilation Beware of draughts which harm the serissa greatly.

Container The serissa can take a fairly flat container, especially if it is in a group style. It can be decorated provided that the pattern goes well with the bonsai. The serissa looks very well in old Chinese pots or copies of them. Old trees need deeper pots, from 7 to 15 cm (2¾ to 6½ in).

Cleaning The serissa has evergreen foliage, but it constantly produces yellow leaves which it is as well to remove. Use clippers to remove any dead branches. It is most important to eliminate any shoots coming from the trunk or the base of the trunk. They are comparable to rose suckers which siphon off all the sap.

Growth Though there is not much difference between the seasons, the serissa does have a dormant period in winter. During the growing season it grows very fast (from April to September).

Repotting In March-April every second year, first pruning the root hairs by half. Repot before the flowers open.

Serissa *(Serissa japonica)*. About 20 years old. Height 25 cm (10 in). 'Neagari' style. Photograph taken in June.

Soil The serissa flourishes in a mixture of ⅓ clayey loam, ⅓ heath mould and ⅓ sand.

Pruning After repotting and root pruning, the branches and side branches are pruned which produces a foul smell. The serissa is not pinched back.
Leaf pruning Unnecessary as the leaves are already very small and so do not need to be reduced.

STYLES

Chokkan   Shakan   Kengai   Bankan   Tachiki   Han-Kengai   Hôkidachi   Sharimiki   Fukinagashi   Neagari   Sekijôju   Ishitsuki   Nejikan   Takozukuri   Sabamiki

Serissa *(Serissa foetida* syn. *Lycium japonica).* 10 years old. Height, 18 cm (7 in). 'Nejikan' style. Photograph taken in October.

Pruning of branches After repotting (between April and the end of October), young shoots are cut back to one or two pairs of leaves as soon as the side branches have got bigger in every way. The serissa must be kept compact and bushy. You should not prune during flowering.

Development pruning It may be necessary to prune the serissa hard right back to the wood every two or three years.

Flower cutting Remove the flowers as soon as they fade to increase blossom.

Wiring The wood of the serissa is soft and the tree lends itself to any style. It is readily wired, working from bottom to top, using fine wire; avoid pressure so as not to wound the bark. The wire is put in position in June and removed in September, and the process repeated annually until the desired shape has been achieved. Apply a wound-sealing compound if you wound the tree.

Watering More water is needed in summer than in winter. Water on a regular daily basis. The serissa is a tree that likes humidity. Its roots dry up quickly. Even so the ground must be allowed to dry out between waterings.

Spraying The serissa which comes from the tropics loves humid heat. Mist-spray the foliage daily – this is very important. However, keep the spray off the flowers as it would cause them to fade. The serissa can be placed in its pot on a bed of gravel. Any excess of water goes down into the gravel, then gradually evaporates, thus creating a humid atmosphere.

Feeding From the start of the growing season until the dormant season once a fortnight, in bottle, powder or liquid form. Do not feed in July-August or after repotting. Give slightly less fertilizer when the tree is in flower. In winter, if the serissa is in a warm place it can be given a little fertilizer.

Pests and diseases

Pests
- **Red spider mites** See p. 28.
- **Aphids** See p. 29.
- **Hard-shelled and soft scale insects** See p. 29.
- **Snails**

Symptoms Shoots and leaves eaten. Less leaves. Presence of a veil of white that protects the snails.

Treatment Collect up the snails. make sure the ground is not too moist. Use a snail pesticide that works by contact or ingestion.

Diseases
- **Root rot** See p. 31.
- **Grey mould or damping off** (fungoid)

Symptoms The leaves show the grey-brown patches associated with grey mould round the lamina, spreading over the whole surface. The leaves wither and fall, the branches become cankered, the flower buds drop off and the flowers wither.

Treatment Keep well aired, guard against excessive water and temperature changes. Cut out diseased branches. Spray with combined fungicide. Be careful that the fungicide does not damage the host plant. NB. It is very important to give just the right amount of water to the serissa. It must have good drainage so that the water does not stagnate, which would entail the loss of leaves and flowers, and so bring about the death of the tree. Good air circulation and really good light are essential to guard against possible disease.

Sôkan   Kabudachi   Korabuki   Ikadabuki   Netsunagari   Sôju   Sambon-Yose   Gohon-Yose   Nanahon-Yose   Kyûhon-Yose   Yose-Ue   Tsukami-Yose   Bonkei   Kusamono   Plantations saisonnières

Type of tree	Repotting	Pruning	Wiring	Watering/Spraying	Feeding
OUTDOOR BONSAI					
● Conifers					
For all trees	every 3 to 5 years				except in July and August
Cedrus	March/April	**shoots:** spring-summer **branches:** spring-autumn	end of autumn for about 10 months	copious: spring-summer; reduce in autumn	from the start of growth until Oct
Chamaecyparis	March/April	**shoots:** growing period **subbranches:** March-April Sept-Oct	end of autumn for about 10 months	copious, especially in summer	April-Oct
Cryptomeria	April	**shoots:** spring-autumn **subbranches:** spring	from late spring to summer	frequent from spring to autumn; copious	April-Oct
Ginkgo biloba	March	**shoots:** spring **branches:** March **structure:** Feb	from autumn to late summer	copious: allow to dry out between waterings	April-Oct
Juniperus sinensis	March	**shoots:** spring-autumn **subbranches:** March-April Sept-Oct	autumn for about 8 months	copious: allow to dry out between waterings	spring and autumn
Juniperus rigida	early April	**shoots:** spring-autumn **subbranches:** March	autumn for 8-10 months	copious: allow to dry out between waterings	spring and autumn
Larix	April	**shoots:** growing period **subbranches:** April **structure:** Jan-Feb	early summer-autumn	copious and frequent	spring and autumn
Picea	April	**shoots:** April **subbranches:** spring-early autumn	late autumn for 9-10 months	copious: allow to dry out between waterings	spring and autumn
Pinus	April	**shoots:** April **branches:** Oct	autumn and winter	regular and copious: happier in a dry atmosphere	spring and autumn
Pinus parviflora	March/April	**shoots:** April **branches:** Oct	Oct-March	regular and moderate: mist in summer	spring and autumn
Taxus	March	**shoots:** spring-autumn **branches:** spring or autumn	Sept-March	regular and moderate	spring and autumn
● Deciduous trees					
For all trees	every 2 to 3 years				except in July and August
Acer palmatum	March/April	**leaves:** June **shoots:** March-Sept **branches:** growing period **structure:** Jan-Feb	end of spring for 6 months; protect with raffia	moderate: allow to dry out between waterings	spring and autumn
Acer buergerianum	March/April	**shoots:** growing period **branches:** growing period **structure:** February	seldom used: June, July, August; protect with raffia	copious: spring-autumn; reduce in winter	spring and autumn
Betula	March	**shoots:** March-Nov **branches:** growing period	spring-summer; protect with raffia	light and frequent: dry atmosphere	spring and autumn
Carpinus	March	**shoots:** spring; **branches:** growing period **structure:** Feb	seldom used; spring-summer	copious: cut down in winter; mist in summer	spring and autumn
Celtis	March	**shoots:** spring-late summer **subbranches:** growing period **structure:** March-April	spring-autumn; protect with raffia	copious in hot weather: allow to dry out between waterings	spring and autumn
Fagus	March	**shoots:** late spring **leaves:** June, every 2nd year **branches:** after repotting **structure:** Feb	spring-autumn for 3 months	copious: reduce in winter; mist frequently	spring and autumn
Quercus	March/April	**shoots:** early summer **subbranches:** growing period **structure:** end of Feb	spring-autumn; try to shape by pruning	copious: spring-summer; allow to dry out between waterings	spring and autumn
Salix	twice a year: start of spring and of summer	**shoots:** early spring **subbranches:** after repotting and late autumn	spring and summer; protect with raffia	copious: keep slightly moist; frequent misting	spring and autumn
Ulmus	early spring-summer	**shoots:** growing period **subbranches:** growing period **leaves:** June **structure:** Feb	seldom used; late June-Oct	copious in summer: reduce mid-autumn and winter; misting: spring and summer	spring and autumn
Zelkova	March	**shoots:** spring-autumn **subbranches:** growing period **leaves:** June; **structure:** Feb	seldom done; from budbreak to Oct	copious in summer; otherwise moderate: allow to dry out between waterings; misting: summer	spring and autumn
● Flowering and fruit trees					
For all trees	every 1 or 2 years according to species and age				except in July and August
Berberis	March/April	**subbranches:** after flowering **shoots:** after flowering to Sept **branches:** growing period	possible throughout the year on lignified branches; wire in position 4-6 months	copious in hot weather: allow to dry out thoroughly; hates damp; mist in summer	after flowering; October-November
Camellia	May/June	**subbranches:** when flowers have withered	late spring-late winter, for 3-4 months; protect with raffia	copious in summer; reduce in Sept: allow to wilt before flowering; mist except when in flower	after flowering and in autumn
Chaenomeles	October or after flowering	**subbranches:** after flowering **branches:** June to Sept	from spring-late summer; for 4 months	regular: moderate before flowering; mist in summer	after flowering until September, very sparing

Type of tree	Repotting	Pruning	Wiring	Watering/Spraying	Feeding
● *Flowering and fruit trees (continued)*					
Cotoneaster	March	**shoots:** June **subbranches:** Sept **branches:** March **structure:** Feb	before budbreak; protect with raffia	seldom; moisten thoroughly and allow to dry out well; misting required	spring and autumn
Crataegus	early spring early autumn	**shoots:** when hardened **subbranches:** June-July **branches:** before flowering or after fruiting	spring-autumn: protect with raffia	copious and frequent; mist in hot, dry weather	after spring growth and in autumn
Enkianthus	March	**subbranches:** after flowering before new shoots have hardened **branches:** Sept	spring-autumn	copious from appearance of leaves to autumn	spring and autumn
Ilex	March	**shoots:** growing period **subbranches:** growing period **branches:** March **structure:** Feb	spring-summer; protect with raffia	copious once flowers have opened till fruit appears, otherwise moderate; allow soil to dry out; mist frequently	spring and autumn
Jasminum	Feb before flowering or after leaf fall	**shoots:** spring and July **subbranches:** after flowering **structure:** Jan	spring-summer: protect with raffia	copious: allow to dry out between waterings	after flowering and in autumn
Lespedeza	March/April	**subbranches:** May-Sept **structure:** Feb	spring-late summer; protect young branches with raffia	more copious when flower buds are forming, otherwise moderate	feed more in spring than in autumn
Malus	March/April	**shoots:** after growth **subbranches:** after flowering – July **branches:** March-April	spring-autumn; protect with raffia	moderate: more copious when flowerbuds are forming; spray except during flowering	after flowering in spring and in autumn
Milletia reticulata	March	**subbranches:** after flowering before shoots appear **branches:** in autumn	spring-summer	copious: can be soaked; spray regularly	feed more in spring than in autumn
Morus	April	**shoots:** spring-autumn **subbranches:** after flowering **branches:** before budbreak	spring-summer; protect with raffia	very copious, but allow to dry out between waterings; mist except during flowering	feed more in spring than in autumn
Parthenocissus	March	**subbranches:** after vernation **leaves:** June	spring and summer	copious; mist except during flowering	spring-autumn
Prunus communis dulcis	either early spring or after flowering	**subbranches:** after flowering **branches:** late summer and Oct	spring and summer	more copious before flowering; spray after flowering	spring and autumn except if in flower
Prunus Mume	after flowering	**subbranches:** after flowering **branches:** 1 month after flowering	from late spring to autumn	copious when budding and in flower; spray after flowering	after flowering: in spring and autumn
Punica Granatum	when foliage unfurls	**shoots:** early spring and late autumn **subbranches:** after flowering-autumn	late spring-summer	copious in summer: light in winter; mist except when in flower	spring-autumn except if in flower
Pyracantha	March/April	**subbranches:** after flowering and in autumn **branches:** Feb	throughout the year; do not leave on tree more than 6 months	copious before and after flowering	spring and autumn
Rhododendron	after flowering	**subbranches:** after flowering **branches:** when repotting	spring-autumn	frequent: keep slightly moist; misting required	except when in flower; sparing; spring and autumn
Spiraea	March/April	**subbranches:** after flowering	do not wire	copious	except when in flower; spring and autumn
Syringa	before flowering	**subbranches:** after flowering; early spring and late autumn **branches:** Feb	spring-summer	copious in summer; reduce when in flower; mist in summer	generous; after flowering; autumn
Wisteria	immediately after flowering	**subbranches:** after flowering and autumn **branches:** after flowering	spring-autumn	copious; misf when flowering is past	generous; spring and autumn
INDOOR BONSAI					
For all trees	every 2 or 3 years according to species and age	remove all yellow leaves and withered flowers		mist daily	once a fortnight; apply liquid and solid fertilizer alternately for most species
Ampelopsis	April	**subbranches:** after emergence of leaves and restart of growth **leaves:** summer **structure:** Jan	spring-summer	very little once leaves have fallen; regular; allow to dry out	spring-autumn
Polyscias	April	**subbranches:** spring-autumn **branches:** spring	seldom used; possible throughout the year; best done during intense heat	copious	spring-autumn; once in winter
Araucaria	April/May	**shoots:** April-May **branches:** when growth begins	possible throughout the year; wire should not be left on more than 4 months	regular; allow to dry out between waterings	spring and autumn
Bambusa	May-Sept	**offshoots:** spring **clones:** before they unfurl	when it is being formed; not wired otherwise	copious and frequent	spring and autumn with lawn fertilizer
Bougainvillea	April/May	**shoots:** after flowering **subbranches:** after flowering **branches:** Jan-Feb	when branches have lignified; 3-5 months	water frequently and regularly but moderately; daily in summer	after flowering and in autumn

Programme of work (continued)

Type of tree	Repotting	Pruning	Wiring	Watering/Spraying	Feeding
INDOOR BONSAI (continued)					
For all trees	every 2 or 3 years according to species and age	remove all yellow leaves and withered flowers		mist daily	once a fortnight; apply liquid and solid fertilizer alternately for most species
Buxus	April/May	**subbranches:** during growing period	possible all year round; no longer than 2 months	copious; allow to dry out between waterings	spring and autumn; once in winter
Caragana	April	**subbranches:** after flowering and throughout growing period	when branches have lignified; for 6 weeks; can be done throughout the year	moderate; withstands drought	spring and autumn
Ehretia	April	**subbranches:** spring-autumn **branches:** Feb	seldom used; when branches have lignified; 2-3 months; can be done throughout the year	copious; allow to dry out between waterings	March-June and September
Crassula	April/May	**shoots:** growing period **subbranches:** growing period **branches:** April-Oct	seldom used; when branches have lignified; for 6 weeks	not much water in winter; moderate in summer; mist	May-June and September
Cycas	April	cut out withered palms	no wiring	not much water in winter; moderate in summer; misting more important in summer than winter	spring and autumn
Dracaena or Cordyline	April/May	**branches:** spring; all branches to encourage ramification	seldom used and not advisable; in the course of the summer	not much water in winter; moderate in summer; daily misting during growing period	spring and autumn
Ficus	April/May	**subbranches:** growing period **branches:** Feb; **leaves:** June	when branches have lignified; 8 weeks at most; can be done throughout the year	moderate; more in summer than in winter	spring and autumn; once in winter
Gardenia	end of spring	**subbranches:** after flowering – Sept	when branches have lignified; protect with raffia	not much water in winter; moderate in summer; give more before flowering	after flowering and in autumn
Murraya	April/ early May	**subbranches:** growing period **branches:** spring	possible throughout the year; 10 weeks at most	keep soil moist; regular	spring and autumn; once in winter
Nandina	April	**subbranches:** growing period	seldom used: spring-summer	moderate: regular	spring and autumn
Podocarpus	late spring	**shoots:** growing period **subbranches:** after a growing spurt	when branches have lignified: 8-10 weeks but can be done throughout the year	regular: moderate	spring and autumn; once in winter
Rhapis	March/April	main stem if there are offshoots; otherwise no pruning	is not wired	not much water	spring and autumn
Sageretia theezans	April/May	**subbranches:** growing period **branches:** early spring	when branches have lignified; 6-8 weeks; can be done throughout the year	more copious in summer then in winter; regular	spring-autumn
Schefflera	March	**subbranches:** spring **branches:** spring	very seldom used	not much water; mist-spray occasionally	spring-autumn
Serissa	March/April	**subbranches:** April-end of Oct except when in flower **development:** every 3rd year in Feb	June-Sept	more copious in summer than in winter; allow to dry out between waterings	spring and autumn; reduce amount when in full flower

GLOSSARY

acicular — needle shaped (as in the foliage of pine trees)

acuminate — describes an organ (leaves, fruit) that ends in a point

alternate — describes leaves or branches placed singly at different heights on either side of the stem

auriculate — mainly used to describe leaves with a rounded extension to the leaf which prolongs it below the starting point of the lamina

axil — acute angle formed by a branch growing out from a stem or by a leaf growing from a branch

bract — a small leaf found near the flower on the stem; it differs from the other leaves in shape and colour

catkin — a curved elongated inflorescence

cupric — describes a copper-based compound or product

dioecious — describes plants in which the male and female reproductive parts are borne on different individuals

eye — describes young buds on trees and shrubs

fasciculate — gathered in a bundle; describes flowers or leaves that grow in bunches

lanceolate — shaped like the point of a lance; describes an ear of corn, a leaf or a petal

lignified — describes a branch which is beginning to harden and turn brown, with eyes forming on it

marcescent — withering but not falling off; marcescent leaves dry out in autumn, stay on the tree in winter and fall in spring when the new buds break

mucro (*pl.* **mucrones**) — a small, thick, pointed projection at the tip of a leaf

obovate *syn.* **obovoid** — shaped like an upside-down egg, wider at the top than at the bottom

pubescent — covered with very fine hairs, like down; a **pubescent** stem or leaf

radicel *syn.* **radicle** — small root branching off from main root

reticulate — marked with veins that form a network; organs covered with fine, interlacing lines like a net

samara — a dry, usually one-seeded, winged fruit, like that of the elm, ash, sycamore, maple etc; similar to a winged achene

spinescent — bearing small, not very prickly, thorns

stoma (*pl.* **stomata**) — a microscopically small opening in the epidermis of the green parts of a tree or other plant through which gases pass out of and into the plant from the atmosphere

systemic — describes a product (pesticide) which is transported into the sap of the tree; the pest at which it is directed is poisoned as it eats its tree 'host'